Advance Prais

"To those of you who are educators, teaching in 'revolting times,' under difficult circumstances, working with students who need you as much as ever, this book is a gift and a life raft."

—From the foreword by Michelle Fine,
distinguished professor at the Graduate Center, CUNY

"This is a terrific book and badly needed at this time when 'grit' has become the magic word in pedagogic thinking about inner-city kids. Goodman rightly notes that 'fixing' children of the poor by fostering their perseverance and persistence—worthy values in themselves—does nothing to address the toxic forces that surround their lives. In tandem with the videos to which the book is linked, it's a vivid and arresting answer to a newly cultish fashion that is doing us no good."

—Jonathan Kozol, education activist and bestselling author

"This book reads like an absorbing documentary; these are stories that need a public response to match the work of EVC."

—Deborah Meier, education reform leader

"It's not about grit, but it is about agency. Nobody knows better than Steve Goodman how to help young people tell their stories and, in the process, empower themselves with research and video skills and an activist sense of justice. In this brilliant book, Goodman shares their stories with us, with a depth and particularity that you'll find moving and also, I hope, stirring."

—Joseph P. McDonald, professor emeritus, New York University

"This is an insightful and moving analysis of how students from marginalized backgrounds use their work with video to tell their stories, develop critical thinking skills, and overcome obstacles. As the founder and executive director of the Educational Video Center, Steve Goodman has years of experience in helping to create powerful learning experiences for young people. In this important new book, he shares these experiences and shows us that beyond working hard and demonstrating grit, low-income students need support and guidance to become resilient."

—Pedro A. Noguera, University of California, Los Angeles

"This wide-ranging, penetrating, and telling book is a marvel that highlights a new and needed direction for American education."

—David E. Kirkland, New York University

IT'S NOT ABOUT
GRIT

Trauma, Inequity, and the
Power of Transformative Teaching

STEVEN GOODMAN

Foreword by Michelle Fine

TEACHERS COLLEGE PRESS

TEACHERS COLLEGE | COLUMBIA UNIVERSITY
NEW YORK AND LONDON

Published by Teachers College Press, 1234 Amsterdam Avenue, New York, NY 10027

Cover photo by Torrance York

Library of Congress Cataloging-in-Publication Data

Names: Goodman, Steven, author.
Title: It's not about grit : trauma, inequity, and the power of transformative teaching / Steven Goodman.
Description: New York : Teachers College Press, [2018] | Includes bibliographical references and index. |
Identifiers: LCCN 2018006578 (print) | LCCN 2018016085 (ebook) | ISBN 9780807776865 (ebook) | ISBN 9780807758984 (pbk. : alk. paper)
Subjects: LCSH: Transformative learning—United States. | Education—Social aspects—United States. | School environment—United States. | Community and school—United States. | Educational Video Center.
Classification: LCC LC1100 (ebook) | LCC LC1100 .G66 2018 (print) | DDC 371.102—dc23
LC record available at https://lccn.loc.gov/2018006578

ISBN 978-0-8077-5898-4 (paper)
ISBN 978-0-8077-7686-5 (ebook)

Printed on acid-free paper
Manufactured in the United States of America

25 24 23 22 21 20 19 18   8 7 6 5 4 3 2 1

Pessimism of the intellect, optimism of the will.

This aphorism is most commonly associated with the Italian Marxist Antonio Gramsci, who adopted it for the masthead of his political newspaper, *L'Ordine Nuovo*, prior to his imprisonment by Mussolini's Fascist regime in 1926. Attributed to the French humanist writer Romain Rolland, the slogan is a call to maintain a dialectical tension between realism and idealism, and between critical analysis and the revolutionary will to change the world.

Contents

Foreword

To those of you who are educators, teaching in "revolting times," under difficult circumstances, working with students who need you as much as ever, this book is a gift and a life raft. *It's Not About Grit* offers readers a pedagogical and ethical life preserver to survive the flood of anti-teacher rhetoric, the demonization of public schools, and the conservative push to move away from teaching "controversy" at a time when your students are marinating in injustice—squeezed at the bottom of wealth gap hierarchies, dangling at the precarious edge of housing insecurity, living a knock away from deportation, anxious about abusive racialized policing, vulnerable to state and interpersonal violence—and yet yearning to be respected, educated, and recognized as creative.

Two kinds of questions animate this book: *questions of pedagogy* and *questions of ethics in the face of trauma*. Regarding pedagogy, the book asks how contemporary progressive educators in the mold of Paolo Freire, pioneer of critical pedagogy, can teach through the Common Core. That is, in times of spiking hate crimes and unleashed protest, when Black Lives Matter, DREAMers, and #MeToo flood our social media and our streets, how can we teach on topics of injustice, inequity, White supremacy, voracious capitalism, gentrification, gendered violence, homophobia and transphobia, aggressive policing, immigrant (in)justice, and state violence—and still keep our jobs (whether in New York City or in Idaho)? On the question of ethics in the face of trauma, this book probes how we as educators respond to the nagging whispers that rumble in our own souls, asking if children living in so much trauma can find the space and desire to learn.

To each question above, Goodman and his stunning crew of students/filmmakers offer a decided "Yes!" Retreat is not an ethical option.

- Yes, we must think at once about Freire and the Common Core, even as we might also engage in educational resistance and organizing.
- Yes, we must address how structural injustice saturates our students' communities and carve delicate, democratic classrooms where we can discuss and study the structural precarities manifest in their everyday lives.
- And, yes, we must honor and chronicle both the pain and wisdom that grow from trauma, building educational spaces where knowledge and creativity come alive at the radical margins.

As his long career and this current text will attest, Steve Goodman is a brilliant storyteller. But more than that, he is a gifted midwife who enables young people to tell their own stories through text and video. With Raelene, Scarlett, Luis, Rob, Muzik, and Makeba, Goodman has now curated a book and series of youth-produced videos that educators can use to scaffold the aesthetic imaginations of students who are at once alienated and vibrant, despairing and relentless, undocumented and queer, anxious and bold, gifted and struggling. In this volume, Goodman and his young colleagues teach us how to create stories and videos from small patches of pain: from mold on the ceiling; a police stop; a school nurse who harasses a student for not wearing a dress; an aunt who threatens to throw a young person out of the house for coming out as gay; the catcalls and harassment of strangers on the street; and bullies in school sustained by homophobic silence and adult complicity. With their collective guidance, we bear witness to documentaries that probe painful memories for important insights. In their hands, trauma is metabolized into aesthetics.

THE GIFT OF MIRRORS

In 2009, Pulitzer Prize–winning author Junot Diaz told a rapt audience:

> You know how vampires have no reflections in the mirror? . . . If you want to make a human being a monster, deny them, at the cultural level, any reflection of themselves. . . . And growing up, I felt like a monster in some ways. I didn't see myself reflected at all. I was like, "Yo, is something wrong with me?" That the whole society seems to think that people like me don't exist? And part of what inspired me was this deep desire, that before I died, I would make a couple of mirrors. That I would make some mirrors, so that kids like me might see themselves reflected back and might not feel so monstrous for it. (quoted in Stetler, 2009)

In this book and at the Educational Video Center, Steve Goodman makes mirrors, and he insists that we, in our classrooms, do no less. For decades, he has sat alongside young people who embody, speak freely about, and/or bury their trauma. And he has them make films. Steve welcomes these overaged and undercredited high school students, in classes and workshops, to lift up and interrogate whatever downstream symptom of inequality afflicts them. He then supports his students as they trace the structural origins, the tangled roots, the tentacles of consequence, and the messy possibilities for action.

It's Not About Grit is a gift, a recipe for radical possibility, and it's actually three books in one. First, it is a secular bible for progressive teachers to consider how we might help young people move from silence about personal problems to engagement through films about structural, public issues. Second, it is a genuinely accessible, textual mirror, stuffed with stories, photos, and reflections of young people once tossed to the educational curb who now teach us as artists and researchers. And third, *It's Not About Grit* offers us a series of compelling videos produced by and for young people so that we may all understand the knotty braid of structural violence and radical possibility.

Dear educators and future teachers, reading this text, you too will learn to slay vampires and monsters. Develop the skills and courage to design mirrors with your students, and you will nurture the next generation to imagine and project their own freedom dreams. Thanks for an outstanding journey, Steve, Rob, Luis, Scarlett, Raelene, Muzik, and Makeba.

—Michelle Fine

REFERENCE

Stetler, C. (2009). Junot Diaz: Man in the mirror. Retrieved from www.nj.com/entertainment /arts/index.ssf/2009/10/junot_diaz_man_in_the_mirror.html

Acknowledgments

The origins of this book can be traced back to a conversation that I had with Carole Saltz at the 2014 premiere screening of *Unequal Education Revisited,* an EVC documentary inspired by Jonathan Kozol's *Savage Inequalities* and first commissioned by Bill Moyers in 1992, and again to revisit that story 2 decades later. We spoke with sadness and anger about the unfulfilled promise of the gifted-and-talented 7th-grade student portrayed in the film who later drops out and is incarcerated, and about the countless other students from low-income communities of color whose life opportunities are foreclosed by poverty, racism, and systemic inequities in schooling, health care, and juvenile justice. Over several more conversations, this book took shape as a response to this crisis—a call to action for educators to uplift their students' voices and collectively interrogate and disrupt these inequities.

I am forever grateful to Carole Saltz for inviting me to write this book for Teachers College Press and for her kindness, encouragement, guidance, and unwavering support throughout the journey. I'm deeply indebted to Peter Sclafani for his sharp editorial eye and detailed reviews of each chapter, and for coaching me to stay focused on what matters most to teachers so they can bring the power of transformative teaching to their students, particularly those in greatest need. I appreciate all the tremendous support that John Bylander provided with the editorial production of both the manuscript and accompanying website, as well as the invaluable assistance of additional Teachers College Press staff, including Kathy Caveney, Michael McGann, Karl Nyberg, Nancy Power, Jamie Rasmussen, and Leyli Shayegan. I owe a huge debt of gratitude to Michelle Fine, whose humor, eloquence, and radical writing and public speaking has greatly inspired me and influenced my work over the years at EVC—at least as far back as the 1980s, when I was changed forever by her essay "Silencing in Public Schools."

This book also grows out of my earlier collaborative thinking and writing with my partner, Carolyn Cocca, whose perspective as a feminist political scientist deepened my understanding of neoliberalism and its relation to educational inequity and the growing gaps in wealth and in political participation in our country. I thank Alexis Carreiro for inviting us to write about EVC student civic engagement in resistance to police abuse for the inaugural issue of *Journal of Digital and Media Literacy.* I greatly appreciate our colleague and good friend Terry Locke for encouraging us to contribute an article on teaching critical literacy, identity and community empowerment for *English Teaching: Practice and Critique.* These online journals gave us opportunities to test out our ideas and experiment using

EVC student video clips to interweave youth and community voices with policy and pedagogical theory, which became the organizing approach for this book.

I'm grateful to Cindy Bautista-Thomas, Ivana Espinet, Jane Quinn, David Tobis, and Natalie Zwerger for so generously giving their time, expertise, and insightful comments, which helped strengthen and improve each chapter. Each in their own way has also supported the students of EVC over the years, whether through funding, teaching, or as an interviewee in student films. I'm also thankful to those inspiring educators and practitioners who shared their knowledge and wisdom with me, and to those who helped conduct research and facilitate those conversations, including Bahar Akyurtlu, Lara Evangelista, Amira Hassan, Tameka Jackson, Betsy Krebs, Jennie Soler-McIntosh, Taeko Onishi, Alberto Luis Ortiz-Garcia, and Alexis Sheets. I also appreciate Susan Katz for the coaching and support she gave me.

Special thanks is due to Lynette Lauretig and Eve Bois of the NYC Department of Education's Office of Postsecondary Readiness; their thoughtful contributions to the video guides and their longstanding support and partnership made it possible for us to innovate and expand EVC's youth participatory action research project on students and police in the transfer schools. I'm indebted to the teachers, principals, and EVC coaches whose time and dedication helped transform student voices into action, including Tyona Washington, Dan Storchan, Cynthia Copeland, Emmanuel Garcia, Lydia Howrilka, Sarah Rodriquez, Sean Turner, Rhys Daunic, Carla Cherry, and Robin Bacigalupo.

Over the years, I have been very fortunate to learn from and work with a range of extraordinary scholars and activist educators whose writing, research on EVC, and various collaborative partnerships have greatly enriched my thinking and practice. They include Maxine Greene, Deborah Meier, Jonathan Kozol, Dixie Goswami, Lou Bernieri, Lalitha Vasudevan, Joe Riina-Ferrie, Ray McDermott, Michelle Fine, Bill Ayers, Norm Fruchter, Pedro Noguera, David Kirkland, Natalie Zwerger, Shelley Pasnick, Bill Tally, John Parris, Cecelia Traugh, Anthony Conelli, Frank Pignatelli, Luisa Liliana Costa, Cathleen Wiggans, Fern Kahn, Linda Levine, Bernadette Anand, Myra Goldberg, Mark Reid, Jeff Share, ML White, David Buckingham, Jenny Grahme, Cary Bazelgette, Kathleen Tyner, JoEllen Fisherkeller, Keith Hefner, Marcie Wolfe, Paul Allison, Meghan McDermott, Hana Sun, Sarah Zeller-Berkman, Lora Taub-Pervizpour, Tom Delgiudice, Marian Mogulescu, Sylvia Rabiner, Charlotte Marchant, Steve Shreefter, Candy Systra, Mark Weiss, Alan Dichter, Olivia Ifill-Lynch, Barbara Cervone, Kathleen Cushman, Joe McDonald, Rosa Riccio Pietanza, Jasmine Ma, Sarah Radke, Michael Rothman, Camille Kinlock, and Paul Forbes. My work has been further enriched through the collaborations and generous support of social documentary producers, editors, and journalists, including Jon Alpert, Karen Ranucci, Amy Goodman, Maryann DeLeo, Eugene Jarecki, Alex Gibney, Sloane Klevin, Farai Chideya, Catherine Gund, Maria Hinojosa, Marc Levin, Ray Suarez, Nina Alvarez, Geoffrey O'Connor, David Murdock, Judy Doctoroff, Judith Moyers, and Bill Moyers.

To be sure, this book is rooted in my work at EVC—in the communities, schools, and students I've been honored to serve since 1984. The student stories rendered in these pages and online are excerpted from longer videos that were the collective effort of a range of EVC youth documentary workshops. I would be remiss if I didn't acknowledge the EVC media artists/educators who so masterfully taught those particular teams of youth producers, including Christina Biddle, Natalie Cosby, Julie Creniere, Tanya Jackson, Joan Jubela, Jessie Levandov, Sonya Lynn, Christine Mendoza, Pam Sporn, Larry Washington, and Andrea Ortega-Williams.

It's been a real privilege for me to work with and learn from the staff at EVC, whose commitment and daily practice exemplifies what transformative teaching really is. They have changed more students' lives than they can ever know. I'm thankful to Laura Scheiber for her comments on my writing, to Gil Feliciano for his help facilitating student and teacher interviews, to Jennifer Proulx for the guides she helped develop, and to all the staff for their support and encouragement, including Meryl Feigenberg, Janelle Galvez, Emmanuel Garcia, Mary Greuser, Raelene Holmes-Andrews, Bria Holness, and Jessie Levandov. I'm especially thankful to EVC archivist Michael Grant for his time and assistance in transferring and editing the student archival footage and images that appear in this book.

I've also been tremendously fortunate to enjoy the support, guidance, and friendship of EVC's board of directors, who have generously dedicated their time and resources to ensuring EVC's continued growth over the years, including Colleen Devery, Steven-Emmanuel Martinez, Rosa Riccio Pietanza, Marlene Roy, Jennifer Spiegel, Sherri Wolf, and Torrance York. I'm thankful for the longtime funders who have generously supported and sustained our work at EVC over the years, including the Robert Bowne Foundation, the Brenner Family Foundation, HBO, the National Endowment for the Arts, the New York State Council on the Arts, the New York City Department of Cultural Affairs, the Pinkerton Foundation, the W. Clement and Jessie V. Stone Foundation, the Wellspring Foundation, and the Milton and Roslyn Wolf Family Foundation.

Our work at EVC simply wouldn't be possible without the generosity and collegiality of City-As-School High School principal Alan Cheng; assistant principals Rachel Seher, Joslyn Pena-Phillips, and Carl Oliver; and the entire school staff. I appreciate Lissa Paulson for her suggestions on the manuscript and E. M. for her resources on restorative justice programs. I'm thankful to them all for the warm, creative, and intellectually vibrant home they have given EVC and for the countless ways their partnership has strengthened EVC's pedagogy and youth services through restorative justice programs, mental health and drug counseling, literacy and library services, internship and college guidance, and more.

Looking back, it's been a great pleasure for me to witness three generations of youth grow and find their passion and their footing at EVC, and see many go on to become successful media professionals, educators, and community activists. I owe a huge debt of gratitude to the EVC students and their family and community members who shared their stories in this book and to those who kindly allowed me to conduct follow-up interviews, in some cases decades after their first videos. Although the identities of some have been hidden by pseudonyms, I would like to acknowledge by their first name those who appear in the videos: Millie, Raelene, Jacklyne, Ana, Annmarie, Mariann, Ricardo, Efrain, Rob, Brandon, Katrena, Scarlett, Luis, Perla, Mohamed, Irene, Muzik, Jennie, Raquel, Andrea, Samantha, Nang, Lailah, Makeba, Adina, and Iesha. I also thank the students who appear on the cover of this book: William Cortez, Iyanna Nation, Orlando Ramos, and Iyleen Torres.

I have been deeply moved by the courage and grace of these students. Their struggles to succeed in school have not been about their individual grit alone, but rather the mutual support and solidarity to challenge the injustices they face, that come from the social bonds they form with family, school, and community. They consistently explain that they tell their stories not only because it is healing and self-empowering but also because it gives strength to others who are struggling and who see themselves in their stories.

I'm grateful to my family for their support throughout my writing and my work at EVC, including my children, Theo, Amelia, and Anna Goodman; my mother-in-law, Anne Swinton; my brother and sister-in-law, Ben and Alison Goodman; and my sister, Jackie Goodman. I'm also thankful to Amelia for her suggestions that helped improve the gender and identity chapter. Most of all, I'm indebted to Carolyn Cocca, my thought partner and life partner, for the editorial and moral support she has so generously given me throughout the process. I can't thank her enough for the copious comments she made on each of her numerous readings of the manuscript and the many insights and improvements she contributed along the way.

This book is dedicated to Carolyn Cocca. Her support has made it possible for me to bring student voices, sociopolitical critique, and transformative teaching strategies to the cause of dismantling the systemic barriers blocking our students from reaching their fullest potential. This book is also dedicated to the students of EVC who, even in the darkest times, remain for me an unfailing source of inspiration and hope.

Introduction

Raelene hasn't picked her head up from her desk all period. There are only 5 minutes left in the class. She says she's not sick, but she just won't sit up. At least she's come to school. She's missed more than 6 weeks this semester. Rob, Scarlett, Luis, and Muzik have missed almost that much as well, though they've attended different schools in New York City recently. They have been out so much and done so few of the assignments, there is little hope they can catch up and pass their classes. They're not the only ones. A third of the class seats are empty today.

This is a familiar scene for teachers of students considered "at risk" or "high needs." When questioned as to what's wrong, where they've been, and why they are failing, our students almost always have a story to tell. They are often stories of trouble, trauma, and transience—of being evicted from their home, or moving into a shelter, or being placed in a foster care family. They may talk about going to court or going to the hospital because of asthma attacks, hypertension, homophobic assaults, or gang violence. Or they may say they were feeling too depressed to get out of bed, mourning the loss of a friend or family member. And as we listen to these stories, and listen with great empathy, we often feel stuck. We know our students are struggling. What we see and understand from a teacher's perspective are their struggles to stay in school, focus on their work, and graduate. What we don't always see and understand well enough are our students' struggles outside of school, at home and in their communities, and how they impact their success in school. We may hear their stories, but rarely do we have time in our busy day to find out much more than that. And so we really aren't able to learn in any depth what it means for them to grow up in poverty, in the wealthiest nation in the world; what it's like for them fighting on a daily basis for respect and dignity and a fair shot at succeeding in what has become a profoundly segregated, unjust, and unequal society.

Now there is a growing body of research that argues that it will be more helpful for our students not to focus on the problems of poverty and equity but rather to develop their individual character. As Paul Tough (2012) describes, what matters most in a child's development is a set of noncognitive qualities "that includes persistence, self-control, curiosity, conscientiousness, grit, and self-confidence" (p. xv). Teaching these character traits to children in poverty is important, he argues, because they experience more toxic stress in their lives than middle-class students—stress that neuroscientists find can hinder their emotional and cognitive abilities. This relates to something that Carol Dweck (2006) calls a "growth mindset." Dweck argues that regardless of one's IQ, talent, or social background, by changing their view of themselves from a "fixed mindset" to a "growth mindset"

1

everyone can change their basic qualities and ability to learn. According to Angela Duckworth (2016; Duckworth & Eskreis-Winkler, 2013; Duckworth, Peterson, Matthews, & Kelly, 2007), it comes down to hard work: developing the necessary stamina, passion, and perseverance to stay the course and stick with things over the long haul, and most of all—grit. *Grit* is the character trait that she has popularized and describes as "perseverance and passion for long-term goals" (Duckworth et al., 2007, p. 1087). She observed that those she called the highly successful and the high achievers all had a combination of ferocious determination and direction. It follows then that if low-income students can better endure their social and economic conditions, through hard work and belief in self-change, they can learn to rise above them.

There is no question that stress and trauma are serious problems for students, particularly those living in poverty. As Jeffrey Duncan-Andrade (2009) notes, exposure to chronic stress and trauma is now considered to be one of the most significant contributors to students' poor health. In fact, the impact of trauma on the educational outcomes of low-income students was recognized to such an extent that a class action lawsuit was brought against the Compton school district in California on behalf of traumatized students alleging the school has failed to meet their needs (Associated Press, 2015). This points to a dire need for more counseling and physical and mental health services in schools and communities to help students cope with trauma.

The grit and mindset theories are appealing in their commonsense simplicity, apparent egalitarianism, and lack of need for social policy or funding to enact. From their perspective, talent and IQ don't count as much as the noncognitive character traits of effort, practice, and learning from mistakes. We know that developing noncognitive social and emotional skills are essential components of school and out-of-school youth development programs, as well.

The trouble is, Tough, Duckworth, Dweck, and other writers in the past who have advocated pull-yourself-up-by-the-bootstraps-type character-building approaches are promoting an essentially individualized solution to what is fundamentally a social problem. Limiting the focus on students' character abilities to delay gratification, learn from failures, and become more "gritty" sidesteps the complex and often debilitating problems that structural poverty and racism create for students.

They paper over the macro-level structural inequities that produce the trauma in the first place.[1] More than four out of five inner-city youth report experiencing one or more traumatic events (Collins, et al, 2010), which may include being a victim or witness to family or community violence,[2] abuse, or sexual assault; or a family's forced eviction, homelessness, or parental separation due to foster care,[3] deportation, incarceration, or death. Significantly, the directing attorney in the Compton lawsuit acknowledged the systemic causes of trauma, noting that students in the district were suffering "from exposure to violence, racism, extreme poverty, and other adverse childhood experiences" (Public Counsel, 2015).

Low-income students experience greater toxic stress and trauma than middle-class students as a result of racialized social policies and systems that need to be critically analyzed and disrupted. Black and Brown students routinely experience fear of violence from random police encounters in cars, on street corners, in parks, or in apartment buildings—encounters that nonminority middle-class students rarely have to face. Even when violence is avoided, the disproportionately high rates of police stops, arrests, and school suspensions often result in the removal from school of those children who are often most in need of academic attention and emotional support (Noguera, 2003, 2008).[4] Black girls in particular must struggle to overcome negative stereotypes that are too often deeply engrained in school culture (Morris, 2016). And for those who still do manage to come to school, these degrading and often abusive encounters with security officers in school and with police officers out of school—experiences that children of more privileged White families have far less often—contribute to a diminished sense of self-worth and increased anger, alienation, and distrust of teachers and other school authorities.

Defining students and their relative grittiness as the problem that needs fixing fails to address the banking and real estate markets that segregate their families in unsafe and unhealthy housing, or the child welfare and justice systems that serve to break up the families of low-income students of color and incarcerate, detain, and deport their parents. It further overlooks the misogynistic, homophobic, and transphobic systems that produce pervasive harassment and assault on female and LGBTQ students. Improving students' disposition to learning won't change these conditions.

The preponderance of evidence shows that for millions of students from underresourced communities across the country, whether they live in inner-city, rural, or suburban areas, they must endure a broad range of social and economic disadvantages that correlate directly with and *create* the conditions for academic disadvantages. The dropout rate for students in the lowest 25% of family incomes is about five-and-one-half times greater than the dropout rate for students in the highest 25% of family incomes (U.S. Department of Education, NCES, 2012). In New York City, the largest and most segregated school system in the nation (Kucsera, 2014), 82% of White students graduated in 4 years in 2015, while only 64% of Hispanic students and 65.4% of Black students did so (Stringer, 2016). The racial/ethnic gap grows twice as large when comparing graduation rates for Black and Hispanic students with advanced designation diplomas across New York State, which are 35% and 31% lower than the rate of Whites, respectively (NYSED, 2018, Slide 11).

Systemic inequities cause real and lasting damage on a community, family, and individual level, which can't be explained away by character flaws. The wealth gap and the Black–White opportunity/achievement gap are inextricably connected, and the causes for this connection are as complex as they are varied. Certainly nutrition and physical health is an important factor. Black children are one-and-one-half times more likely to have lead poisoning than Whites because of substandard housing conditions, and a child poisoned with lead is seven times more likely to drop out of school than other children (Jones et al., 2009; McCoy, 2015). Students are at a disadvantage in school if they can't see the board well, and children from impoverished families suffer from severe vision impairment at twice the normal rate (Rothstein, 2004). Students' ability to work hard and concentrate on their classes is limited if they are chronically hungry or ill, and poorer students are in general less healthy than middle-class students due to their nutrition, housing, and more-limited access to health care. There were 17.5 million "food-insecure" households in 2013 that could not provide enough food for all members of the family (Coleman-Jensen, Gregory, & Singh, 2014). Malnutrition increases the risk of illness, and chronically ill students are also chronically absent from school. Chronic absences increase the likelihood that these students will repeat grades, lose social networks, and drop out of school.

Raelene, Rob, Scarlett, Luis, Muzik, and Makeba (students whom we meet in the following chapters), and all those students whom we classify as at risk, overage and undercredited, off-track from graduation, special education, English language learners—all have struggled to stay engaged and succeed in school while also struggling on the home front. These struggles take a heavy toll on their physical and mental health and well-being. We know well the damaging impact on students who live in homes with lead paint or black mold, experience or witness gang and gun violence, are forced to leave their homes due to their sexual orientation, live in shelters and foster care homes, live in homes with drug-addicted parents, or have parents who have been incarcerated or deported. These children and young adults often suffer from some form of trauma, chronic stress, sleep deprivation, hypervigilance, abandonment, abuse, neglect or violence that can lead to depression, anxiety, and a range of other mental health problems, all of which negatively affect their academic performance.

Over and over, we can see the heavy price that the least fortunate students must pay for growing up in inequitable conditions of segregation and poverty that, through no fault of their own, get in the way of their academic success. Just as other students born into families of privilege are rewarded for success in school that they didn't have to earn, evident in the tutors, travel, after-school and summer enrichment, and social networks for college and employment that their parents can provide. Yet, although the link between poverty and diminished educational outcomes for low-income students of color is well documented (Kozol, 1991; Oakes & Rogers, 2006; Orfield & McArdle, 2006; Rothstein, 2004), there has been neither the political will required to change these underlying social conditions, nor the broadscale change in educational practice that would take this research into account. As Richard Rothstein (2004) put it:

> For nearly half a century, the association of social and economic disadvantage with a student achievement gap has been well known to economists, sociologists, and educators. Most, however, have avoided the obvious implication of this understanding—raising the achievement of lower-class children requires amelioration of the social and economic conditions of their lives, not just school reform. (p. 11)

This book takes this "obvious implication" as its point of departure, and uses student voices to ground our understanding of the links between race, poverty, and academic achievement in their lived experiences. These student voices are documentary stories of their trauma, resilience, and moral courage in the face of adversity.

But it's not about grit. Sure, hard work, determination, practice, and perseverance make a difference, and might even be a determining factor if all things were equal. But they're not. Perseverance, effort, and dogged determination weren't a problem for Luis, who as a 10-year-old boy made his way to the border on foot through the Mexican mountains and desert six times before he finally succeeded in crossing and reuniting with his family in New York. But his grit wasn't enough to make him a highly successful high achiever in school. After his father was deported, he ended up leaving school to earn money for his family. Anti-immigrant policies, wage theft, overpolicing, poverty, inequity, and the trauma of losing his father were among the systemic barriers he faced. His is just one of countless cases of smart, hardworking, and gritty students with strong character whose school and life chances are undermined by inequitable and unjust systems.

Listening to their video stories in this book reminds us that the students we see struggling to pass our classes are also struggling outside of school. Their often abusive and racially biased treatment at the hands of "street-level bureaucrats" (Lipsky, 1980), including border patrol agents, housing eviction marshals, corrections officers, and school resource officers, teach our students harsh and lasting lessons about race, class, gender, and the power that these authorities use to regulate poor people.

But educators have a power of a different kind to make a lasting difference in the lives of students. Ours is a power of transformative teaching that works to counter these dehumanizing experiences with lessons of compassion, dignity, empowerment, and "critical hope" (Duncan-Andrade, 2009) that help students critically analyze the systems that oppress them and create new possibilities for social justice. Engaging students in personal and community inquiry, they not only learn the history behind these unjust systems but also develop the resilience, agency, and collective voice needed to bring about more equitable and just futures for themselves and their local communities.

This is a book for teachers and school leaders, and for guidance counselors, social workers, and youth practitioners—all of us who care deeply about the students we teach—who are looking to take up this kind of teaching: a transformative teaching. It calls for a pedagogy anchored in social justice that is both student centered and community based. In our classes and schools this means creating vibrant spaces where students, too often silenced in stress and trauma, can feel safe and included, and know their ideas count and their voices matter. Listening to and learning from our students, we see the scope of systemic change that is needed and recognize that transformative teaching cannot stop at the schoolhouse door. It requires the more wholistic notion of community schools, which provide students with multiple resources, opportunities, and partnerships in the community. In this way, we can be that much stronger standing with, and advocating for, our students and their families to dismantle those oppressive systems.

Transformative teaching is attuned to the nuances and details of students' lives as well as the broader context of racial and economic inequities that so many struggle against every day. From this perspective, the sense of fatalism, alienation, hurt, and anger that many students bring into the classroom is not viewed solely as a problem of personal character, but also as a product of their experiences living under oppressive and dehumanizing conditions. Understanding that many of our students too often suffer alone in silence, turning social issues in their lives into a subject of study is a powerful strategy for breaking that silence, for creating community in our classrooms, and for opening pathways to resilience. Connecting the personal and the political in this way, students can find renewed purpose in their learning and develop stronger habits of reading, critical research, and creative expression.

The chapters in this book are divided by themes that students I have worked with over the years have identified as urgent social problems that have undermined their opportunities in school and more generally in life. They were among the recurring issues that several classes of students chose, after intensive study and deliberation, as the central focus of their semesterlong documentary inquiries. Although they are discussed separately for the purposes of our analysis—health and housing, police and juvenile justice, immigration, gender and identity, and foster care and child welfare—in reality, our students and their families experience them as intersecting and overlapping systems and institutions in their lives. We should understand them that way, too.

Reading and screening the stories in each chapter will help educators come to see the world through their students' eyes and bring greater compassion and critical understanding to their teaching. It is self-affirming for students who are struggling with similar problems to see themselves in those stories, to see that they are not alone and feel empowered to speak up and share their own experiences. Such discussions will also develop a greater sense of empathy and understanding in those students who have never had those experiences.

We must work to provide safe and inclusive spaces for our students who may have been stereotyped and stigmatized, whether these spaces are an advisory or academic class, restorative justice program, DREAMers club, Genders & Sexualities Alliance (formerly called Gay-Straight Alliance and still known by the abbreviation GSA), girls club, youth participatory action research project, a foster care youth publication, or other program. Taking time to discuss the microaggressions (Nadal, 2008)—those brief, sometimes unintentional verbal slights and behavioral indignities that they may experience in their daily lives—helps create a more inclusive space regardless of their status, whether they might be sick, hungry or homeless, court-involved, undocumented, queer, pregnant or parenting, foster youth, or other. Developing such safe spaces requires intentional community-building activities, strategies, and protocols (McDonald, Mohr, Dichter, & McDonald, 2013) to facilitate inclusive conversation where everyone is heard and respected, and where we educators can also make ourselves vulnerable. This work is most effective when teachers can partner with one another to problem-solve and share ideas and lesson plans.

In such spaces, students not only feel safe and supported but also feel *needed* as agentive participants learning about and working to disrupt the inequitable systems that are oppressing them and their communities. This kind of teaching is transformative, not because it develops individual mindsets and grit, but because it promotes and is only possible within compassionate communities of practice that link personal healing to social transformation. Inspired by a Freirian pedagogy (Freire, 1970), we work to create openings of authentic dialogue with our students and strive to teach with a sense of humility and love.

In these spaces, students grow critical academic skills and social–emotional resilience while also moving toward collective social justice. Students surviving trauma are able to thrive in these spaces because they form strong and enduring relationships with their teachers and peers, who provide them with mutual support to develop personally and academically. It's worth underscoring this point about transformative teaching: that students develop individual academic skills and rigorous habits of study as well as social–emotional resilience when they are part of a compassionate, collective, and generative process of dialogue and action—when they are making their voices heard on social justice issues of consequence to them and their larger community. It is healing for students to know that it's not their fault that they live in inequitable and impoverished conditions in their community or attend underresourced schools, and that these conditions do not define them. It is empowering for them to learn that there is a history of economic forces and racialized public policies that have created these conditions, as well as movements of people who have long struggled to change them.

I have seen struggling students experience this transformation in project after project, semester after semester, in my nearly 35 years of work at the Educational Video Center (EVC) in New York City, where I am the founding director. Nearly all the EVC students whose stories appear in this book have experienced such resilience from trauma through storytelling and active civic engagement. Some of the key ingredients of this transformative pedagogy are that students feel supported and needed by their peers in the group, have a close relationship with their teacher, learn with a purpose, make their voices heard by creating real work for real audiences, and see their social justice films used as tools for dialogue and change in their school and community (Goodman, 2003).

At EVC, we teach struggling newcomer and overage and undercredited high school students to collaboratively research, shoot, and edit documentary stories that critically examine social, emotional, and cultural issues in their lives. Using art and storytelling, they organically link personal and social change. Through their experiences in EVC's after-school workshops and in school-based academic classes, students come to see the deeper social causes for their sense of hopelessness, fear, shame, or anger—whether from abuse by police, bullying of LGBTQ students, sexual harassment, homelessness, or a broad range of other issues. Teaching them to become critically literate in analyzing, questioning, and talking back to these systems, they develop a greater sense of purpose and power in their learning, as well as control over their lives. They learn to tap into their family and community "funds of knowledge" (Moll, Amanti, Neff, & Gonzales, 1992) and broaden their social networks by conducting oral histories and interviews with family, community elders, and grassroots organizations struggling with the same problems and working to change them. Their documentary making becomes a step toward channeling anger and frustration into political action against a collective injustice (Goodman & Cocca, 2013). They find power though the process of storytelling, learning that their stories matter and that spreading them out into the world can lead to change. Within this context, we can understand their storytelling as a radical political act.

Over the years, EVC students have created a rich library of extraordinary, award-winning films of student, family, and community portraits and inquiries that have been shown on television and in museums, libraries, schools, and film festivals. Excerpts from many of these EVC student documentaries are discussed throughout this book, with screenshots and simple hyperlinks to the video clips themselves on the Teachers College Press website (www.tcpress.com/goodman-video-clips) and the EVC website (www.evc.org/its-not-about-grit). The students who appear in the videos are named, and pseudonyms are used for those who have been interviewed for this book but who don't appear in the videos. The intercutting of written, spoken, and visual texts across book and documentary makes this what might be called a "book-umentary."

EVC's method of transformative teaching can be applied in nondocumentary school-based settings as well, where student and community voices are celebrated through art, inquiry, and storytelling. As the renowned philosopher Maxine Greene describes, such an approach develops students' *social imagination*, where they learn "to name the obstacles in the way of their shared becoming" (1988, pp. 126, 133) in order to imagine a realm beyond those obstacles, and to develop the capacity "to think about things as if they were otherwise" (2001, p. 65). This not only entails a change in students' ways of seeing and thinking about the world, but a change in the kind of person they are—a change in their sense of identity.

This approach shares much in common with what Gloria Ladson-Billings (1995, 2009) calls a "culturally relevant pedagogy," one that develops students' learning, cultural competence, and critical sociopolitical consciousness. She (2017) describes the importance of teaching about real-world social justice issues, and linking learning

> to the challenges the students are confronting . . . racial profiling, mass incarceration, or inequality in suspension may be impacting students directly. These more politically volatile topics are the ones that teachers may want to hold at arms length. But failure to engage them is exactly why students do not trust schools to be places that deal honestly and forthrightly with the issues of their lives. (p. 146)

More than being culturally relevant, or "culturally responsive," as Geneva Gay (2010) describes it, Samy Alim and Django Paris (2017) call for a "culturally sustaining pedagogy" (CSP). This is a pedagogy that reimagines "schools as sites where diverse, heterogeneous practice are not only valued but *sustained*. In fundamentally reimagining the purpose of education, CSP demands a critical, emancipatory vision of schooling that reframes the object of critique from our children to oppressive systems" (p. 3).

Teaching students to critically analyze unjust and inequitable conditions in their lives means having hard but necessary conversations about poverty, race, trauma, and oppression in their lives and the actions needed to change them. However, talking about poverty as a structural problem of policy and discrimination goes against stereotypes about poor people held by those more privileged, as well as by working-class and poor people themselves, that blame the poor for their condition and stigmatize them as lazy and undeserving of our help. Poor people are particularly stigmatized when the source of disadvantage is perceived as controllable, as compared with an uncontrollable cause of poverty such as natural disasters (Williams, 2009). As educators, we too carry our own assumptions and implicit biases about race and poverty that impact our teaching. As Paul Gorski (2013) writes, "What we believe about poverty and why it exists even affects our expectations of and attitudes toward low-income students. . . . [W]e need to challenge common myths about poverty and develop robust understandings of the experiences of poor and working-class families both in and out of school" (p. 27).

Teachers may feel that, with all the requirements they have to meet and papers they have to grade, they barely have time to eat their lunch, let alone develop such an understanding and discuss social issues with their students. There is no question that teaching is demanding and stressful work, with competing priorities and never enough time or support to take care of them all. But teachers and school leaders must also recognize what an urgent priority it is to invest time and space to reach and teach all our students, particularly our most troubled among them. That's what makes teaching so challenging and also so rewarding.

Some educators may be concerned that by focusing on social problems of poverty we risk pathologizing low-income students of color and their communities and reinforcing negative stereotypes about them. To be clear, in this book when we discuss problems such as high rates of incarceration or low rates of graduation in poor communities of color, we are naming social problems but not defining our students by them. We are not promoting a deficit model or generalizing trauma for all poor students. As Gay (2010) writes, "while school failure is an experience of too many ethnically diverse students, it is not the *identity* of any" (p. xxiv). Drawing from Paulo Freire's (1970) problem-posing critical pedagogy, in analyzing oppressive systems we learn that they are historically created. That is a hopeful and empowering idea for students because it means these problems are not intractable but are subject to change, and we all can play a role in changing them.

Whether in an academic or extracurricular program or student club, exploring social justice issues in students' lives must be embedded within a process of compassionate community building. Learning about one another's personal histories and exploring social issues in their lives validates students' experiences, counters negative stigmas and stereotypes and deficit views of them and their community, and makes possible greater empathy and compassion among all students. It leverages students' family, community, and culture as valuable resources for learning. And it creates the basis for stronger, trusting relationships with teachers.

As Deborah Meier (1995), founder of the small schools movement, writes:

> This close knowledge helps us demand more of them; we can be tougher without being insensitive and humiliating. It also means we know their moods and styles—whom to touch in a comforting way and whom to offer distance and space in times of stress. It means that every adult in the school feels responsible for every kid and has insights that when shared can open up a seemingly intractable situation to new possibilities. Knowing one's students matters, including—and perhaps especially—those who are hardest to know. (p. 111)

Knowing our students well and developing trusting relationships with them takes time, but investing in our students is time well spent. These close and stable relationships with adults are absolutely essential components in student resilience. Such relationships develop when our students feel respected and listened to by us, and when they have shared experiences with us in projects and activities with a purpose that they find meaningful and relevant.

One such meaningful and relevant project is participatory action research. Educators and community partners are increasingly engaging students in such projects to help them learn to critically investigate and peel back the layers of the often invisible institutions and policies that wield power over them. Though these school- and community-based spaces have been described variously as "counter publics," "youth participatory action research," "countercultural communities of practice," and "spaces of action" (Cammarota & Fine, 2008; Duncan-Andrade & Morrell, 2008; Goodman & Cocca, 2014; O'Donoghue, 2006), they share a common approach that calls for collective, not individual, research into the root causes of the inequitable conditions in their lives that undermine their academic and human potential. Armed with these new insights, students learn to search for solutions that will strengthen their own and their community's health and well-being.

From this perspective, the boundaries between what is considered cognitive and noncognitive are not so neatly divided as Tough, Dweck, Duckworth, and others assert. The interdependence of efficacy and agency shows that, in order for people to take independent action, they need to develop the belief that action is in fact possible and is worth the effort. This is especially important for young people who have been historically marginalized from the mainstream social and political institutions. Imagining new possible futures for themselves, and believing that change is in fact possible and is worth the effort, helps students break free of the hold that past patterns of thought and action may have on them (Emirbayer & Mische, 1998; Oyserman & Markus, 1990).

Participatory action research and other popular education projects provide evidence that the very process of engaging in cognitive activities of research and writing, of creating and sharing new knowledge, and identifying methods of political influence through community action also build noncognitive qualities. That is, these rich experiences of sociopolitical learning, of making even small changes in the most local terrain of school and neighborhood, can develop their of sense of self-worth, hope, and efficacy, believing that they as students are not simply subjects to change, but agents who can themselves make a difference in the world (Beaumont, 2011; Cammarota & Fine, 2008; Duncan-Andrade & Morrell, 2008; Oakes & Rogers, 2006).

Powerful examples of such social justice popular education efforts can be traced to the educator-activists who organized the 1950s and 1960s civil rights–era Citizenship Schools and student-led Freedom Schools for literacy and voting rights in the South (Carson, 1981; Cobb, 2011; Horton, 1990; Lynd, 1965). Septima Clark, Myles Horton, Charles Cobb, Bob Moses, and other radical educators well understood that there could not be improved educational achievement in the poorest, most oppressed African American communities without also changing their economic and political conditions. Their courage and bold vision of education for freedom and democracy continue to be a great inspiration for us all.

Each of the following chapters in this book begins with a student's story, as told by the EVC youth documentary makers, giving us intimate portraits of often marginalized or misrepresented communities, with the fine grain and texture that comes from their daily life. The context for each case draws connections between how the student's living conditions and private problems have been impacted by that particular history of public policies, and the role each student plays in his or her educational achievement. These clips are powerful documents of life for students in neighborhoods across New York City. Some are like time capsules from the 1980s and 1990s, and others date from 2000 up to 2016. The clips show us the connections between the private problems and traumas the students struggle with, the public debates that shape them, and the grassroots leaders and organizations that resist them.

Seeing video stories made by other students who look like them and who are sharing experiences that connect to theirs motivates students to share their own stories and think more deeply about the issues they raise. This is why the book provides teacher guides with suggested activities for using the EVC video clips to spark student discussion, writing, interviewing, creative expression, and action research projects on the social issues. Strategies for creating safe spaces in the class and for addressing student bias and stigmatization are also included. The social, political, and historical context in each chapter, as well as the statistical and related information in endnotes are critical resources to enrich these activities. The full EVC documentaries and EVC video production curriculum (Baudenbacher & Goodman, 2006) are also available online at www.evc.org/store.

Through their documentary stories, this book gives voice to those students in our schools who come to class unprepared, behind in their work, and with failing test scores, feeling some combination of disengaged, distracted, disrespected, depressed, confused, lonely, hurt, afraid, angry, hungry, or sick. And they will give voice to the yet untold stories of those students who just go missing, those empty seats in the classroom where the students are lost for days, weeks, and even months at a time. In one way or another, they have been tangled up in the web of interconnected systems and oppressions—whether through health and housing, police and juvenile justice, immigration, gender and identity, foster care and child welfare, or most likely some combination of the above. Although these hard-to-reach students are the ones who need us the most to listen to, stand with, and advocate for them, all students will benefit from a more inclusive and empathetic understanding.

As Raelene, Rob, Scarlett, Luis, Muzik, Makeba, and the other students open their homes and neighborhoods to us, we are invited through their videos to bear critical witness with empathy for their struggles and trauma, and solidarity in their art and resistance. They are sharing with us some of the spirit and rhythm of their life in New York City's most impoverished neighborhoods, and by extension in urban communities like them across the country. By accepting that invitation, and by examining the relations between poverty, race, gender, inequity, and educational achievement, I hope that you will bring the power of transformative teaching to inspire a multitude of personal and social transformations that will help our students realize their potential with dignity, hope, healing, and well-being.

CHAPTER 1

"Unlivable Conditions"
Health and Housing

Where students live can have a deep and lasting impact on their physical and mental health and well-being, and on their abilities and opportunities to succeed in school. Housing, health, and education are all intertwined. Although teachers surely take notice of students' work habits, class behavior, grades, or attendance, the deprivation of students' living conditions and the history of systemic discrimination and upheaval of their residential communities remain largely invisible and uncounted. The impacts of hazardous and toxic indoor environments, disrupted family and social networks, and segregation on the physical health, emotional well-being, and educational achievement of low-income youth of color are structural, not individual (Fullilove, 2004; McKoy & Vincent, 2008; Rothstein, 2004). Yet schools are arranged so we must give low or failing grades to students who are chronically absent or unable to concentrate on classwork as a measure of their poor attendance and academic achievement. What rarely is measured is the toxic mold, lead paint dust, rat infestation, lack of heat or hot water, and other damaging conditions that many students must endure growing up in impoverished housing that might affect their attendance. As a result, these students must struggle with a range of physical and mental health problems, including chronic asthma, childhood lead poisoning, fatigue, hypertension, anxiety, depression, and traumatic stress—problems that their peers in a more affluent community with better-quality housing stock and greater access to affordable health care do not have to face. The collateral damage of the wealth gap (substandard and inequitable health and housing conditions) on the achievement gap (low graduation rates) for mainly Black and Brown children living in poverty have intergenerational consequences and can last a lifetime (Orfield & McArdle, 2006).

This chapter will make visible students' experiences at home—private struggles that students too often carry alone, unspoken and unknown in the schoolhouse. Through their stories, we see how mostly African American and Latino families living in impoverished neighborhoods have suffered the consequences of landlord neglect, segregated housing policies, disinvestment in public housing, and forced displacement through foreclosures and gentrification. These and other housing policies have systematically undermined the health and education of students from poor communities of color, though youth and community groups continue to organize to resist these policies. As educators, we can make an important difference by bringing a critical understanding of these systemic injustices into our classes. We can practice a culturally sustaining pedagogy that challenges negative stereotypes about poverty and engages students in projects that value their experiences and community assets and strengthens student voices for change.

In *2371 Second Avenue: An East Harlem Story* (Educational Video Center, 1986), Millie and her classmates document conditions in her rat-infested apartment without heat or hot water. We watch her cousin as she heats water on the stove in order to give her baby a warm bath and Millie as she leads the tenants on a march to read a petition in the landlord's office. In Raelene's video, *Breathing Easy: Environmental Hazards in Public Housing* (Educational Video Center, 2013), she keeps a video journal documenting the infestation of black mold in her public housing apartment and her struggles with asthma. In *Mortgage Mayhem: Living Inside Fraud* (Educational Video Center, 2011), Annie reports on her family's struggle to save their house from foreclosure in the face of predatory lending and recession. In *As the Sun Comes Up, the Bricks Fall Down* (Educational Video Center, 2010a), Ricardo describes the gentrification of his Bronx neighborhood brought on by the building of Yankee Stadium, while Efrain explains how landlord withholding of services and increases in rent have forced his family out of their Brooklyn neighborhood undergoing gentrification.

These are individual cases, drawn from particular poor and working-class neighborhoods spanning over 25 years in four New York City boroughs. These students and their families give us a close-up, street-level perspective of the larger trends and problems that millions of other low-income students are grappling with at home and bringing with them to schools across the country.

Part of practicing a transformative and culturally sustaining pedagogy means bringing an understanding of the whole student into the classroom, including both their school and out-of-school community experiences, and the systemic interconnections between housing, health, and education that shape them. This requires a shift in perspective from a punitive approach for students' absences and missed assignments to one of greater empathy, support, and inquiry to uncover the deeper roots of the problem. This will look different depending on the student. But it may involve a combination of health- and academic-related responses such as ensuring that students have access to the medical and psychological resources they need, while also engaging them in activities such as spoken word, arts, or action research projects that explore these issues and advocate for improved housing conditions.

Looking for signs of students' environmental-related illness is important, just as is looking for signs of students' strength and capacity for resilience. Students develop a greater sense of hope and possibility when they can see their peers as active youth leaders. And in all of the students' stories there are examples of this, where students have raised their voices against "unlivable conditions," seeking environmental justice from landlords—clean, safe, healthy living conditions in their homes—and nonpredatory treatment from banks. As educators who care deeply about the students we teach, learning about the often dehumanizing conditions they and their families face in their community enables us to be more compassionate, knowledgeable, and supportive of our students when they come to class—not always feeling in full health and ready to learn.

"WHERE THE RATS COME OUT": SLUMLORD NEGLECT

Millie was a thin, quiet student who wore large glasses and liked to wear pastel-colored bows in her hair. She was absent often and sick a lot. But when the class began discussing the topic for our documentary, she became animated, suggesting we should make a film about housing. It had been weeks now since her apartment building had any heat or hot water, she told us. Her parents and the other tenants had complained to the super, but nothing had changed. They had difficulty reaching the landlord, and weren't sure where the landlord's office was. The temperature at night was dropping as fall approached. She said she would ask her parents for permission to be interviewed about it.

The next day, she told us they agreed to be interviewed and we all went up to her building in East Harlem to meet Millie's family and document the conditions there. She narrates the opening of her documentary:

> I live in a building with broken windows, garbage, rats, and no hot water. This is a documentary I made with other teenagers about my family, my neighbors, and how we struggle to survive under these conditions. . . . My family came to New York from Puerto Rico almost 30 years ago for a better life, but this is what they found. (Educational Video Center, 1986)

The camera zooms in on the wall as her father points to gaping holes in the plaster. Millie interviews her father in Spanish and translates his answers to English: "He's telling us about how the rats have eaten up all the wall, and that's where he had to fix. And that's where the rats come out through. That's why there are so many holes there. . . . Yes, he has seen rats before." Next, she interviews her mother and translates, "You have seen rats before. You have to wake up in the middle of the night, to protect your food because of the rats."

They walk into the bathroom, where her father turns on the bathtub faucet so the students can record evidence that there is no hot water coming out. Millie continues, "That's the hot water and there isn't any coming down through the pipe now. He says that this is not the only apartment that's this way. There are more in the building that's this bad."

Millie then brings the crew upstairs to visit with her cousin and narrates, "My cousin Marta Sanchez lives upstairs in apartment 11 with her 1-year-old son, Fernando. Marta is one of the many in this building that does not have hot water. So in order to give her son a bath, she has to boil water." The students film her as she boils water in a pot on the stove and gives her son a bath.

The students next speak with Angel, an elderly resident in the building, and ask, "Angel, why are there so many rats in this building?" He answers in Spanish and they translate, "La basura? The garbage outside?" They record shots of the piles of uncollected garbage in the courtyard below.

Later, Angel comes into Millie's apartment with a large garbage can. Millie narrates, "To prove how bad the problem really is, Angel showed us a rat he caught." He leans into the can and everyone gasps as he pulls out a huge dead rat, holding it up by the tail for the camera. Millie retells his story of what happened: "The rat fell into the garbage can. And since there is no hot water, he had to boil some water so he could throw it in the garbage can so the rat could die." She continues interviewing him about it: "I asked him if he's not scared living in this apartment like this. And he says he is because if a rat was to jump on me and bite me, I don't know what would happen to me. Something bad might happen to me."

This is a slice of life of the housing and health conditions for a student and her family living in East Harlem in 1986. Dickensian in its narrative, the video leaves little to the imagination, and clearly shows how living in a rat-infested apartment with nearly 100 building code violations, without heat or hot water, must have impacted Millie's health and well-being and her ability to regularly attend, focus, and succeed in school. The literature on poverty and low-income housing gives ample evidence that conditions that could be avoided by better-quality housing and access to afford-able health care—such as the overcrowding, lack of waste disposal, rodent infesta-tion, dampness, and cold that Millie and her neighbors experienced—have long been identified as routes for infectious disease transmission (Krieger & Higgins, 2002). There may have been several causes for Millie's illnesses and absences from school, her feeling distracted, and dropping out of her comprehensive high school and en-rolling in an alternative school. But surely, we can see how the appalling conditions

Garbage, Rats, and No Hot Water

 View the clip online: www.tcpress.com/goodman-chapter-one#v1.1

of her unhealthy home environment were clearly an important factor. Consider the magnitude of this impact on the education of countless other students like Millie over the years as slumlords are still, 3 decades later, renting unhealthy, rat-infested apartments to low-income tenants of East Harlem (Ransom, 2014).   ⌐ *Quote* ⌐

The correlation between students' poor health and low educational outcomes is also well documented. Low-income students are less likely to have regular eye, ear, and dental care. Vision problems interfere with schoolwork and hearing problems lead to difficulty in understanding teachers. Dental problems and dental pain, exacerbated by lack of dental care, lead to difficulty concentrating in the classroom. Poor nutrition also causes difficulties in concentration and, along with dental problems, may negatively influence test performance and academic achievement of low-income children (Meier, 2009; Rothstein, 2004).

In addition to these myriad physical health problems, poor housing can also affect behavioral and mental health outcomes. Exposure to lead through lead-based peeling paint, several times higher in low-income communities because of older and substandard housing stock in cities, affects neurodevelopmental functioning in children and contributes to hearing loss and often lifelong brain impairment. Housing quality (structural quality, level of privacy, indoor climate, hazards, degree of cleanliness, and children's resources) is also related to psychological distress and a behavioral index of learned helplessness. The rat infestation in Millie's building was a clear source of anxiety, psychological stress, and sleep loss for her and her family. Higher incidents of crime and violence, arson, and abandonment, combined with unresponsive or abusive police—common features in neighborhoods with housing in decline—also contribute to increased levels of emotional stress (Acevedo-Garcia & Osypuk, 2008).

However, the number-one reason for chronically missing school is asthma. Nationally, it accounts for an estimated 14.4 million absences each school year, which is about one-third of all school days missed (Attendance Works & Healthy Schools Campaign, 2015; Meng, Babey, & Wolstein, 2012). Rates of asthma are especially high among Latino and Black children in low-income urban communities (Myers, Walters, & Perez-Rivera, 2012). Associated with chronic exposure to allergens in the indoor environment from mold, cockroach and rodent infestation, and dust mites, asthma not only can affect educational achievement but also parental work attendance (Acevedo-Garcia & Osypuk, 2008).

"SILENT KILLERS": MOLD AND ASTHMA IN PUBLIC HOUSING

Asthma, lead poisoning, and unhealthy housing conditions was the subject of an EVC documentary produced 25 years after Millie made her film by a student who also lived in East Harlem some 30 blocks north of Millie's apartment. Born and raised in the Polo Ground Towers, a 30-story public housing development with about 4,200 residents, Raelene made a film called *Breathing Easy: Environmental Hazards in Public Housing* (Educational Video Center, 2013) that documents the toxic living conditions of her apartment.

Through their documentary research, Raelene and her crew members learn that the toxic mold she's been living with can lead to permanent respiratory illness, and that children living in New York City public housing are nearly three times as likely to suffer from asthma as those in private family homes. She explains the situation to Ana Parks, a public health advocate with West Harlem Environmental Action: "My ceiling looks ridiculous at home and in my bathroom. The bathroom ceiling looks really bad. It's covered in mold and the paint is falling off and everything. When you take a shower, you got paint falling on you! If you sit on the toilet, you have paint falling on you." In her video diary, she describes her health problems and the black mold, which she calls "silent killers," that has spread in her apartment: "My environment is not a very healthy environment. I have all these issues that are affecting my health. And I don't even notice it. They're like silent killers" (Educational Video Center, 2013).

The video crew documents Parks's inspection of their apartment. Raelene's mother tells her, "I don't know where to turn. I don't know what else to do about this!" Parks notes in her report, "You stated to me before that you took them to court 2 years ago." The camera pans the room revealing the extensive mold covering the bathroom ceiling. Visibly disturbed by the condition she sees, the advocate says, "It is a very bad case of mold. I haven't seen a case of mold like this in some time. So, I'm concerned about you and the children's health, which is very important." Ms. Holmes responds, "Naturally, not only was I always back and forth in the hospital, but my daughter Raelene. We both are asthmatic" (Educational Video Center, 2013).

Studies show that children in high poverty endure four times more hospitalizations for asthma than those living in low poverty, and are three times more

My Ceiling Looks Ridiculous

 View the clip online: www.tcpress.com/goodman-chapter-one#v1.2

I Don't Know Where to Turn

View the clip online: www.tcpress.com/goodman-chapter-one#v1.3

likely to miss 10 or more days of school per year (Attendance Works & Healthy Schools Campaign, 2015). The class disparity is even more stark when considering that children in East Harlem are almost 13 times more likely than children in the more affluent Upper East Side to visit emergency rooms for asthma-related illnesses (Myers, Walters, & Perez-Rivera, 2012).

Raelene's own experiences exemplify the statistically high rates of chronic school absence due to asthma. She recounts the story of her illness and struggles in school:

> I had my first asthma attack when I was 5 years old. It occurred 1 month before I started kindergarten. . . . Whenever I would go to the ER, it was recommended that I stay home for *at least* 3 consecutive days from school following my visit. . . . I was out of school for 1½ weeks every month between kindergarten and 7th grade because of my asthma. It was that bad! . . . I went to school in 8th grade, I just got tons of suspensions. Many of them were in-house suspensions, so I'd be in detention *all day*. In the beginning of 9th grade I started suffering a bit with sleep apnea, which led me to skip school to sleep, then later dropping out. . . . During that period of time I'd stop breathing in my sleep. As time progressed, I would begin to wake up gasping for air, choking or coughing. . . . I discontinued going [to school] for about 2½ years before getting up and attending the high school equivalency program. During that large gap, I stayed home, skipped school, and was constantly annoyed at life. (personal communication, August 13, 2015)

With each successive year of chronic school absences, students such as Raelene are at higher risk of falling further behind their peers in reading and other critical academic skills and developing social–emotional and behavioral problems in school. Students not only struggle to catch up from all the school they miss but must struggle to stay focused and engaged when they are in class. Health and educational problems are compounded for many students with asthma who also suffer from obstructive sleep apnea, such as Raelene, and come to school exhausted after another sleepless night.[1]

Chronically absent students who suffer from illnesses and sleep deprivation and are most in need of health care are also most likely to attend underfunded schools in low-income communities without on-site nurses or health clinics. Too often, they end up falling through bureaucratic cracks in school and dropping out, as Raelene did. But as busy as teachers are, they can make a big difference by carving time out to meet with other teachers to discuss the status of chronically absent students. They can then share their attendance data with one another as well as with social workers, and school nurses to map the patterns of particular students' absences, investigate the underlying causes, and connect the students and their parents to the health resources they need. The health and well-being of each student is then taken up as a schoolwide concern.

Sometimes, educators have misconceptions about frequently absent students, believing that their parents allow their children to miss school because they don't value education. The fact is, low-income parents like Millie's and Raelene's want what's best for their children, just as middle-class parents do. With a deeper understanding of how poor housing conditions can harm both health and academic outcomes for their students, teachers can have a better chance of developing stronger relationships with their students' parents. Rather than coming from a place of judgment or blame, this approach situates the students' interconnected problems of health and schooling within the broader systemic context of environmental justice. Then teachers and school counselors can problem-solve in partnership with parents to collectively advocate for their children's education, health, and well-being. This may involve everything from helping students make a plan to prepare for the next time they get an asthma attack, to inviting a public health specialist on mold and lead poisoning to give a presentation about it in school, to advocating for a health clinic on site in the school.

The infestation of toxic mold in Raelene's apartment was not an isolated problem, nor were her chronic asthma-related absences from school. In fact, mold and other health hazards in the aging buildings run by the New York City Housing Authority (NYCHA) are rampant and systemic, putting thousands of residents and their children at great risk. Serving more than 400,000 residents, NYCHA is the largest landlord in New York City, and the largest public housing authority in North America (New York City Housing Authority [NYCHA], 2017, 2018). For thousands of low-income New Yorkers, public housing is an affordable alternative to living in the more expensive and often deplorable conditions of a privately owned building. As Raelene's mother, who has been a resident for 44 years, explains, "I basically moved into this development when I was

6 and a half years old. . . . It's not that I chose to stay, but financially this is where I had to stay since I was a single parent."

Though it may be an affordable option for both unemployed and working poor people (nearly half of NYCHA families have a working member), public housing is often not a healthy alternative. Investment in NYCHA repairs has reached a crisis. In fact, the problem became so bad that, based on the claim that NYCHA violated the rights of tenants with asthma as part of the Americans with Disabilities Act, the federal courts ordered NYCHA to remedy the mold conditions for residents with asthma. Even that failed to force NYCHA to fix the problem, as *The Daily News* reported in 2014: "Exclusive: Mold still a growing problem for hundreds of NYCHA tenants a year after promise of fixes" (Abramo, Hogan, & Smith, 2014).

NYCHA's mismanagement is not only ethically corrupt but also criminal. As the New York City Department of Investigation (2017) reports, NYCHA has for years not only failed to inspect for lead-based paint in its apartments in violation of federal and local laws; it has also filed paperwork falsely certifying to federal authorities that such inspections had been completed.

Though the mismanagement and criminal negligence of public housing is often in the headlines, far less reported is the chronic federal underfunding for public housing capital and operating costs that has for decades been the underlying cause of this housing crisis. This is both a political problem of federal funding priorities not sufficiently serving low-income urban communities, and a bureaucratic problem of inequitable power relations between the government institution of housing and the low-income residents who live there.

However, the root of both problems is not just about class; it must also be viewed through the lens of race and gender. Hispanic or Black female-headed families make up 93% of all the families in NYCHA public housing (NYCHA, 2015). And Raelene's family is one of them. It strains the imagination to believe that children of middle-class families headed by White males would ever be put at such risk of toxic mold and lead poisoning in housing that fails to comply with mold, smoke, and carbon monoxide detection and other health and safety regulations, with years of falsified claims of lead inspection, and decades of government disinvestment. Or that such children would ever be allowed to attend schools that penalized them for absences and missed work due to environmentally caused illnesses.

Not only has this disinvestment in Black and Brown communities resulted in unsafe and unhealthy public housing, but it has worsened conditions in the surrounding low-income neighborhoods as well, all of which can affect students' psychological health and well-being, and educational achievement. Teachers of students who live in public housing developments know that gang and drug-related violence can create a heightened and ever-present tension that pervades the physical and cultural space of school. As students have expressed in EVC documentaries over the years (Educational Video Center, 1990, 1992, 1997, 2017), they experience great emotional stress and trauma living in public housing projects and neighborhoods with highly concentrated unemployment, crime, and violence. Research shows that living in such high-poverty communities is associated with a loss of learning among Black children equivalent to a full year of school (Reardon & Bischoff, 2011).

As we bring to our classrooms a social understanding of the impact these conditions can have on our students' attendance, participation, and achievement in school, we also need to maintain high standards and expectations for them as individual learners. Holding both perspectives at once means we need to challenge our students to learn about often complex issues drawn from their lived experiences, while also ensuring that those who may be struggling with physical illness or emotional trauma feel safe and supported discussing those issues. Breaking the silence about housing, health, and community issues means challenging the stigma, shame, and self-blame that many of our students may feel regarding their family's impoverished housing conditions, and teaching them to think and act critically to change them. This can include engaging students in environmental justice research projects where they can survey their peers on lead paint, lack of heat, potential allergens and other asthma triggers in their homes, and the frequency of students' health-related absences. Students can also learn to conduct tests for lead in apartments if there are public health environmental justice advocates or medical experts in the community willing to partner with the class and share testing kits. Students can write letters and request meetings with local authorities to present their findings. They can also learn about the origins of public housing in their area and the larger history of residential segregation in this country.

Far from being accidental or the natural result of the free market, the fact that so many of our students now live in such stressful, densely populated, segregated areas with high rates of violence and unemployment is one outcome of a history of government-sponsored race-based policies, a caste system of institutional housing discrimination (Rothstein, 2017) in both private and public housing, dating back to the 1930s.[2] We are still feeling the impact decades later in our schools and classrooms.

Ta-Nehisi Coates (2014) describes how the government's Federal Housing Administration (FHA) policies worked in his powerful essay, "The Case for Reparations":

> From the 1930s through the 1960s, Black people across the country were largely cut out of the legitimate home-mortgage market through means both legal and extralegal. . . . On the [FHA] maps, green areas, rated "A," indicated "in demand" neighborhoods that, as one appraiser put it, lacked "a single foreigner or Negro." These neighborhoods were considered excellent prospects for insurance. Neighborhoods where Black people lived were rated "D" and were usually considered ineligible for FHA backing. . . . Black people were viewed as a contagion. Redlining went beyond FHA-backed loans and spread to the entire mortgage industry, which was already rife with racism. . . . As late as 1950, the National Association of Real Estate Boards' code of ethics warned that "a Realtor should never be instrumental in introducing into a neighborhood . . . any race or nationality, or any individuals whose presence will clearly be detrimental to property values."

As government "urban renewal" policies and highway construction were implemented that cleared out poor Black neighborhoods, public housing projects were typically built to house as many families as possible that had been displaced on the cleared land within or near existing Black neighborhoods (Massey, 2008; Massey & Denton, 1993; Schwartz, 2010). The very *design* of public housing—its high density, extreme segregation, and spatial isolation—increased and concentrated rates of unemployment, crime, violence, and poverty, creating a set of mutually reinforcing spirals of decline for poor urban communities of color. By 1970, public housing projects in most large cities had become what Douglas Massey and Nancy Denton (1993) called "black reservations, highly segregated from the rest of society" (p. 57). The segregation of Blacks and Latinos has continued in the decades since; however, the concentration of people living in severely impoverished neighborhoods has greatly increased, with the number of people nearly doubling between 2000 and 2015 (Jargowsky, 2015).[3] This is the legacy that has been handed down to our students, which weighs so heavily on them as they struggle to succeed in our classes.

Teaching students about this history helps them understand the discriminatory housing policies and practices that created conditions of poverty and segregation in public housing and elsewhere in their communities while also learning about those who fought to resist them. To learn more about their local situation, they can conduct oral history interviews with family members and local residents. They can also interview mortgage brokers, urban studies professors, and housing advocates and present their class findings to the local community or town board. In many cases, these projects require context and scaffolding of vocabulary and concepts such as *mortgage, restrictive covenants, redlining,* and *reverse redlining* to explain some of the more complex legal and financial issues involved.

"WHERE ARE WE GOING TO WIND UP?":
THE TRAUMA OF FORECLOSURE

Just as poor conditions within the home can cause students' physical and emotional health and academic achievement to decline, so can *not having* a home. One in every 10 New York City students—more than 111,500 students—was homeless at some point in the 2016–2017 school year. Placed in transitional housing, doubling up with friends or family, or moving from one temporary living situation to another, these students end up changing schools and missing school more often than their nonhomeless peers. A third of homeless students miss up to 30 days of school. And like students with chronic asthma and other illnesses, frequent absences and disrupted schooling causes homeless students' grades to suffer (Harris, 2017). Homelessness can also negatively impact students' physical and mental health putting them at "a much greater risk of illness, injury, malnourishment, abuse, neglect, violence, separation from family, and delays in cognitive and language development than housed children" (Crowley, 2003, p. 23).

Housing foreclosure is a major cause of homelessness and was especially common during the Great Recession of 2008. The process is traumatic for both the students and their families. Students' attendance and grades often suffer as well when their families are experiencing severe financial stress in the home. But the underlying political and institutional practices that are widening both the wealth gap and the achievement gap—including reverse redlining and predatory lending—are often hidden from view.

When millions of families across the country lost their homes to mortgage foreclosure, a disproportionately high percentage of New York City students living in those homes facing foreclosure were Black.[4] They were concentrated within a small number of schools, mostly located in north-central Brooklyn and southeastern Queens. At the time, the Mortgage Bankers Association estimated that one child in every classroom in America was at risk of losing his or her home because parents were unable to pay their mortgage (Federal Deposit Insurance Corporation, n.d.).

Annie was one of those students. She and her fellow EVC video students made their documentary, *Mortgage Mayhem: Living Inside Fraud* (Educational Video Center, 2011), about Annie's family's struggle with foreclosure in Queens, and the housing crisis that was impacting families and communities across the country in 2010. Annie narrates the opening of the film: "When we think of this country, we think of the American Dream. The idea of buying a house and raising your children. But sometimes having a house can cost you a place to live." The camera follows her from her front stoop into her kitchen, where she introduces her parents. Her mother works as an office manager, and her father has been on Social Security disability for 25 years due to chronic back pain. She goes on to describe her living situation:

> While my family was going through foreclosure, I didn't know the extent of how bad things were. All I knew is that we didn't have the extra money for the little things. And in order to help get money, we would have to move from my upstairs apartment where I lived my whole life to my grandma's downstairs apartment. That way, we could gain an income from tenants.

Annie comes from a White working-class family that had been sold a subprime mortgage they couldn't afford. Over dinner, her mother shares her fears about their finances:

> When you're facing foreclosure it's really, really stressful. I feel really responsible for what happened. And everyday you're thinking about how am I going to be able to pay the bills. Pay the mortgage. What if I can't do it? Where are we going to wind up? If I had to move, where would I go? The rents are almost as high as what a mortgage could be. (Educational Video Center, 2011)

Annie had been repeatedly absent from school and was suffering from migraine headaches, depression, and emotional distress. Studies have shown that

I Didn't Know the Extent of How Bad Things Were

 View the clip online: www.tcpress.com/goodman-chapter-one#v1.4

family financial troubles and the experience of housing foreclosure can negatively affect students' social relationships and behavioral development, physical and mental health, and academic performance through increased school change and instability (Pribesh & Downey, 1999). Children in foreclosed homes must move to poorer neighborhoods and often poorer resourced schools, changing teachers and curricula, and having their friends and social networks disrupted.They are more likely to repeat grades, not receive special education, and perform less well on standardized tests than stable students. In some poor schools the mobility rate can be as high as 70%, meaning only 30% of the students enrolled began and ended the school year at the same school (Crowley, 2003).

There can be little doubt that the financial and social–emotional stress and continual upheaval and mobility for children living through foreclosure are disruptive to their social relationships, emotional well-being, and academic achievement (Pettit, 2004; Pettit & Comey, 2012; Pribesh & Downey, 1999; Scanlon & Devine, 2001). As much as parents may try to protect their children from adult problems, children and youth still do suffer when their families must endure frequent unplanned or unwanted moves, doubling up in apartments, family separation, and homelessness, whether caused by eviction or foreclosure due to soaring home and rental prices, divorce, sudden parental unemployment, or illness (Been, Ellen, Schwartz, Stiefel, & Weinstein, 2010; Crowley, 2003; McKoy & Vincent, 2008). The impact of foreclosure is often traumatic and long lasting (Bowdler, Quercia, & Smith, 2010).

We need to be mindful of how stressful and traumatic these conditions are for students whose families are experiencing foreclosure or living in shelters and other transitional housing. We also need to be sensitive to students who may be stigmatized for their condition by peers and others, and may internalize the stigma and sense of shame. Sharing stories about homeless and transient families will help them know they are not alone, provide opportunities to counter negative stereotypes, and help the rest of the students become more empathetic and understanding. Researching the problem further, students may interview financial journalists or housing advocates to learn more about foreclosure, or talk with residents of shelters to hear their stories.

"AS IF THEY'RE PASSING AWAY": GENTRIFICATION

The continual relocation of individual children and their families is part of the larger history of housing for low-income people of color in this country since the 1930s, as noted above. This has led to a process of what Mindy Fullilove (2013) calls the "serial displacement" of communities. *Serial displacement* is "the repeated dispersal of low-income communities of color by environmental processes such as violence, segregation, redlining, urban renewal, planned shrinkages, gentrification, and the foreclosure crisis . . . forcing communities to involuntarily move out and start over" (Fullilove, as quoted in Stern, 2013, p. 8).

The process of gentrification, the replacement of low-income with more affluent residents, has been a central driver of this displacement and the trauma that results from it. As discussed with high student mobility due to housing foreclosure, increased displacement, changes in schools, and disruption of social ties due to gentrification can also hinder student achievement.

Gentrification also increases income segregation in housing, which has doubled overall since the 1970s. According to Reardon and Bischoff (2011):

> Higher-income neighborhoods often have more green space, better-funded schools, better social services, and more of any number of other amenities that affect quality of life. Income segregation creates disparities in these public goods and . . . limits opportunities of low-income children for upward social and economic mobility and reinforces the reproduction of inequality over time and across generations. (pp. 5–6)

Efrain and Ricardo, two other EVC students whose families, like Millie's, also came from Puerto Rico, tell their stories of gentrification. They both attended New York City transfer schools for students struggling to graduate high school, but Ricardo lives in the Bronx and Efrain lives in Brooklyn. Their documentary, *As the Sun Comes Up, the Bricks Fall Down* (Educational Video Center, 2010a), opens with stop motion animated pencil drawings set to a salsa beat showing Efrain's Brooklyn neighborhood as they experience it—with bodegas, a church, basketball court, and Puerto Rican flag on a wall. It changes as the mother playing with a baby on the stoop disappears, a moving van takes away their things, and Starbucks and other chain stores move in.

Ricardo lives in the Bronx and tells the story of how the new Yankee Stadium is displacing his family and friends—his social and emotional ecosystem:

> I see a lot of people move, a lot of people who was dearly close to me that I basically grew up with, who can no longer afford the rental who are slowly moving out. So I'm just losing everybody who used to be family to me.

They're Passing Away

 View the clip online: www.tcpress.com/goodman-chapter-one#v1.5

So, it's like, it's like almost as if, to me, I see it as if they're passing away. (Educational Video Center, 2010a)

In addition to gaming the system by collecting rent and not investing in desperately needed repairs, landlord neglect can also be understood as a tactic of gentrification. Efrain revisits the Brooklyn apartment building where he grew up, and finds that it has been renovated since he left. He explains how landlord neglect, harassment, and increases in rent forced his family out of that neighborhood when it was being gentrified:

> I lived there for 15 years. And I had to move out because the conditions in my apartment were unlivable. We often had roaches, water bugs, and mice coming out of the holes in floors and walls. But the last straw was the carbon monoxide. Every winter when the heaters were on, we had to open up all the windows just to prevent carbon monoxide poisoning. This went on for three winters, despite our complaints. . . . When we finally decided to move out, we discovered that it was way too expensive to stay in Carroll Gardens, or to move into similar neighborhoods. (Educational Video Center, 2010a)

His family then was forced to relocate to East New York, which, as he describes it, is a neighborhood "at the end of Brooklyn" with drugs, violence, and prostitution. As he explains, "This is where I live, but this is not my neighborhood." In 2010, *New York Magazine* ranked Carroll Gardens, the first subway stop in Brooklyn, as one of the top 10 most livable neighborhoods in Brooklyn. East New York is the last stop on the train, and was not ranked in *New York Magazine* (Educational Video Center, 2010a).

Had to Move Out

 View the clip online: www.tcpress.com/goodman-chapter-one#v1.6

Tenants rights advocates explained to Efrain and the crew that the landlord's restriction of services in Efrain's family's Carroll Gardens apartment was effectively a form of harassment. It forced his family to leave for a more impoverished and violent community in East New York, and enabled the landlord to increase the rent of their old apartment.

The experience of gentrification has become so common and normalized in New York City and in communities across the country that it is a phenomenon almost beyond questioning. It is often characterized as bringing about urban regeneration with reduced crime and so creating a common good for the community. The building of Yankee Stadium is an example of this. Gentrification has been framed as being a natural process, driven by free-market forces, not by political and economic decisions, government partnerships, and tax incentives that privilege real estate developers over the community they are "developing," and profits over people (Fullilove & Wallace, 2011; Maeckelbergh, 2012).

Efrain and Ricardo, and countless students much like them, have been uprooted and moved out of neighborhoods that their families could no longer afford, and as a result experienced emotional loss and damage to their social relationships. Being sensitive to students' sense of dislocation and loss, we need to create openings in our classes to talk about the impact of gentrification in their students' families and communities. Naming the problem is an important first step in validating students' experiences and assuring them they are not alone.

Reading and responding to stories and poems about housing issues can motivate student discussion, research, and creative writing on this theme. For example, students can read Langston Hughes's powerful protest poem "The Ballad of the Landlord," which he wrote when evictions of African American tenants were common in Harlem in the 1930s. Then they can read, watch, and discuss Ricardo's spoken word performance on gentrification at the end of his documentary (see lyrics below).

As the Sun Comes Up, The Bricks Fall Down (Lyrics for Spoken Word)
By Ricardo "Luss" Nigagliani

As the sun comes up, and the bricks fall down,
I look up at somethin' that used to be my town.
I just sit back and ask myself, how did it get this way?
This beautiful place, that is now just simply a shadow of something it used to be.
You see, 'cause what used to be was a community full of happy people.
Until they came in and took everything.
And made it more comfortable for their people.
So far from me, took advantage it should be a sequel.
But who's to blame for that?
When they come around and change my community.
Just 'cause we're predominantly Latino and Black.
Separating the lies from the facts.
How we supposed to react?
When the landlords are corrupted.
Building equals destruction, developers are constructed.
Please take it all back.
And our rents are getting higher, condos on the fliers.
My people are getting tired. Please take it all back.
They speak their minds. Most are afraid.
Gentrification was happening 20 years ago.
So why's it still happenin' today?
Cops got us on the frame.
Because they feel it's an obligation to protect those who put us all under our grave,
Traded over like slaves.
'Cause we can't even afford half of what we living in,
So how you expect us to maintain?
This is far from a positive change.
'Cause the community is going through a so-called improvement,
Unfortunately, you're not part of the movement.
And it hurts my soul!
'Cause even though I don't want to, I know one day I must let go. Go.
'Cause this is all different.
It used to be more than a place I used to call home.
It was a family, but right now it's all business.
Lost one, just to give it I paint the pictures of business.
It was all worth it, the can was spilling. Deception.
We got cameras on every corner now, so we feel rejection.
We say wait a minute, this must be some type of misconception.
But they say, there's no mistake about this once we start playing the funerals and
     the receptions.

Well your honor, I have an objection!

Why don't you put yourself in our position?

Think about that single mother who was forced out of her home.

And now lives in a shelter trying to keep warm.

Think about the teenagers with no place to go.

With so much talent they never have a chance to show.

So back on top of them cars, corners, and the stoop they go.

Think about the parks that are being knocked down and turned into stadiums.

Think about so little for the public housing, but so many condominiums.

Think about that homeless person that once had a place to live, and now lives in
 the street,

No food to eat,

Rides the subway to sleep.

So many opportunities for the rich, but not enough for the poor.

You need help fixing a disease, then our voice could be the cure.

Will we finally have peace, or should we take you to war?

They yell, "Order in the court!"

Hold up, you listen while I report.

I have my people walking with me,

I have their support.

'Cause it ain't hard to tell.

We used to be living in a place similar to Heaven, but now we're living in hell.

So go ahead, your honor. Handcuff the community.

Put us in jail.

And we'll continue to tell gentrification that we're not for sale!

As the Sun Comes Up

▶ *View the clip online*: www.tcpress.com/goodman-chapter-one#v1.7

Facilitating community action projects can give students a greater sense of empowerment and control in their lives. Such projects might include conducting oral histories with family members, interviewing local residents and shopkeepers, mapping changing patterns of affordable housing and resident income levels in the community, and writing letters to local authorities with their findings. Students can also invite guest speakers or interview local or regional housing rights organizations to learn from the research they have gathered and see that fighting for decent housing and resisting the displacement of low-income communities is possible.

It is worth noting that when students were given opportunities to access their family and community "funds of knowledge," when they opened up their homes for their class documentary projects, not only did their peers and EVC teachers get to know them better, but their parents developed a respect for and trust in the crew and the project they were creating. A strong and long-lasting relationship developed between the EVC staff, the students, and their parents, rooted not only in the problems they struggled with but also in their strength to challenge and overcome them.

Teachers can also develop closer relationships with their students and parents when they facilitate and publicly present class projects (whether or not they involve video) on community issues of importance to their students and their families. Through these public presentations, students can then feel valued for their success in school as well as for the art, research, and new knowledge they are contributing to their community. The fact that these projects are not just about a grade, but also are about improving conditions in the students' community, is a powerful idea for both students and parents alike.

"WE HAVE A PETITION": SPEAKING OUT AND TAKING ACTION

In each EVC project discussed in this chapter, the students not only documented their conditions of health and housing, connecting their own and their family's individual problems to the structures and systems that shape them, but also found ways to take action to address those problems. As young witnesses to the health and housing crisis in low-income communities, their journalistic and artistic expression not only amplified their voices, but gave them opportunities for collective support, intergenerational solidarity, and healing.

The youth who worked on the gentrification documentary partnered with housing rights activists who unpacked its multilayered economic and historical context, and also provided models for what it means to be active in the community. Raelene and her mother joined a class action suit against NYCHA, claiming their negligence in eradicating mold in their apartments violated the Americans with Disabilities Act by discriminating against people with asthma. They continue to work as housing and welfare reform organizers, screening their film and speaking out about their story to city council members and NYCHA officials as well as at environmental justice housing conferences. Annie and her classmates uncovered a scam in their community, one of many fraudulent companies that was targeting low-income residents, who had already been victimized by predatory lending.

Annie and the crew handed out leaflets on the streets of Jamaica, Queens, warning residents about these scams and filed a complaint about the company with the Better Business Bureau.

Returning once more to Millie's story, *2371 Second Avenue: An East Harlem Story* (Educational Video Center, 1986), her classmates documented her efforts to organize her neighbors to petition the landlord. She narrates:

> I went door to door getting my neighbors to sign a petition which we would then present to the landlord. . . . It was hard to track down the landlord Simon Rubinov, since he worked out of an office that sells air conditioners, but we went in anyway.

With the youth camera crew in tow, she led the march on the landlord's office to make their demands heard. She became a spokesperson,[5] advocating not just for her own family, but also for her neighbors in the building who had difficulty speaking English.

Entering the landlord's office, Millie says, "We would like to speak to Simon." Taken by surprise, the woman in the office asks, "What is it about?" And Millie responds:

> We have a petition from some of the tenants and it states: "That the tenants of 2371 Second Avenue have been living in rat-infested apartments without hot water, and demand that these and other 95 violations be corrected immediately. If there is nothing done to change these conditions, we will withhold the rent starting October the 1st." (Educational Video Center, 1986)

We Have a Petition

 View the clip online: www.tcpress.com/goodman-chapter-one#v1.8

Unfortunately, there is no resolution. The landlord never appears, and they are all thrown out of the office. However, the power of the film and of Millie, a student/documentary filmmaker/youth activist with the courage to literally speak truth to power, continues to resonate with audiences 3 decades later with screenings in schools and in national and international museum exhibitions.[6]

Millie, Raelene, Annie, Ricardo, and Efrain's stories shine a spotlight on their struggles with poor health and housing conditions, and on the systemic constraints and community strengths that countless other students living in marginalized communities in New York City, as well as across the country, also have. We see what it can mean for our students and their families to inherit the bitter legacy of discriminatory housing policies that perpetuate transient, segregated, impoverished, and toxic conditions in the home, and poor academic performance in school. Whether they suffer from rat bites, asthma, hypertension, depression, anxiety, or trauma, it is clear that our students' pain and dislocation and poor performance on standardized tests in school is a result of oppressive systems and not a lack of intelligence or grit on their part.

Significantly, these students chose not to acquiesce, lose hope, stay silent, or be shamed into accepting those conditions as fixed or given. Through their collective inquiries, they found the courage to question, document, speak up, and talk back to more powerful individuals and institutions of domination. Opening up their homes and neighborhoods to the camera, they bore witness to their family's unhealthy, stressful, and often traumatic conditions, and rendered stories of community strength, struggle, and action.

As educators, we are asked every day to teach through and around our students' pain and trauma. And this teaching must be done amid growing lists of requirements and demands on our time, and only so many hours in the school day to meet them. However, we can't allow ourselves to lose focus on what matters most—our students, and their health and well-being. We can use these stories in our classes with the context provided, as powerful springboards to move students to critically discuss, research, and act on these problems and counter the stigma of students experiencing them. Just as seeds of cultural resistance and activism were planted in the EVC filmmakers, when students in other classes break the silence and begin telling their own stories about health and housing, they too will make their voices heard for change and healing in their communities.

CHAPTER 2

"They Put Us Down When We Already Down"

Police and Juvenile Justice

By the fall of 2015, there had been a wave of police murders of unarmed Black youth, young men, and boys: Eric Garner choked on a sidewalk in July 2014; Michael Brown shot in the street in August; Tamir Rice shot in a playground in November 2014; Freddie Gray dead from injuries in a van, and Walter Scott shot in a park, both in April 2015. Shocking videos had been recorded of some of their deaths, and they had gone viral. Black Lives Matter became the rallying cry and a protest movement. Angry and shaken to the core by these deaths, high school students at EVC feared that they could be next.

They had good reason to fear for their lives. According to a ProPublica analysis of police deaths between 2010 and 2012, Black teenage boys were a staggering 21 times more likely to be killed by police than their White peers (Gabrielson, Grochowski Jones, & Sagara, 2014). Like students of color across the country, the EVC video crew members had come to feel that they, too, were at constant risk of attack by police, fearing that their Black or Brown skin gives law enforcement enough of a probable cause to be stopped and targeted for violence. Repeatedly stopped and questioned in their neighborhoods because they're told they "fit the description" of a criminal suspect, they bring an anxiety and fear of authority with them into their school day. Students of color are targeted for discipline in school as well, and are much more likely to be suspended and arrested than their White peers (New York City School-Justice Partnership Task Force, 2013). A state of vigilance, in some cases hypervigilance, is the new normal for many children and youth in our schools.

This disturbing reality not only raises questions of students' civil liberties, but of their human rights. Just how well our students survive, and even thrive, in our schools and communities depends largely on how strongly we as principals, teachers, school counselors, and social workers are committed to standing with our students in the face of this harsh reality. This includes having a critical understanding of how the school-to-prison pipeline works to discipline and remove students of color from within too many of our schools, and of the very real existential threat our students face on a daily basis outside of our schools. Even though White educators among us may enjoy the privilege of not being under constant surveillance and risk of violence by police in the streets and safety officers in their school, we need to develop an empathy and heightened awareness of how the disproportionate use of punitive power over our students marginalizes them by race, class, gender, and zip code. We then need to apply this awareness and understanding to create culturally sustaining classes and schools where our students can feel safe, respected, included, and nurtured.

Interweaving EVC student documentary stories to illuminate these issues, this chapter will explore further how low-income students of color have been disproportionately criminalized and had their academic and life opportunities diminished through a history of mass incarceration and the overpolicing in their schools and communities. In *Policing the Times: Youth Perspectives on Police Brutality* (Educational Video Center, 2015b), Rob describes the abuse he has experienced from police in his community and safety officers in his school. In *Growing Apart: The Politics of Family Separation* (Educational Video Center, 2015a), Scarlett tells of her confusion from growing up without her father and not knowing that he was incarcerated since she was an infant. In *Life Under Suspicion: Youth Perspectives on the NYPD's Stop and Frisk Policy* (Educational Video Center, 2012), Brandon shares his experiences being repeatedly stopped and frisked by the police. In *Another Part of Me: Youth Views on Drugs and Incarceration in Our Community* (Educational Video Center, 2009), Katrena shares her harrowing experiences incarcerated as a teenager in Rikers Island.

As degrading and dehumanizing as treatment at the hands of police and the carceral system can be for students, with transformative teaching, we can create opportunities for student hope and self-empowerment. In some schools, this may involve forming restorative justice (RJ) practices to improve school culture, reduce school suspensions, and disrupt the pipeline. Other schools may engage students in classroom action research projects where they analyze the history and causes of these urgent problems, create dialogue with the police, and take action to make a positive change in their schools and communities.

"HE STARTS GRABBING ME": STUDENT PERSPECTIVES ON POLICING IN AND OUT OF SCHOOLS

After all the stories that appeared in the news in 2015, it wasn't a surprise that the EVC students decided that semester to make their documentary an inquiry into police brutality. To start their research, they recorded their conversations about their own encounters with police, how they always felt watched and in constant risk any place, any time of being stopped—harassed, humiliated, abused, and possibly worse. Housing police monitor them through hallway cameras as they leave their public housing apartment buildings on the way to school in the morning. Transit police dressed in civilian sweatshirts lurk around corners watching as they go through the subway turnstiles. The street police cruise by as they walk down the block or stop in to get breakfast in the corner bodega. And officers in vans greet them as they wait in line outside the school, regardless of the weather, ensuring that they pass through the metal detectors. After school, street police watch them hanging out in the park. Store security guards watch them as they shop and socialize with friends in the mall on weekends. As Michelle Alexander (2012) describes it, this regime of surveillance and overpolicing of urban youth creates "a perpetual class of people labeled criminals" (p. 236).

These were not easy conversations to have. Our staff first worked to create a safe space where there was sense of trust and mutual respect among the group members. Only then could the students open up about their often painful memories of personal encounters with the police. Only then could these traumatic emotional stumbling blocks be turned into stepping-stones for their project of documentary storytelling, inquiry, and action.

When the students began telling stories of their encounters with police, they also talked about how the harassment and abuse didn't stop outside the schoolhouse door. Some students told stories about the abuse they suffered in school at the hands of school resource officers (SROs), or School Safety Agents, as they're called in New York City. Watching the EVC documentary *To Serve and Protect?*, made in 1991, the students learned that there is a long history of police violence in communities of color. They decided to intercut archival footage from that film with a contemporary interview with their EVC classmate, Rob, in their documentary *Policing the Times: Youth Perspectives on Police Brutality* (Educational Video Center, 2015b).

The dark, grainy video from 1991 begins with Michael, a young man, telling a story that is both contemporary and familiar to the students while also out of time, coming from the Harlem streets of their parents' childhood. When the shot later pulls out, you can see his mother is standing next to him.

> We were coming from a store . . . me and three other friends, came through, gettin' ready to leave all of us about to disperse to go home when we were pulled over. Asked why we were there. We were asked for ID, which one of my friends did not have. So I explained to the officer that we was coming to sit back on my steps. . . . I showed him my ID and explained to him this is a private house, I live here. He threw my ID back in my face and proceeded to curse some more at me. Asked me do I have a fucking problem. To where he told me I had 2 seconds to get my Black ass in the house.

The 2015 video starts with Rob talking outside, leaning on a railing overlooking the East River in Manhattan. As he tells his story, it cuts to a shot of him walking and then sitting in a school lunchroom. "I remember being at FDA [Frederick Douglass Academy]. I came in the lunchroom and I'm waiting for my friend. And the School Safety Agent is like, 'You can't wait in here.' So he's—he starts counting down from 10."

Back to Michael. "And he counted, 'One, two.' And he proceeded to hit me."

And then back to Rob again. "He gets down to five. And he's like, 'Four, three.' And he's like, 'One.' And he starts grabbing me up. And I have like, long hair. So my Afro was out. And he's like grabbing my book bag and my hair at the same time. So he's like pulling me. And he starts pushing me, he pushes me through the staircase door" (Educational Video Center, 2015b).

We Were Coming from the Store

(▶) *View the clip online*: www.tcpress.com/goodman-chapter-two#v2.1

In just those one and a half minutes of video, they managed to capture some of the key problems in the policing crisis. First, perhaps an obvious but important point to underscore, both are young men of color bearing witness to the blatant abuse of state power used against them. They are the demographic most heavily overrepresented as victims of abuse in all stages of the juvenile justice system. Second, they juxtapose the capricious police violence that is done to students in schools with violence done to community members out on the streets, all part of an interconnected system of policing. Third, neither of the young men was really breaking a rule, or law. And that is the point. In both cases, they were criminalized and assaulted for sitting where they were—on steps in front of their house or in a lunchroom in their school—and more fundamentally, for being *who* they were.

These video clips bridge a span of nearly 25 years between when the two stories were recorded. These years are essential to understanding the history of urban policing and juvenile justice that make up the world our students have inherited. They include the "broken windows" and tough-on-crime NYPD tactics in the early 1990s with its roots in the War on Drugs, which spread into the schools as zero-tolerance policies and in the streets as stop-and-frisk.

Over decades and generations, these policies have led to the mass incarceration and fragmentation of communities and the breakup of families. Students are directly affected when they themselves are caught up in the justice system, as well as when they grow up with incarcerated parents and guardians. Those who have suffered trauma from juvenile detention or growing up in broken families with incarcerated parents have had to struggle that much harder to relate positively to teachers and other adult authority figures and focus on the daily demands of school. In some cases, it's important to know that an angry student pushing back against a teacher's authority is also fighting with painful memories of encounters with authorities in the justice system.

"IT'S A MEMORABLE MOMENT": STOP-AND-FRISK POLICING OF STUDENTS IN THE COMMUNITY

The NYPD's stop-and-frisk policy became controversial and was a big story in the news leading up to the city's mayoral election of 2013, and again in the presidential election of 2016. The policy was criticized for the disproportionate targeting of young men of color on the streets. What was less discussed was the negative impact it had on students in school, who suffered the cumulative effect of near-daily stops and harassment by police.

In 2012 another group of EVC students produced a film about this problem, which they called *Life Under Suspicion: Youth Perspectives on the NYPD's Stop and Frisk Policy* (Educational Video Center, 2012). The NYPD's stated goal for what was called the stop-question-and-frisk program was to take guns off the streets. It was mostly used, however, to crack down on low-level crimes such as loitering, public urination, and graffiti. Through their research, the students found that this policy resulted in nearly 700,000 street stops in 2011. Over half of those stopped on the streets were 14-to-24-year-olds, which mostly includes students in middle school, high school, or college. Nearly 90% were African Americans and Latinos, and were innocent of any wrongdoing. As New York Civil Liberties Union executive director Donna Lieberman told the students, "If the goal is getting guns off the street, then a success rate of 0.15 percent is an abysmal failure" (Educational Video Center, 2012).

The students wondered whether the program actually had another goal: to spread a climate of fear and abuse that criminalizes poor young Black and Brown men in the community. If that was the case, then their documentary showed that it has been a great success.

This sense of being criminalized impacts our students in multiple dimensions: Legally, when they are given summonses or arrested, they are detained, fingerprinted, filed, and sorted by the justice system. Psychologically, when they are surveilled, tracked, and subject to repeated interrogations in public spaces, they are demeaned, demoralized, and dehumanized. They begin to internalize a heightened sense of stress and a diminished sense of self-worth. Academically, when their attendance and grades suffer and their emotional feelings of anxiety and self-doubt continue unabated, as school resource officers, metal detectors, and zero-tolerance policies reproduce within schools the culture of street policing.

The EVC crew brought their cameras to film a discussion at the Umoja Network for Young Men, an initiative designed to support Black and Latino middle and high school male students that was founded by Erik Nolan at Forsyth Street Satellite Academy and inspired by the late Sarah Blos, who was director there. Here's what Brandon, one of the high school students in Umoja, had to say about it in *Life Under Suspicion*:

They just stop us out of nowhere. We could be walking as a group, and they stop us out of nowhere. And we be like, you know, "What happened? What we did?" "Oh, we heard some suspicious thing in the neighborhood." And it'll be outta nowhere. We didn't even know what the problem was. But we all go down. We all get frisked. No matter what. If you have a bag of weed. And we have something small and minor that we could all get tickets for. And we all go down. And we all gotta go through the process. And it's like, it's a memorable moment for us. We remember that the most, because like, they put, they put us down. When we already down. We not even doing nothing. (Educational Video Center, 2012)

These experiences were not only humiliating and time-consuming for students, but they also negatively impacted their school performance. Students described how these negative encounters with police caused them to miss school to answer a summons in court for a minor infraction and fall behind in their classes. Others described missing weeks of school because they were in jail and had no one who could afford to bail them out.

The cumulative effect of repeated stops by police can be demoralizing if not traumatic for students, causing them to become bitter, alienated, and distrustful of teachers and other authorities. This, of course, makes it difficult for teachers and school leaders who are working to create a more positive school culture. As Nolan put it in *Life Under Suspicion*, "It creates an atmosphere of hostility that causes some type of breach in trust. As one student told me, 'I'm on my way to school. Cops stop me. Then when I come here, you're on my case about following rules,

We All Get Frisked

▶ *View the clip online*: www.tcpress.com/goodman-chapter-two#v2.2

and why I'm late.' So whatever goes on before they get into the building, they bring in and they project it onto us" (Educational Video Center, 2012).

Adopted by police departments across the country, the same kind of tactics target students and poor communities of color for low-level infractions, such as driving with a broken car taillight, possession of small amounts of marijuana, or selling "loosies" (individual cigarettes). Though abuses continue, New York City has been working to reform its stop-and-frisk program and numbers of police stops have declined since the high of 2011. Although the U.S. Justice Department under President Obama has investigated and pushed reforms of police departments in nearly two dozen cities, those reforms have been rolled back by the Trump administration. Without oversight or accountability, these departments are unrestrained to continue these deeply disturbing zero-tolerance policing policies that diminish the future life chances of students in these communities and in the schools they attend there.

"ALL MY YOUTH WAS LOCKED UP IN PRISON": JUVENILE INCARCERATION AND THE WAR ON DRUGS

The struggles that students have when they are caught up in the juvenile justice system through stop-and-frisk and zero-tolerance policies can be traced to the decades-long War on Drugs and the mass incarceration of African Americans and Latinos it produced. It has had devastating consequences for the individuals sent to prison, as well as for the families that they left behind on the outside—consequences that can be felt for generations. The end result in almost all cases was strained or entirely broken family relations, with decreased academic performance and damaged life chances for children and youth.

More than half of children with incarcerated parents have had school problems such as poor grades and instances of aggression. Some exhibit hypervigilance, such as the case of the student who avoided school because he feared the security guard. Often internalizing their emotional pain due to a lack of social support for their grief, students with incarcerated parents often avoid others, spend time alone in school, and have been found to become unresponsive when feeling upset and called on by their teachers to talk. Many had troubled relationships with peers and few if any caring adults in their life who could help them cope with their stress and trauma (Bocknek, Sanderson, & Britner, 2009).

While the *Policing the Times* (Educational Video Center, 2015b) student film crew discovered that zero-tolerance policing dates to at least the 1990s, an earlier EVC team that produced the documentary *Another Part of Me* (Educational Video Center, 2009) about mass incarceration found that its roots can be traced further back to the 1970s. That was when President Nixon launched the War on Drugs, effectively abandoning the federal government's War on Poverty of the 1960s, and replacing it with a permanent campaign of law and order.[1] This War on Drugs was greatly expanded under President Reagan in the 1980s and President Clinton in the 1990s.[2]

Over the years, getting "tough on crime" was politically popular for politicians as social and economic conditions deteriorated in inner-city communities.

Black and Brown students suffered not only as children of the unemployed in abandoned communities, but also as targets of this war when they turned to drugs as users and dealers (Alexander, 2012).

Treating the drug problem as a crime instead of an unemployment and public health crisis, the War on Drugs and "tough on crime" Rockefeller drug laws in New York State ruined hundreds of thousands of lives of young people living in depressed urban communities who were incarcerated for working in the underground drug economy. In *Another Part of Me: Youth Views on Drugs and Incarceration in Our Community* (Educational Video Center, 2009), Katrena tells her story of getting caught up in the world of drug dealing as a young teenager:

> I'd say I started selling drugs when I was 13, 14 years old. I really was unaware that I was selling drugs. I just thought I was just watching the mailbox and giving out little brown bags. . . . 'Cause that was the "in" crowd. that's what they was doing. Whatever they was doing, that's what I wanted to do. I wanted to be part of that gleam, that hustle. I wanted to be a part of that. I wanted to be—I wanted that sense of feeling of belonging. . . . I did a great substantial time of my life in prison. All my youth was locked up in prison. I was convicted under the Rockefeller Law.

Ongoing communication and outreach with students and their families is critically important. When youth in underresourced communities become disconnected from their homes and schools, they, like Katrena, can more easily become attracted by the promise of easy money and fall into the underground drug economy and into the justice system. The War on Drugs brought about a staggering 1000% increase in the number of people incarcerated for drug offenses, from 41,000 in 1982 to nearly 470,000 in 2015 (The Sentencing Project, 2017).[3]

My Youth Was Locked Up

▶ *View the clip online*: www.tcpress.com/goodman-chapter-two#v2.3

The human toll of the War on Drugs can most certainly be counted in the hundreds of thousands of incarcerated nonviolent drug offenders. However, the collateral damage of this assault on poor communities spreads even further. Even when they are not themselves incarcerated, students are still vulnerable to at least three levels of punishment by this assault. First, they are punished emotionally by the loss of friends, parents, and other relatives who are incarcerated. Second, they are punished economically when public funds desperately needed for more equitable schools, health clinics, job training, and other community youth services are siphoned off to pay for more police, school security technologies and resource officers, and prisons. Third, they are punished academically when the social and emotional trauma from the loss of resources, friends, and parental relations slows or derails their progress in school.

Although government is increasingly abandoning poor neighborhoods and affordable housing to market forces and deepening poverty in those communities as a result, there is no shortage of funds for maintaining order and warehousing poor Black and Brown people in prison (Simon, 2007; Vitale, 2017). Public schools are forced to operate in a permanent state of scarcity as teachers and counselors educate and care for marginalized students of color who are struggling to overcome the odds and succeed.

"HE NEVER GOT TO MEET ME": GROWING UP WITH INCARCERATED PARENTS

One clear measure of the direct impact that the War on Drugs has had on schools is the estimated 1.5–2 million minor children with parents in prison, approximately double the estimates from 1991. Behind these statistics are the actual students in classrooms across the country who are struggling to stay focused on learning, while coping with the loss and separation from their parents behind bars. The disrupted family and stigma that students experience contributes to a range of psychological problems, including feelings of guilt, rage, sadness, depression, and anxiety; disrupted and insecure attachment patterns; chronic sleeplessness; difficulties concentrating; and symptoms consistent with posttraumatic stress disorder. The academic impact of these psychological problems is well documented. Students with incarcerated parents, both mothers and fathers, are more likely than their peers to be absent from school, fail classes, get suspended, and fail to graduate (Bocknek et al., 2009; Eddy & Reid, 2003).

Taking a deeper look at the interconnected issues related to children of incarcerated parents, there is a range of factors that contribute to these behaviors. Incarceration can lead to increased family instability, including changes in living arrangements, strained marriages, and separation of siblings from one another. Whether they have suffered the loss of a sole caregiver, or an already absentee parent, children will experience a dramatic disruption in their daily lives.

How students experience and process this instability and disruption varies depending on the circumstances leading up to and following their parents' incarceration. For example, in her EVC group's documentary *Growing Apart: The Politics of Family Separation* (Educational Video Center, 2015a), about teen experiences living in broken families, Scarlett tells how her father was incarcerated when her mother was 5 months pregnant with her. As she explains it, "He never got to meet me. No photos, or any of those things."

Growing up, Scarlett struggled with depression, anxiety, and other mental health problems. Her family underwent further upheaval when her stepfather committed suicide, and her mother left her to live with relatives. That separation from her mother hit her hard: "I never got to see her. I got a severe depression at 6, and I wanted to kill myself. So they had me in therapy from like the age of 6 to the age of 10" (Educational Video Center, 2015a).

Scarlett's parental loss and subsequent struggles with depression and anxiety all contributed to her falling behind in school. Though this is just one case, teachers across the country must in fact teach and care for the nearly 2 million students with incarcerated parents. The challenge for all of us who teach such vulnerable students is to give them the time and personalized attention that they, like Scarlett, deserve and need.

As Scarlett says in her film:

> I like to say that I'm a proud weirdo. What it was like growing up—it was, like, on and off. Bad days. Good days. . . . It was sad because the people I loved the most, were either, you know, not there, or, you know, treating me the way I didn't like to be treated. I like to say, I was raised by a village. Although at times it was a corrupted village, it was a village nonetheless. I grew up with a lot of family. (Educational Video Center, 2015a)

Raised by a Village

 View the clip online: www.tcpress.com/goodman-chapter-two#v2.4

After her mother left, Scarlett was raised by her aunts, uncles, and her grand-mother, living with 14 different family members throughout her 18 years of life. Though being separated from both her parents left deep emotional scars, Scarlett also developed a sense of resilience through her relationships with these fami-ly members, particularly her grandmother. In Scarlett's case, as with many other students who grow up with alternative caregivers, she benefited from her grand-mother's loving support and involvement in her schooling that her mother and father were not able to give.

This is not to say it was easy for her grandmother and other relatives to care for her. Scarlett and other students across the country who have lost a parent to incarceration, regardless of whether it was before or after birth, are also more likely to suffer from financial hardship than those students who have not. One contrib-uting factor is that nonresident fathers can't provide child support while in prison and children may also lose welfare support from a previously unemployed (now incarcerated) parent, because these funds are difficult to transfer to a new caregiver. The additional financial burden of caring for new children in the household can also put retired grandparents and other caregivers at risk of using up their retirement savings, and in fact, high rates of children living with a grandmother live in poverty (La Vigne, Davies, & Brazell, 2008).

In Scarlett's case, even though her extended family members all worked, the limited income from their minimum-wage jobs as home health-care workers and other service jobs meant they had to struggle to put enough food on the table and keep a roof over her head. Scarlett recounted the many times when her family was threatened with eviction from their apartment when one or more members were laid off from their jobs.

Another destabilizing factor for children of the incarcerated is that many caregivers often don't openly discuss the incarcerated parent's whereabouts or sta-tus with children. As Alexander (2012) describes it:

> Imprisonment is considered so shameful that many people avoid talking about it, even within their own families. . . . Remarkably, even in communities devastated by mass incarceration, many people struggling to cope with the stigma of imprisonment have no idea that their neighbors are struggling with the same grief, shame, and isola-tion. . . . Lying about incarcerated family members is another common coping strategy. (pp. 166–167)

Whether because of adults' shame, fear, or not knowing how to talk about it, this silence in the home creates a sense of ambiguous loss and confusion for chil-dren about their incarcerated parent. Scarlett experienced this kind of confusion regarding her father:

> When I was a kid, I didn't even know—I thought some kids had dads
> and some didn't. I just thought, Oh, I'm just that one kid that doesn't. . . .
> Everyone [my friends and I] thought that my dad was dead. My last name
> comes from my stepfather, and he killed himself. So everyone thought my

dad was dead. . . . My mom was hiding it from me. . . . Once I met my father, that's when things changed. Oh well, why weren't you in my life? 'Cause I didn't even know he existed. Like he just showed up one day. On Christmas. I think I was 13. Oh! I have a dad. Cool. I don't know who you are, but . . . (personal communication, January 29, 2016)

Showing clips of Scarlett and Katrena's stories can provide openings in classes for students, who otherwise may feel stigmatized and silenced because they have incarcerated family members, to share their own stories in journal entries, spoken word, and other forms of creative expression. Bringing transformative teaching activities into the classroom in this way not only validates these students' experiences and counters the negative stereotypes other students may have about them, but it also creates a more inclusive and empathetic class for all students.

These class conversations are especially important to have, given the high number of students with incarcerated parents who are struggling to stay in school. From 1997 to 2007, the number of incarcerated fathers and mothers respectively increased by 76% and 122%. Though incarceration of both fathers and mothers increased the risk of educational failure, maternal incarceration has been found to be a particularly strong predictor of dropping out of high school. One study found that adolescents with incarcerated mothers dropped out at an astonishing four times the rate of their best friends whose mothers were not incarcerated (Huynh-Hohnbaum, Bussell, & Lee, 2015; Trice & Brewster, 2004).

These trends in dropout rates of students with incarcerated mothers can be attributed to the larger caregiving role that mothers tend to play in their children's upbringing and also because students are then more likely to experience changes in living arrangements such as being placed in foster care (see Chapter 5), or in the care of relatives. This puts a burden on relatives who usually don't know how long they will have to care for children and youth without their mother and usually do so without the financial and emotional support they need to cope (Bocknek et al., 2009).

The capacity of children and youth to cope with the impact of these complex sources of trauma often depends on their maintaining ongoing communication with incarcerated parents. Phone calls are the most common communication, because most incarcerated parents are in prisons located over 100 miles from their home and visits can be expensive and time-consuming. But the exorbitant fees charged by private phone companies, which can be as much as 10 dollars a minute for in-state prison calls (Kang, 2017), limit the healing that children from poor families can experience by maintaining bonds with their parents behind bars.

Not only is the child–parent relationship strained during the period of incarceration, but the damage can remain even after parents return home and attempt to reunite with their children after spending years apart. As an incarcerated mother, Katrena was separated from her daughter for over a decade. In the video *Another Part of Me: Youth Views on Drugs and Incarceration in Our Community* (Educational Video Center, 2009), she describes her struggle to reunite and attempt to rebuild the broken bonds of her family:

You know my incarceration, we speak about family. It really damaged my family a lot, to the point where I never had a relationship with them and I don't think that I will ever get one with them. . . . I go through mad crazy stuff about my daughter, like right now. It hurts me. . . . It's hard to cut out certain ties, like my, my kid. I don't want to cut her out of my life. But I have to keep her at arms distance if I want to get better. Because if I allow that to come too close to me, it's gonna affect me. Her reaction. . . . I've been a ward of the state all my life! Since 15. That's all I knew! That's all I knew was how to survive in there. I didn't know how to do time out here.

"THEIR WRISTS ARE TOO SMALL, SO YOU HAVE TO HANDCUFF THEM UP BY THEIR BICEPS": ZERO-TOLERANCE POLICING IN SCHOOL

Schools ought to be places of refuge and support for students who are struggling to recover from the damage done by their own or their family's involvement with the justice system. Some school leaders are conscious of the added burden placed on their staff and address it with counseling and guidance that aims to heal their students' emotional wounds and build their resilience and sense of hope. Some work to build restorative and trauma-sensitive school cultures that seek to de-escalate violence, conflict, and punishment through restorative justice programs, which will be discussed below..

But unfortunately, the much larger trend is still in the opposite direction. Once separate domains, criminal justice policing in the streets became the model for policing in schools. Increased scanning, metal detectors and other technologies of surveillance, heightened police presence, and excessive force have become dominant features of a zero-tolerance culture of control in schools.

It Damaged My Family

 View the clip online: www.tcpress.com/goodman-chapter-two#v2.5

This is not accidental; the policies for policing communities and schools share threads of a common history. Clinton's 1994 crime bill was sweeping poor men and women of color off the streets and into prisons as "zero-tolerance" policies that spread to schools during this period were appropriating the criminal justice system's "broken windows" ideology of social control.

Kelling and Wilson popularized the "broken windows" theory in a seminal article (1982) asserting that serious crime is a result of social and physical disorder in neighborhoods. New York City mayor Rudolph Giuliani and his police commissioner William Bratton led the way in putting this theory into practice, calling for targeted and punitive policing in poor communities and subways, arresting people for low-level "quality of life" violations such as panhandling, graffiti, sleeping in parks, loitering, and sitting on sidewalks in the belief that it would reduce overall crime rates. Schools developed the same broken windows–type of punitive cultures where students were suspended or expelled for even minor infractions. According to the New York Civil Liberties Union (NYCLU), "Fighting in the hallway is classified as assault; swiping a classmate's pencil case can be classified as a property crime; and talking back to an SSA or being late to class is disorderly conduct" (Mukherjee, 2007). Like in the community, these quality of life campaigns become a strategy for moving poor students of color along the school-to-prison pipeline.

The police assault on poor minority youth was also framed as moral poverty, rather than economic poverty, when criminologist John J. Dilulio Jr. (1995) wrote about a new kind of inner-city juvenile criminal, a "super predator" roving "in wolf packs" who "kill or maim on impulse, without any intelligible motive." By branding urban teens of color as "super predators," Dilulio used the language of race without explicitly referring to race, as Presidents Nixon and Reagan had successfully done before. It was a "dog whistle" that criminalized and built popular hostility against inner-city youth and marshaled public support for a range of crime control laws aimed at urban youth, including curfews, strict truancy laws, and antigang loitering ordinances (Nolan, 2011).

It was no surprise that as adult incarceration rates exploded, rates of juvenile incarceration also rose. Infractions that once might have merited a call home, like shoving another student or cursing, increasingly became grounds for suspension (Dominus, 2016).

Instead of bringing greater safety and security for the school community, the law and order culture has increased fear and anxiety among the student body. Students who need academic and emotional support the most—students with incarcerated parents, like Scarlett or perhaps Katrena's daughter, or students who have experienced abusive treatment from police and SROs such as Brandon or Rob—are too often the ones taken out of the classroom. Once removed, students of color and those with learning disabilities are then likely to receive the most severe disciplinary consequences, including suspension and expulsion. African American students are disproportionately suspended at nearly four times the rate of White students, increasing their likelihood of dropping out, or more accurately, of being pushed out. With each suspension, a student's odds of graduating high school decrease by an additional 20% and the odds of enrolling in postsecondary school decrease by 12%. Thus are students of color pushed along through what has become widely recognized as the school-to-prison pipeline (Losen, 2015; Noguera, 2003; Nolan, 2011; U.S. Department of Education, National Center for Education Statistics [NCES], 2016).

Expanding the metaphor to be more gender inclusive, Monique Morris (2016) describes the punitive experience for disproportionate numbers of Black girls as being pushed into "school-to-confinement pathways." Not necessarily only confined in prisons, girls are often placed in "house arrest, detention centers, electronic monitoring, and other forms of social exclusion" (pp. 12, 69).

Even though school crime rates are much lower than they have been for over a decade, there were still 1,555 students arrested in New York City schools during the 2014–2015 school year. Almost 700 students were handcuffed during the first quarter of 2016. And nearly all of these interactions that took place in schools across the city involved students of color[4] (City of New York, 2015; NYCLU, 2016).

School cultures that criminalize students have led to large investments by districts in security staff and technology. With the increased privatization of public schools, the security technology and hardware first developed by the Pentagon that found its way into the prisons and to police departments are now being sold by hundreds of security companies recently formed with the purpose of selling safety to the vast education market (Casella, 2010).

In New York City, where the NYPD reports that schools are safer than they have been in a decade, more than 200 schools still require their 100,000 students to remove their shoes, send their belongings through X-ray machines, pass through metal detectors, or have SROs wand their bodies before they are allowed to cross the school threshold and go to their first class to start their day. As with nearly all other aspects of the school policing and security apparatus, it's disproportionately students of color who must endure this daily ritual. A ProPublica survey found that African American and Latino high school students are nearly three times more likely to walk though a metal detector than their White counterparts (Reyes, 2016). Nationally, 93% of public schools have controlled access with locked or monitored doors and 89% of high schools and combined schools use security cameras, according to the National Center for Education Statistics (NCES, 2016).

In the late 1970s, there were fewer than 100 police officers in our public schools (Nance, 2016). There are now more than 43,000 school resource officers and sworn police officers and an additional 39,000 security guards working in the nation's 84,000 public schools (NCES, 2015). The presence of law enforcement in schools continues to grow, particularly as mass shootings in schools have become more common. Four out of the 10 largest school districts in the country—New York, Chicago, Houston, and Miami Dade County—including three of the top five, have more security officers than school counselors (Barnum, 2016). It is deeply disturbing that 1.6 million students across the country attend a high school with a police officer but no school counselor (NCES, 2016).

This massive investment in SROs, policing technology, and zero-tolerance practices has created school cultures with a disproportionate focus on the social control, discipline, and punishment of students of color. The involvement of law enforcement officers in schools has become normalized and accepted by students and adults alike. Teachers and administrators end up deferring to SROs those student problems that, with sufficient training and support, they used to resolve themselves. Troubles with classroom and lunchroom management become redefined as criminal justice problems, and poor students of color with academic, social, and emotional problems become overidentified as dangerous to the safety of the school. It increases the likelihood that overpolicing will result in an escalation of minor offenses into violent disciplinary encounters ending with student suspension, expulsion, or arrest. Further, it increases the likelihood that excessive force will be used against them in the process (Kupchik, 2010).

It's difficult, but more important than ever, for us to make time to advocate for those of our students who are the most troubled and in need of support, even when this conflicts with the prevailing zero-tolerance school culture. Making time for those needy students means we will have less time for something else. But it's well worth it. In the long run, when students know you are treating them with respect and dignity and are committed to supporting them through their troubled times, it will lead to less conflict and greater healing between students and their peers, teachers, and school resource officers.

It's no surprise that violent and disturbing incidents abound in school cultures where such responsiveness and care for the most vulnerable students is absent. There are now a growing number of videos captured on cell phones by fellow students and bystanders that have gone viral recording students in high school, middle school, and even students as young as preschool age variously being maced, pepper-sprayed, choked, body-slammed, and arrested by SROs. They are indeed horrifying to watch.

There was the case of the 6-year-old African American girl in Avon Park, Florida, who was handcuffed and charged with a felony—battery on a school official—after she had a tantrum in her kindergarten classroom (Herbert, 2007). In Los Angeles, a school resource officer broke a high school student's wrist while arresting her in her school lunchroom after she dropped a piece of birthday cake and didn't clean it up to the satisfaction of the school resource officer (Nolan, 2011).

Then there have been instances where the police abuse of students was captured on video by students' cell phones. In Columbia, South Carolina, a school resource officer was called into a classroom to remove a high school girl who refused to give up her cell phone. Video of the incident shows the officer grabbing the African American student by the neck, flipping her backwards, and then dragging her from her chair and throwing her on the floor past rows of desks (Blad, 2017; Fausset & Southall, 2015). One-hundred-pound, 15-year-old Jasmine Darwin suffered a concussion when a school resource officer, who is also a member of the local police department, picked her up over his head and slammed her to the concrete floor. Jasmine had been trying to protect her older sister who was in a fight in the Rolesville, North Carolina, school cafeteria (Yan, 2017).

The victims in these reports of violent and degrading assaults are overwhelmingly African American students—and in these cases, African American girls. The disproportionately high number of school suspensions, expulsions, and arrests of African American students compared with White students is well documented.[5]

Black students are suspended and expelled at a rate three times greater than White students. Black girls are 16% of girls in schools but make up 42% of girls receiving corporal punishment, 42% of girls who are expelled, and 45% of girls with at least one out-of-school suspension. In New York schools, Black girls are expelled at 53 times the rate for White girls (Morris, 2016).

Evidence shows that excessive force or singling students out for punishment and removal for these minor infractions do not improve school culture and learning or make schools any safer. Data from several studies have shown that these zero-tolerance suspension and expulsion policies do not deter bad behavior and most likely feed it by alienating students from the school community. When these students are removed from school, they are much more likely to become tangled up in the juvenile justice system (City of New York, 2015; Nance, 2016; Noguera, 2003).

"I WAS 15. CAME HOME AT 25":
JUVENILE DETENTION IN RIKERS

Whether students are arrested through systems of stop-and-frisk policing in the streets or zero-tolerance policing in schools, they are moved out of a law and order education system and into the justice system. This marks the end of the metaphorical school-to-prison pipeline. With its culture of pervasive violence and excessive force, it is built as an institution of punishment and not of rehabilitation or healing that might provide a pathway for students to return to school and graduate.

There are about 48,000 juvenile offenders held in residential facilities across the country on any given day, and 69% of them are youth of color (Office of Juvenile Justice and Delinquency Prevention, 2017).[6] Although they may be high school age, over half of the inmates read below 6th-grade level at intake.

The systemic criminalization, dehumanization, and excessive force those students have experienced by police on the streets of their communities and by SROs in the classrooms, lunchrooms, and hallways of their schools is realized in all its naked brutality when they enter Rikers, the largest penal facility in the world. Rikers is notorious, the subject of numerous investigative reports and documentaries (Gonnerman, 2014; Moyers, 2016; Schwirtz, Winerip, & Gebeloff, 2016). A 2014 investigation by the U.S. Department of Justice revealed disturbing findings:

> A deep-seated culture of violence is pervasive throughout the adolescent facilities at Rikers, and DOC [Department of Corrections] staff routinely utilize force not as a last resort, but instead as a means to control the adolescent population and punish

disorderly or disrespectful behavior. . . . As a result of staff use of excessive force and inmate violence, adolescents have sustained a striking number of serious injuries, including broken jaws, broken orbital bones, broken noses, long bone fractures, and lacerations requiring sutures. . . . Use of force was particularly common in areas without video surveillance cameras. (pp. 3, 4)

Youth in Rikers are at constant risk of violence. Inmate-on-inmate violence in Rikers is, of course, not a new problem for incarcerated teenagers. A casualty of the war on drugs, Katrena told of her own experiences early in her time there in the late 1990s:

> I was 15. Came home at 25. It was hell for me in there, you know. At 16 you know, I got jumped. They put a sheet over my head. I got a quarter plate in my head as a result. You see the incision there. They beat me up in the shower. The second altercation in prison I was 17. I got burnt up in my bed. I heard people screaming around me. "Get up! Get up! Get up! Get up!" (Educational Video Center, 2009)

The outcome of this brutal violence can be seen not only in the physical damage but also the lasting social and emotional trauma that incarcerated teenagers suffer. This trauma often leads to substantially worse outcomes later in life. Research demonstrates that formerly incarcerated youth are very unlikely to ever return to, or graduate from, school and are that much more likely to become incarcerated again as an adult. If they do return, they are more likely to be classified as special education students for emotional and behavioral problems rather than cognitive ones, and be at greater risk of being removed from school. For example, in the 2014–2015 school year, students with special needs were suspended 2.6 times as frequently as students without disabilities (Aizer & Doyle, 2015; City of New York, 2015).

Get Up!

 View the clip online: www.tcpress.com/goodman-chapter-two#v2.6

Though prison education programs were decimated on both the state and federal levels in the "tough on crime" era of the 1990s, there is currently renewed support for in-facility and alternative-to-sentencing educational and career training programs for incarcerated and court-involved students. There has been progress on rolling back some of the most pernicious laws still in place from the 1970s War on Drugs and reforms. There have also been reforms in New York City and elsewhere to improve school culture and reform zero-tolerance discipline codes, making it harder to use physical restraints on students under age 12 and preventing suspensions for minor infractions. And the use of restorative justice programs has been spreading in schools across New York City and more broadly across the country as a strategy for disrupting the school-to-prison pipeline.

"ON THE SIDE OF THE KIDS":
RESTORATIVE JUSTICE AND STUDENT ACTION

Rooted in indigenous practices of community building and restoration, these practices are now applied as an alternative, nonpunitive, problem-solving approach to practicing discipline in schools. As such, restorative justice (RJ) practices bring people together in order to maintain the integrity of the community rather than expel them from it, to promote empathy and bring about healing from the harm that has been done instead of managing through surveillance, control, and punishment. In this way, the students and staff are solving the problem themselves rather than calling on police or school resource officers to resolve it.

Through the process, the student victim or victims sit in a circle with the offender or offenders, along with mediators and other relevant parties, and engage in a facilitated conversation about what happened and how they felt. After these reforms were begun, between July and December of 2015, New York City schools documented a 32% drop in suspensions, as compared with the same period a year earlier. The New York City Department of Education believes strongly enough in this that it has invested in training and resources to roll out restorative justice methods in 100 schools (City of New York, 2015; Dominus, 2016; Fronius, Persson, Guckenburg, Hurley, & Petrosino, 2016; Teachers Unite, 2012).

With EVC support, students in one New York City school created an instructional video to teach other students and teachers about the culture of restorative justice that they have been building there for about 8 years. In their school, students take restorative justice classes where they learn to conduct peer mediation and facilitate support circles. As the principal describes it, their philosophy is to build a student-centered culture in the school where the students learn to take responsibility for their actions:

> It's about getting people in the same room and having a conversation, about building a culture of caring and accountability. It's a long process. You have to start small. Everyone's going to learn better if they are happy to be there.

You have to make them feel part of the community, not ostracize people. (personal communication, October 13, 2017)

An important feature of their approach is to engage students as peer mediators who have themselves had discipline problems in the past. With an emphasis on social–emotional development and youth leadership, there is a payoff for the students who are having harm restored in some way, as well as for the students mediating the process. Julian, who described himself as one of the kids who had a bad temper and would get into fights in school all the time, changed when he had the opportunity to be trained and became an RJ mediator. As he said:

RJ isn't about letting people go after they've done something wrong. Every action is because of a reason. Every reason is about a feeling. If you lash out mentally or verbally, or physically, the point is not to let them go. It's to have them talk. (personal communication, October 13, 2017)

Another student, Mateo, described how it took him some time to see the value in it:

At first I didn't want to be in it. I would skip the class. Or sleep. I didn't see the point of restoring other people's problems. After a while, once we were doing it, I could see how conversating with other people brings out the peace in everyone else. (personal communication, October 13, 2017)

Implementing this approach to discipline depends so much on building a strong sense of community, a schoolwide culture of belonging through storytelling, listening, and empathy with students and teachers. The principal reflected on a memorable support circle she has participated in:

There was a student who was really, really struggling in school. So, we decided to do a support circle. His mom, dad, his best friend were all there. He complained and said, "My dad won't talk to me." His dad said his son was just coming home and running into his room and wasn't talking to anyone. After more discussion, it turns out that the reason the kid had fallen apart was because he had broken up with his first girlfriend. Then everyone went around the circle to talk about the first time they fell in love. Even though his parents were divorced, they still talked about when they first fell in love with each other, and it was good for him to hear this. His dad said, "Oh! You're just in love! That's why you're acting like a knucklehead!" (personal communication, October 13, 2017)

So much of restorative justice is about storytelling, collaborative problem solving, and building on students' strengths. The principal wondered out loud, "After hearing a story, how can you not help but be more empathetic to what they are going through? . . . How do we, as educators, position ourselves to be on the side of the kids?" (personal communication, October 13, 2017).

Part of the answer is for educators to create curricula with student-led projects and spaces in their classes and schools that advocate against police violence and work to shut down the school-to-prison pipeline and confinement pathways. In addition to integrating restorative justice practices in the school culture, being "on the side of the kids" means actively engaging them in discussion and inquiry into the way these pipelines and pathways work, the impact of overpolicing, mass incarceration, and zero-tolerance policies, and the ways they can be changed. Whether in academic or advisory classes or extracurricular clubs, students may want to study data on police stops of students and school and district suspensions and arrests with student race and gender. They might be interested in researching district expenditures on metal detectors and police safety officers as compared with costs for school counselors and social workers. They may coordinate student correspondence with other teens in juvenile detention facilities. They may critically analyze media reporting on police–youth relations, and write their own letters to the editor. Or they may interview their peers and tell their own stories of the stigma they experience in school as court-involved youth or as children of incarcerated parents.

In each case, it means having difficult conversations among students and staff about race, power and privilege, and embedded attitudes and practices of institutional and individual bias. There are no easy answers. But it is an empowering process for students to learn with a purpose and to study social justice problems directly connected to their lives. In this way, knowledge is linked to action with the goal of combatting those problems, even in small and local ways—and knowing their teachers are on their side.

Returning to the story of the *Policing the Times* documentary project (Educational Video Center, 2015b), the purpose and power of the students' work became evident not only when they documented their stories about police violence in their film but when they screened it and led "know your rights" discussions for their peers at their schools. Like with the restorative justice student mediators, they were doing their part to disrupt the school-to-prison pipelines and pathways.

But it turned out not to be a simple or straightforward process. Many of their peers were resistant, and some felt hopeless, believing that knowing their rights wouldn't reduce the threat of violence or make them any safer. In fact, the students feared that telling police that they know their rights might cause them to be even more angry and abusive.

When the students screened their film and shared this story with teachers and principals at the citywide Transfer School Conference, a teacher in the audience argued that teachers have a responsibility to address this problem, to stand with their students and their families. It echoed again the principal's question of how educators can be on their students' side, how can they commit to being allies and advocates for their students and use their privilege and as they negotiate and navigate systems of power.

If ever there was a need for a restorative justice mediation or support circle, this would be it. But the police officers and safety agents weren't in these school conversations. And so EVC, participating principals, and the NYC Department of Education's Office of Postsecondary Readiness began planning to engage more students and teachers in another collaborative inquiry into school and community policing. This would be a youth participatory action research project that could also involve police in the dialogue. (This project is described in more detail in the Conclusion.) As with the RJ student mediators, students who may have previously felt alienated or hopeless would be invited to participate in school in a new way, and with a greater social purpose than passing a test. Their questions, ideas, and experiences with police would be needed, and *they* would be needed for the collective task of solving urgent problems for the well-being of their schools and community. And teachers would be facilitating, collaborating, and standing with them all along the way.

CHAPTER 3

"The Legal Right to Be Somebody"

Immigration

ICE

Home raids by armed agents early in the morning or in the dead of night are the new normal for immigrant communities in our country. Families are torn apart as children lose their parents, and many children are left unsupervised without knowing where their parents were taken, or who will take care of them. These raids not only impact those who are arrested and deported, but disrupt and destabilize their families and create panic among far greater numbers of immigrants in surrounding communities who fear they will be next. Some terrified families have remained indoors, even hiding in closets and basements for days after large raids (Thronson, 2008).

Tracked by local police and the U.S. Immigration and Customs Enforcement (ICE) agents, those members of the community who are branded as rapists and murderers by President Trump and other anti-immigrant politicians are also the students who sit in our classes and are the parents and family members they go home to. Labeling students *immigrants* can include those who are legal immigrants, undocumented (also called unauthorized), or naturalized citizens. Students may be in the process of changing from one status of immigration or citizenship to another or may be U.S.-born children of immigrant parents living among millions of what are called "mixed-status" families. So, nearly 26% of children and youth now growing up in the United States are children of immigrants or are themselves immigrants. And 5.1 million children and youth under 18 live with at least one undocumented immigrant parent, representing 30% of all children of immigrants (Capps, Fix, & Zong, 2016; U.S. Department of Health and Human Services, Health Resources and Services Administration, Maternal and Child Health Bureau, 2014).[1]

In addition to the challenges of learning another language in a hostile climate of persecution and discrimination, many new immigrant students whose parents have been deported must struggle to succeed in school while being raised by older siblings or fending for themselves. This chapter will make visible their often hidden stories of family immigration, reunification, and deportation, and discuss ways teachers can support immigrant students' academic self-efficacy and advocate and be culturally sustaining in solidarity with them and their families. In *Growing Apart: The Politics of Family Separation* (Educational Video Center,

2015a), EVC student Luis tells his story (translated from Spanish) of multiple attempts to cross the U.S. border from Mexico, and then losing his father to deportation weeks after being reunited with his family. Perla also shares her struggles emigrating from Mexico and adjusting to school. In *New Visions: A Deeper Look at the American Dream* (Educational Video Center, 2016), Mohamed describes his difficult and complicated reunion with his family after more than a decade of separation living in the Ivory Coast.

"FEARFUL OF ANY INSTITUTION": CHALLENGES FACING EMERGENT BILINGUALS

Studies of prolonged parental absence, particularly for Latino immigrant youth, and the fracture of networks of support at home or in school for first-generation immigrant students show a negative impact on students' school performance and on students' own expectations for their educational achievement (Suárez-Orozco, Suárez-Orozco, & Todorova, 2008; Wright & Levitt, 2014). In the country's two largest school systems, Los Angeles and New York City, nearly 25% and 15% of all students, respectively, are English language learners (Ruiz Soto, Hooker, & Batalova, 2015). These students are also referred to as *emergent bilinguals*, a term that recognizes students' "strengths—their home language and cultural practices . . . [and] children's potential in developing their bilingualism; it does not suggest a limitation or a problem in comparison to those who speak English" (Garcia, 2009, pp. 322–323; see also Garcia & Kleifgen, 2010).

The anti-immigrant climate they are living in causes unauthorized students and those in mixed-status families to live in constant fear of losing their parents and other family members in raids and random stops. Some undocumented parents in New Mexico and other border states keep their children home from school for fear of being arrested when they drop them off at school, or being stopped at border patrol checkpoints on the roads along the way there.

One New York City high school principal described the increased fear she has witnessed in her students and their families:

> I've been doing this work over 20 years, only now am I seeing families that are afraid to bring their child with emergency situations to the hospital. They are afraid they will be deported, and their child will be deported. We have a student who tore his ACL (anterior cruciate ligament). He actually borrowed crutches and braces from someone else because his family was afraid to bring him to the hospital. . . . There are serious health issues, including domestic violence, now that they won't report. They are fearful of any institution—hospitals, schools. . . . Students are coming to us if they have a parking ticket. They are afraid. . . . ICE is showing up at courts. . . . I want to say nothing is going to happen. But I can't assure our students that they will be safe. (personal communication, October 17, 2017)

Sightings of ICE agents at courthouses across New York State have surged, with a 900% increase in ICE arrests or attempted arrests reported between 2016 and 2017 (S. R. Brown, 2017). Seeing a growing anxiety and drop in school attendance that follows raids or rumors of ICE sightings, superintendents and other school leaders are alerting staff to watch out for their immigrant students and writing letters to parents in an attempt to reassure them (Seelye & Bidgood, 2017). One was moved to write a letter to the Department of Homeland Security about "the devastating impacts [of ICE raids] . . . on the academic, social, and emotional well-being of all our students" (Blitzer, 2017).

The fear of deportation and hypervigilance that newcomer students carry with them to school each day are all the more difficult for teachers to address, as students often adopt a sense of invisibility and silence about their status, as a strategy for survival. This situation is further complicated by a range of other challenges that their U.S.-born peers don't have to contend with. Perhaps most obvious is the new language that they are required to learn and the new culture and monolingual school system they have to adapt to with its own set of rules, norms, and graduation requirements.

Emergent bilinguals experience a dissonance between their home and school environment that becomes increasingly difficult to overcome. They not only have to learn to speak socially in a new colloquial language, but perform with proficiency in a context-reduced academic language; researchers say it can take emergent bilinguals 5 to 10 years on average to reach the proficiency of their English-speaking peers. It is no surprise that they struggle in a high-stakes testing environment that is unforgiving to newcomers and their particular challenges. They score an average of 20–50 percentage points below their native-English-speaking peers, not only in English language arts tests, but also in other subjects such as math (Menken, 2013).

In addition to these linguistic challenges, many immigrant students also struggle with social and emotional problems rooted in the trauma and upheaval of their migration and postmigration experiences. These may include the violence, bleak poverty, or family tragedy from religious, ethnic, or political persecution they left behind in their homeland, as well as the long family separation or permanent breakup, their undocumented status, or their family's impoverished living conditions when they arrive.

We as teachers, school leaders, counselors, and social workers need to build close and trusting relationships with our students and get to know them well. Using their students' home languages as a resource is an effective bilingual strategy for developing strong relationships with their students and their families and for gaining insight into the multiple factors that can shape students' attitudes, emotional engagement, and academic performance in school (Garcia, 2009; Suárez-Orozco, Bang, et al., 2010).

The problems for many of our newcomer students are further amplified by conditions of unemployment and gang and drug-related violence prevalent in their communities, with few pathways to college and well-paying jobs (Suárez-Orozco, Bang, et al., 2010). When schools aren't able to meet their social–emotional needs, the lack of community resources and additional stressors of their immigrant experience become formidable barriers to their academic success. It's therefore no surprise that many immigrant-origin students perform poorly on academic indicators such as achievement tests, grades, and dropout rates (Suárez-Orozco, Bang, et al., 2010). Although Latino graduation rates have improved over the years in New York City (New York City Independent Budget Office, 2012), students from Mexico—the largest immigrant group by far—were found to have the lowest graduation rates of immigrant students of any region.[2]

Although we will routinely note changes in our immigrant students' class attendance, test scores, and graduation rates, the continued trauma that they experience in the aftermath of their journey to America too often goes underrecognized and unrecorded. Ranging from the distracting to the debilitating, our students may experience sleeplessness, loss of appetite, an increase in aggression, fear, and anxiety, particularly around police.

Finally, what is perhaps the most devastating outcome for immigrant students is their more general loss of hope. Without hope, students lose the capacity to envision a future for themselves in school, or after graduation. This can happen when their emerging identity as a student with a life full of discovery and possibility ahead of them is eclipsed by a racial, ethnic, and legal identity externally imposed on them as an immigrant, an alien, or as "illegal." Licia, an undocumented friend of EVC students, described this powerfully when she recalled her own loss of hope:

> I didn't make any plans for my future when I was leaving high school. Because I was illegal. I didn't know what plans I was allowed to make or not allowed to make. So as far as, when everyone else in high school was making plans that they are going to be doctors and lawyers, I knew that I wanted to be somebody, but I didn't know what I wanted to be. Because I didn't have the legal right, I feel, *to be somebody.* (Educational Video Center, 2005)

We know that our students' time in our classrooms is only a small part of the larger picture of their family's experiences caught between national systems of border and interior law enforcement and global forces of war and labor regulation. Whether trekking through the mountains and deserts of Mexico, parenting themselves at home, or struggling to learn a new language in their new schools, their struggles reveal the underlying courage, tenacity, and resilience that so many of our newcomer students carry silently within them.

"IN THE DESERT, THE MOUNTAINS, THE COLD— WITH ONLY WATER": BORDER CROSSING STORIES

Practicing a transformative and culturally sustaining pedagogy means, in part, taking time to get to know our students' diverse cultural experiences that may bring them pain and trauma, as well as those that enrich and sustain them and bring them joy. There are nearly one million children in the United States who have at least one undocumented parent and are also themselves unauthorized. The greatest percentage of these students attend middle or high school. They struggle academically to overcome the systemic obstacles and double disadvantages of their parents' and their own undocumented status (Capps, Fix, & Zong, 2016).

These students come from diverse newcomer communities with a range of personal and family stories of crossing into this country without legal documentation. But because of the threat of deportation, they most often remain silent about their status. And so, their stories of struggle, courage, and grit go untold. When teachers get to know their students' stories, it opens up new possibilities for teachers to tap into their students' strengths and support their needs. This can only happen when we create trusting relationships with our students, and when they feel they can count on us to be their allies and advocates. Creating lessons and activities that elicit writing and storytelling about their experiences can provide openings for such trusting relationships, while remaining sensitive to their vulnerability.

One principal of a school serving immigrant students described a "numbers project" on family separation that her teachers use to open up such conversations and build such relationships: "Each student is asked to pick a number representing the amount of time in months or years they were separated from a loved one. They then write about it and share it with each other. Everybody has some story to tell. Then they hang up their numbers and post their stories in the class" (personal communication, October 17, 2017).

Luis and Perla are two such students with stories of separation. They both attended EVC's high school documentary workshop and produced a documentary called *Growing Apart: The Politics of Family Separation* (Educational Video Center, 2015a) about students who grew up separated from their parents. Both Luis and Perla grew up in Mexico and were unaccompanied minors—10-year-old children traveling without their parents—when they made the perilous trip to cross the border into the United States.

As Luis explains in this film, he walked for weeks across the rugged terrain of Mexico, only traveling under the cover of night. He shivered and froze at night in the mountains. He was exhausted and in pain from the wounds he sustained stumbling and falling as he was trying to keep up with the adults in the group. He tells his story in Spanish, with subtitles in English in the video and in this text below:

> I came here [to the United States] when I was 10, almost 11 years old. The reason my family came here was because of the money. We didn't have enough in Mexico. So what they did was earn money and they sent for me. . . . I remember I had to walk for about a week and a half, or two. In the desert, the mountains, the cold—with only water. Because with food—well, you don't get hungry. You get thirsty. So you had to drink a lot of water, so you can walk. The first time I was okay. It was like a new adventure. The second and next time, I was a lot more tired. Because I had to walk in the nighttime and I was a child. Even if I didn't want to, my body was tired. My

In the Desert, the Mountains, the Cold

Because I had to walk in the night time and I was a child.

 View the clip online: www.tcpress.com/goodman-chapter-three#v3.1

body wanted to sleep. I kept tripping and I hurt my leg. When I got here, I had to go the hospital urgently. (Educational Video Center, 2015a).

When he finally made it to the border, he was captured by immigration border patrols and sent back to Mexico. But he didn't give up; he tried again. In fact, he tried crossing six times. Finally, on his seventh try, he made it across without being caught. By then, he was almost 11 years old. He survived the ordeal but was in bad shape when he arrived. He was immediately hospitalized for a severe ear infection and bruises and lacerations and thorns that had to be removed. Reflecting back on it all, in his narration he said, "I didn't care about that. The important thing was seeing my family again. That's why I tried so many times and didn't give up" (Educational Video Center, 2015a). When he was finally reunited with them, he said that was the happiest time he could ever remember.

Perla was about the same age as Luis, another unaccompanied minor from Mexico attempting to cross the border to join her parents in the United States. She described her journey coming to America this way:

At first the coyotes [people who smuggle immigrants into the United States] came to pick us up. They picked up other people and then we had to travel to the city of Puebla. From Puebla we gotta take a bus to Mexico City. From there, we gotta take an airplane to Nogales, Arizona. It was all day traveling. I feel like it was kind of a special day for me. I was gonna see my mom. Finally I was gonna be with my family. (personal communication, December 22, 2015)

But she was also caught and detained at the border:

> We were the only two kids on the bus that they were taking us to the
> detention center. And the day was so cold, so cold. We had to lay down on
> the floor of the bus, since the motor makes it warm. We had to lay down
> over there. We were in a jail, and we could look through and see kids playing
> outside in houses. And I was thinking, when am I gonna see my mom? . . .
> 'Cause in Mexico we didn't have the opportunity to be together. I was living
> with my grandma since I was 7 years old. My little brother was living with
> my aunt. So we were always separated. And finally here we were gonna get
> back together, you know? . . . It was a special day for me. Until I got to the
> border. (personal communication, December 22, 2015)

It was not only a special day for Perla because she thought she was going to see
her mother, but it was also her birthday. So, Perla turned 11 in a detention center.

When Perla was finally reunited with her family in New York City in 2009, she
was joining an estimated 5.1 million other children under 18 who were living with
at least one undocumented immigrant parent, and nearly one million children who
were themselves unauthorized. New York was a common destination for them. In
fact, over half of the roughly 11 million unauthorized immigrants in the country
are highly concentrated in New York and just four other states: California, Texas,
Illinois, and Florida (Capps, Fix, & Zong, 2016). And Mexicans make up more than
half of all unauthorized immigrants. Like Perla's and Luis's families, more than three-
quarters of these Mexicans are long-term residents who have lived in the United
States for 10 years or more (Gonzalez-Barrera & Krogstad, 2017).

Students like Luis and Perla who have had such traumatic experiences leaving
their extended family to join their parents are likely to keep their immigration stories to themselves for fear of being deported for revealing their citizenship status.
Yet we need to give them extra care and attention, and make sure those students
know they are safe and are welcomed in their classroom. Sometimes that might
involve simply hanging a poster in the class in multiple languages saying, "All students are welcome here"—or inviting the students to write and illustrate it themselves. As one principal put it:

> Ultimately, the goal is to make the child or young person feel like they
> belong. They may not feel at home in this country right way, or may never
> feel it with their family here. The question then is how do we establish
> a culture of belonging here in our school. . . . Being a trauma-informed
> school means knowing the students well and understanding what might
> trigger them and how. . . . Every teacher is also an advisor. We have a social–
> emotional focus and an instructional focus. (personal communication,
> October 17, 2017)

This inclusive and welcoming approach includes bringing what is called a
"translanguaging" pedagogy to curriculum, language, and teaching techniques in

the classroom. Rather than projecting a sense of foreignness or ignorance of academic English on immigrant students, teachers can leverage their strengths—their home culture and repertoire of home language practices—to build bilingualism. Recognizing the fluidity of language to make meaning, they can help emergent bilinguals feel more at home by engaging them in speaking, writing, and reading in their home language as well as in English (Hesson, Seltzer, & Woodley, 2014).

"I WAS DOING REALLY BAD": A DOWNWARD EDUCATIONAL SPIRAL

Early adolescence is a time of heightened developmental vulnerability for middle and high school students in general, and all the more so for the half of those new immigrant students who arrive during those years as Luis and Perla did. The emotional trauma they experience from extended parental separations and complicated reunification puts them at increased risk of falling into what Eccles and colleagues (1993) call a "downward spiral" for adolescents of declining academic motivation and self confidence, school attendance, and performance in school (p. 90).

Families are pulled apart as migrants desperate for work leave their children behind with relatives in search of a better life in the United States, to do the least desirable work for the lowest pay. It is common for children of parents who have emigrated to live separately from one or both their parents for many years in nontraditional arrangements in the care of an aunt, uncle, grandmother, or other extended family members. Often, it's the men who leave first, and send home remittances for their families. Increasingly, the demands of the global service economy have meant that it is women who are on the move, leaving their children behind in their home country to take care of other families' children, homes, and aging parents as nannies, maids, and home health aides (Ehrenreich & Hochschild, 2002; Suárez-Orosco, Todorova, & Louie, 2002).

Mexican and Central American women are among those who risk crossing the border illegally to take on this work and are expected to form close physical and emotional bonds of affection with their more privileged employers' children or elders in their care, while relations with their own children left behind grow weaker. As a result, their children develop strong social and emotional bonds with their caregivers while their parents work in the hope of earning enough money in the United States to bring them over. Perla's mother followed this trend in migration, coming to the United States to work as a nanny and leaving Perla in the care of her grandmother and aunt, both of whom she grew very close to.

These complex family circumstances put immigrant children in the difficult position of experiencing two breaks in emotional attachments: first when their parents leave them for America, and second, when they leave their caregiver and extended family, to whom they have grown close, to be reunited with their parents. After a separation of sometimes 10 or more years, parents are often not prepared to relate to and support their newly reunited teenage children in school or at home. Not fully understanding the larger context of immigration, children experience a double loss of attachment and the absence of parents and caregivers, which can lead them to resent and withdraw from their parents whom they have come to America to live with. Some parents may feel guilty for leaving their children with other relatives, while others may expect their children to be grateful for all their sacrifices. On the other hand, their children may feel ambivalent or disoriented, or may not fully trust or respect their parents' authority, as patterns of rejection and counter-rejection between children and parents may emerge (Suárez-Orozco, Todorova, & Louie, 2002).

The reunification process is emotionally stressful and fraught with complications for parents and children alike. For some students, this can trigger a renewed sense of loss and abandonment, as well as emotional and academic disengagement in school. Students may present this disengagement in school as acting out, being more withdrawn, and performing poorly on assignments and tests.

Here, Perla gives voice to this sense of double abandonment and longing for family left behind which contributed to her downward spiral of disengagement from middle school:

> In 7th grade I was doing really bad. I was doing really bad because I always
> told my mom, I want to go back. I don't want to stay here because this is not
> my home. . . . I wanted to go back with my grandma, I wanted to go back
> and be with my aunt. You know, it's two people that were there for me. They
> wanted to take care of us when my mom came to the United States. And for
> me, I appreciate them a lot because they took care of me since I was like 4
> years old and my mom had to come here. I think leaving them was really
> hard. Really, really hard. That's one of reasons why I wanted to go back to
> Mexico, because I didn't feel like this was my home. This was not where I
> wanted to stay, you know? In school, it was really hard to communicate with
> the students. Because I didn't know English. (personal communication,
> December 22, 2015)

Newcomer students like Perla and Luis are especially likely to fall into this downward educational spiral if their schools don't provide a socially welcoming and academically structured and scaffolded environment that can meet their particular emotional and developmental needs. To bridge the disconnect that such students may feel between their lives at home and in school, teachers and other school support staff need to bring a sensitivity to the cultural and psychological transitions they may be struggling with in both environments.

Drawing on the emergent bilinguals' experiences and prior knowledge with a translanguaging pedagogy, educators can have them view, read, and analyze how various domestic and international news sources report on immigrant issues and events, and then write their own editorials or interview one another to add their news commentary. Teachers can have students read and respond to poems, short stories, and novels with prominent immigrant characters and themes. They can be strategically paired to help one another grow in English and their home language through brainstorming and joint writing and revision activities of their own poems, spoken word, and other projects. This engages all students no matter their proficiency in challenging subject matter, giving emergent bilinguals the opportunity to contribute to their group in multiple languages (Hesson et al., 2014).

Having regular informal ways to check in with students is also important, particularly to address the emotional needs of those students who may have experienced trauma. This might include having students keep journals and periodically asking them to draw pictures or jot down how they are feeling on a given day, and taking time to respond in writing, and with a private conversation as needed, with those students who express a sense of loss, loneliness, or sadness.

One significant area of emotional stress for many newcomer students is the complicated process of reunification they likely experience with their parents. They often have to rebuild relationships with their parents, getting to know them again, or sometimes getting to know them and possibly new siblings for the first time. The relationship can feel further strained when, after all the anticipation and emotional buildup of living with their family again, immigrant students' parents are not able to be physically available because they are forced to work long hours to make ends meet. Perla had high hopes for her new life with her mother in Queens. But when she arrived, she barely saw her mother, who worked 10 hours a day at a nail salon. "My expectations in this country was like, having a lot of freedom and being able to see my mom every day in the mornings waking up. So it was kind of like, a disappointment. . . . [Now], I don't have that much of a relationship with my mom. We don't have time for each other" (The Babel Project, 2016).

The process of reunification with their family is further complicated for many immigrant students by the wildly unrealistic dreams they often have of what life will be like for them in America. Images and stories of a luxurious American lifestyle that they consume from U.S.-produced movies and television programs create a jarring disconnect for youth when they actually arrive to their new homes in the low-income and marginalized communities.

As Perla describes it, "Back in Mexico . . . almost all the TV shows were from New York. So I used to watch a TV show that there were two boys that lived in a hotel. And I thought I would live in a hotel. The doorman would open the door for me. I would get my luggage up in my room. That didn't happen" (The Babel Project, 2016).

Like Perla and Luis, Mohamed lived with extended family members apart from his parents while he waited to join them in the United States. Also like them, he had high hopes for what his life would be like when he got there.

He was raised by his grandfather in the Ivory Coast, was only 1 year old when his father moved to the United States, and was 5 when his mother left. In his EVC documentary about his experience immigrating to the United States, he recalls watching countless hours of television depicting the affluence of life in America filled with images of palatial houses, lush lawns, and sports cars, with young men of color like him wearing expensive watches and jewelry. He was convinced that this was the lifestyle that awaited him when he finally reunited with his family at JFK airport at age 19.

Upon arrival, his dreams were dashed not only because meeting his father and siblings for the first time and his mother after 14 years was far more disorienting than he had thought, but also because he was further confused when his parents took him to their small apartment in an economically depressed section of the Bronx that he was convinced was not his home. He kept asking them when they were going to take him to their real home—one of the extravagant ones he had seen in the videos:

> For the first time I met my dad, it was very awkward for me. I didn't grow up with him. I didn't feel connected. When I saw him, you know, we just hugged. After we took some pictures. And we went home after. . . . When we got home, I saw my mom. She was very, very happy to see me. I felt like, maybe tomorrow we would go to our own house. I thought maybe this was just for today. And tomorrow we would be going to our fancy home. Over time I realized that this was actually my house. My home. There was no home somewhere else. We never moved. (Educational Video Center, 2016)

Mohamed, like many other immigrant students, not only had to struggle to build new relationships with parents whom he never or only barely knew growing up and lower his inflated expectations to the reality of a poverty-level standard of living, but he also had to learn to live with nativist and anti-Muslim discrimination in America, which have been on the rise. Because of this, he was afraid of making his religion publicly known for fear of the discrimination. Even though he is Muslim, he intentionally left the box unchecked indicating his religion on the college application form he submitted. So, in addition to providing curricular support assisting newcomer students who are struggling to learn English, teachers also need to attend to their struggles with identity, as well as the humiliation and fear they may experience in school from other students' anti-immigrant and anti-Muslim taunts, and in some cases violence.

This means first of all to name it as a problem, and publicly acknowledge and make visible the hurtful experiences immigrant students may have of being dismissed, demeaned, or marginalized, experiences that are often invisible to others. Addressing this with antibias activities that challenge racial, religious, and ethnic stereotypes can build a safer and more inclusive learning community and help bring those students back into the full group. This includes raising awareness of microaggressions that immigrant students may experience in their daily life at school, such as when peers or teachers refer to them as illegal, repeatedly mispronounce their name even after they have been corrected, or make jokes that degrade or diminish their religion or race. Classes can brainstorm their own lists discussing the underlying assumptions and messages they send, and also share a time they experienced, heard, or witnessed microaggressions. They can then generate a new list where the microaggressions are reworded to communicate more inclusive messages.

Noting these patterns of declining student attitudes and expectations is in no way meant to individualize the problem or blame the victim for their poor academic achievement. Nativist, racist, and anti-immigrant attitudes that stigmatize students can lead students to internalize a sense of shame and also erode their

The First Time I Met My Dad

I was born and raised in Ivory Coast,

 View the clip online: www.tcpress.com/goodman-chapter-three#v3.2

sense of self-worth and academic efficacy. External to a students' individual grit or mindset, there are structural forces, within national systems of law enforcement and global economies of labor, that undermine parental support and family stability and set the conditions for such a decline of attitude and educational achievement in motion.

"SHE'S BARELY HOME":
LABOR EXPLOITATION AND PARENT–SCHOOL ENGAGEMENT

Newcomer students' struggles in school to overcome linguistic and social–emotional disadvantages are compounded by the impoverished material conditions in which they are likely to live. This is the case, regardless of whether they reside in urban, suburban, or rural communities, and especially for students growing up in families with undocumented parents. Over half of children of all immigrants live in poverty, and an astounding three-quarters of children of undocumented parents like Perla and Luis live in families below the poverty line[3] (Capps, Fix, & Zong, 2016). This means they are substantially more likely than students with U.S.-born parents to live in crowded housing, suffer from inadequate food security and poor health, and lack health insurance (Thronson, 2008). These conditions all have a negative impact on their capacity to actively engage in school.

These conditions of poverty for immigrant children persist in spite of the fact that their parents often work long hours in minimum- or subminimum-wage jobs, with no benefits, 6 and 7 days a week. With little or no English proficiency, many of the jobs they find are low-skilled at either below minimum wage or have off-the-books wage levels that are hard to enforce, such as day laborer, landscaper, gardener, nail-salon worker, restaurant worker, domestic worker, or nanny.

Immigrant parents' unauthorized or mixed-status family (including members with differing citizenship status) makes them particularly vulnerable to exploitation by unscrupulous employers who force them to work in hazardous conditions and engage in illegal labor practices such as wage theft. Wage theft includes paying workers less than minimum wage, cheating them out of overtime pay, or refusing to pay them at all. These practices are rampant across the county. A U.S. Labor Department study of wage theft in New York and California found that more than 300,000 workers experience minimum-wage violations in those states every month. That represents 38% of the income of the victimized workers in New York and 49% in California (Eastern Research Group, 2014). Eight out of 10 workers in Los Angeles reported experiencing wage theft. Seventy percent of low-wage workers surveyed in Chicago, Los Angeles, and New York City who worked overtime did not receive any pay for the work they did outside their regular shift. This exploitation is especially widespread for women, who are significantly more likely than men to experience minimum-wage violations, and foreign-born workers are nearly twice as likely to experience violations as their U.S.-born counterparts (Bernhardt et al., 2009).

Isolated in their employers' home, immigrant women who are employed as domestic workers are at particular risk of being threatened by employers to be reported to ICE and sent home if they complain about nonpayment of wages or even in some cases physical or sexual abuse. Beyond domestic workers, this threat of retaliation affects the entire industry of low-wage workers. According to a survey of low-wage workers in New York City, Chicago, and Los Angeles, 43% of those who filed a complaint to their employer or attempted to form a union experienced some form of illegal retaliation from their employer (Bernhardt et al., 2009).

The labor exploitation and abuse of these most vulnerable workers directly impacts the health and educational well-being of their children who are enrolled in school. The minimum or subminimum wages, unstable and unpredictable work hours, and lack of reliable child care these parents are able to provide are associated with poor health, developmental delays, and high levels of stress that all contribute to their children's low educational achievement (Brabeck & Xu, 2010; Capps, Hooker, et al., 2015). The lack of health benefits and paid sick leave and vacation time off makes it even worse for the children of those families. Immigrant children tend to fall even further behind their U.S.-born peers socially and academically when their parents can't afford to pay for them to attend costly after-school, weekend, and summer educational and cultural enrichment activities that middle-class parents provide for their children.

In addition to the disadvantage of missing out on enrichment activities, long work hours and exploitative employers can hinder parents' ability to help with their homework after school and advocate for their children's academic achievement. As Perla explains, her mother is forced to endure such conditions, working 10 hours a day, 6 and 7 days a week, breathing hazardous chemicals in a nail salon. Perla's mother explained that complaining about them to her boss was not an option, despite the fact that these industry-wide wage and health violations have been investigated and publicized by *The New York Times* and the New York State Labor and Health Departments (Nir, 2015a, 2015b, 2015c). "I did know that whatever thing I did bad she [the boss] could call the police. I knew that I was . . . in danger that they would deport me" (The Babel Project, 2016). Not only was she forced to report to work on days when she was sick, but she was also prohibited from taking time off to attend the parent–teacher conference at Perla's school.

As teachers of immigrant students, we need to be conscious of the long hours and often exploitative labor conditions their parents work in when they may show up late, or not at all, for parent–teacher conferences. Immigrant parents care just as deeply about their children's academic well-being as any other parent, but are often prevented from participating more fully in their children's schooling. The result is that they are deprived of critical opportunities to learn about their children's academic performance and any particular problems their children are having (Suárez-Orozco, Suárez-Orozco, & Todorova, 2008). In addition, these missed opportunities for parent–teacher conversations also deprive teachers of the chance to learn more about their students from a parent's perspective, particularly if their students are struggling with feelings of parental loss and disconnection with school and their family at home (Suárez-Orozco, Todorova, & Louie, 2002). The lack of English fluency, combined with the labor conditions of the working poor, therefore makes it all the more likely they will be intimidated and misunderstood by teachers and administrators, and that much more difficult for them to guide and advocate for their children amid a complex and foreign educational system.

As Perla explains:

> I think the only time that I see my mother in parent–teacher conference was when I was in 9th grade. And it was only one time. And I think it's something that, all my teachers ask me, "Oh, I want to meet your mother." You know, but my mother's not able to go to a parent–teacher conference. Even though I want her to go. Because I know I'm putting a lot of effort in school to have good grades. But she's not—she's not able to go. Like, I would like that the teachers to tell her, "Oh, your daughter's having, is doing good in school. She's keeping up with all the homeworks," and things like that. But she's, she's not able to go. I think that it's because they can't go. It's not that they don't care. It's just that, maybe, sometimes parents, for example my mom, she gets out of work at 10 p.m. She gets home at 11:30 at night. (personal communication, December 22, 2015)

Knowing the very long hours many immigrant students' parents must work just to feed their families, we need to be creative and flexible in scheduling their parent–teacher conferences. We can ask our students' parents what time they leave work, or when they can get time off from work and then set the meetings based on the parents' schedule. If that is not possible, such as in the case of Perla's mother,

longer
line

we can ask the parents to send another relative or even a sibling to meet. It's worth noting that such meetings do not replace, but rather are in addition to, the continued need to build a close relationship with the students, and know what is going on in their home lives, as well as in school. As Perla says:

> And the only thing she wants to do is to rest. To work what? Almost 10 hours, almost 11 hours? And when she gets home, she goes, gets home, and goes to sleep. Because that's all she wants to do. She's had a long day at work. She's not able to ask me, "How was school? Want to eat something?" . . . I think that's something, like my little brother always tells me, "I think that mom doesn't care about me 'cause she never asks me how was my day." But she's never there. She's barely home. I only see her in the morning. I sometimes see her in the night. Because I go to sleep let's say at 12 o'clock. And she gets home at 11:30. So I only see her for a half hour. And then I go to sleep. (personal communication, December 22, 2015)

The long hours that immigrant parents must work to meet even their family's most basic needs not only creates barriers to effective communication with their children's teachers, but can also cause their emotional relationship with their children to suffer. Without money to pay for a babysitter or a nanny as middle-class parents do, children often end up being raised by older siblings. In some cases when older siblings also have to work, the children are left alone to simply fend for themselves for many hours after school and into the evening. They have to feed themselves, check their own homework, keep themselves company, and put themselves to bed.

"NOT HAVING A DAD": DEPORTATION AND FORCED SINGLE-PARENT HOMES

The deportation of an immigrant parent,[4] most often the father, has devastating consequences for their children financially, emotionally, and academically. And often, these parents are arrested and deported in retaliation for complaining about wage theft or other illegal labor practices and conditions in their workplace.

Kids alone

The loss of one or both of their parents forcibly tears apart the family, and robs the children of all the financial, academic, and emotional support, guidance, and love they would have otherwise received. Although two-parent homes are more likely to provide more time and resources, a father's deportation suddenly transforms the family into a single-parent, single-wage-earner, female-headed household with less time and fewer resources available for students' emotional and educational well-being. It is exceedingly difficult for students to shut this family upheaval and trauma out of their minds and come to school fully ready to learn.

Luis recalled what happened in his family after he had finally made his way to New York to be back together with his parents and siblings. He had just celebrated his 11th birthday with everyone, and thought he had never been happier. Then, 3 weeks later, everything changed after his father got into an argument with his boss at the restaurant over money he said his boss had cheated him out of. As he tells it:

> One day my mother arrived late at night because she works late. She came home at midnight saying that my dad got arrested. Because he fought with his boss in a restaurant here in the city. I don't really know what happened at that moment. The only thing I know is that he got deported and that he didn't want us to get involved because he was scared that it would affect us. . . . Three weeks after my birthday, they deported him. I have a lot of questions of why they had to deport my dad. If the only thing he did was to defend himself. Because what he was arguing, that I know of, was, because of a week of work that his boss didn't want to pay him. And I saw that as really unfair. I still have questions of why? . . . . Why him? If the only thing he wanted to do was to work. Because he worked hard so he could sustain us. (Educational Video Center, 2015a)

Another EVC student, Jean, who comes from a Haitian family, tells of when ICE agents arrested his father, taking him before Jean could say goodbye. He also explains the additional financial and emotional burden his detention caused his family:

> I remember they came into the house in the morning. Early, early. My mom answered the door. I just remember there were of four or five of them. They were asking about my dad, or whatever. We were all very quiet and respectful to them. . . . They were saying he'll come back in a while. Bring a couple of dollars, $20 for travel money. But he didn't come back. He was gone. Locked up for months. . . . We were always in a rough financial spot. Him being gone put an extra strain on us. Phone calls for him to call us, and the commissary were very expensive. . . . I remember when he was confined, we all had to write letters to the judge. It was a deep emotional investment. I had to write about why he should stay in the States. We all had to plead our case why he was important to us. . . . It was heartfelt. I cried while I was writing it. I said I want him to be able to see me graduate. (personal communication, October 6, 2017)

Students like Luis and Jean experience the damaging economic and emotional consequences of their parents' detention or deportation in a range of ways that can negatively impact their school performance. These short- and long-term social–emotional effects may include increased feelings of abandonment, symptoms of trauma, anxiety, isolation, and depression, increased frequency of crying, loss of appetite, sleeplessness, clingy behavior, and fears of law enforcement officials. These changes in behavior can be caused by witnessing the arrest of parents, not knowing what happened to them, unstable caregiving arrangements, or onset of depression among parents. In some cases, mothers even lost custody of their children when they were unable to provide for their families after the deportation of the father, who was the main breadwinner (Capps, Hooker, et al., 2015; Dreby, 2012).

They Deported Him

▶ *View the clip online*: www.tcpress.com/goodman-chapter-three#v3.3

Of course, not all students respond in the same way to the financial and emotional trauma of losing a parent. In Jean's case, he said he kept his feelings to himself and never spoke to any of his teachers about witnessing his father's arrest or the subsequent hardships his family was facing. But it took a toll on his achievement in high school, nonetheless. "I was just falling further behind. I'm like a rock. I suppressed a lot of my feelings. I was on the path of dropping out. I had to get out of the school I was in to better myself" (personal communication, October 6, 2017).

Men who leave their families to work in the United States and then leave their family, and particularly their wife, with an economic burden after being deported often feel humiliated and emasculated. So their communication with wives and children in many cases diminishes or stops altogether (Dreby, 2012). For the children who remain, the abrupt severing of their relationship with the deported father can have a deep social and emotional impact. But unlike with a death of a parent, the children often don't know whether the separation is temporary or permanent, and so there is no finality to this kind of loss. When students suffer a painful loss like this that goes unrecognized by teachers and others, they aren't given permission to grieve (Suárez-Orozco, Todorova, & Louie, 2002). Luis shares his feelings on his father's deportation:

> At that moment I wanted to cry. I knew that that would be a great change for me. Because not having a dad is a big difference. Since that moment, I was 11–12 years old, I had to take [on] a really big responsibility. Even though I didn't agree. Even though I didn't want to. With my mom, I didn't have enough trust. I trusted my dad more. Because it's supposedly—it's between

men. There are things that I have [done] but haven't told my mom, because I think she is going to think wrong about me, or things like that. I also lost the relationship with my dad, I barely talk to him. There are things that happened to me. . . . Well, there were moments I needed him. And I didn't have him by my side because he was in Mexico. (Educational Video Center, 2015a)

We need to understand what a terrible shock it is for our students and their entire family—not only emotionally but also financially—when a family member, usually the father, is deported. They experience a precipitous drop in income from one day to the next when they are already struggling to pay for their basic needs. One study found a 70% average drop in family income during the first 6 months following the arrest of a parent (Capps, Hooker, et al., 2015). Unlike when a husband is laid off or hurt at work, women who are suddenly forced to become single and responsible for earning the total family income alone are unable to rely on income from unemployment or worker's compensation. Being conscious of the social and emotional impact that this deep financial and emotional loss has on our students will help us be that much better equipped to support those of our students who are experiencing such family upheaval.

We need to bring transformative teaching and multiple strategies to support newcomer students' instructional, social, and emotional needs in multiple spaces across the school day. In addition to academic classes, these spaces can be advisory classes, where teachers also serve as advisors, restorative justice programs, and after-school clubs. Engaging them in inclusive, bilingual, and student-centered

I Needed Him

I also lost the relationship with my dad, I barely talk to him.

▶ *View the clip online: www.tcpress.com/goodman-chapter-three#v3.4*

spaces gives students important social networks for them to know that they are not alone in struggling with these problems, that they have peers experiencing similar difficulties and adults who are there to support and advocate for them. With additional resources, schools can provide students with individual academic assistance, as well as legal and social service referrals in the community.

"HE NEVER WENT TO SCHOOL": A CLIMATE OF FEAR

ICE raids of homes are intentional and strategic tools of immigration law enforcement to create a pervasive and ever-present climate of fear among children and families in undocumented communities. These raids are also designed to maximize the fear of deportation throughout immigrant communities far beyond those who are actually directly affected. Agents are usually heavily armed, wearing bulletproof vests, and pound on the front door in the early morning or dead of night without a warrant. Children suffer stress, depression, and anxiety disorders after witnessing their parents taken away by armed agents in their home. In some cases, they are unable to go home if their parents have been arrested in workplace raids. This sudden loss can cause them to see danger everywhere, carrying an anxiety and pervasive loss of safety into their daily life at school.

Not only are the thousands of children who have seen one or both parents arrested affected, but the impact is much more magnified as fear spreads throughout the community to those who hear about it. This spreads the message that speaking out against wage theft or for rights as a worker to organize unions is an illegal and deportable offense. Because many occupants subjected to raids include children and adults who are citizens or lawful permanent residents, it creates a hyperawareness of legal status, and confusion—even among those who are U.S. citizens but may have family members, friends, or neighbors who are not—as to who is at risk of arrest. In this way, all immigrants become criminalized, and everyone feels that he or she is a target with a fixed identity as "deportable." As a result, immigrants go into hiding, and hide their children, as well (Thronson, 2008).

The parents' legal vulnerability, such as their legal status and history of detention, has a direct relation to their children's emotional well-being and academic performance. The greater their legal vulnerability, the greater the reported impact on children's perceptions of their parent's emotional well-being and ability to provide for them financially. As the children's emotional well-being suffers, there is greater likelihood that their academic performance in school will suffer as well (Brabeck & Xu, 2010).

However, it's not always a family's actual legal status or the deportation act itself, but the *questioning* of their status and the *possibility* of deportation, that has affected an even greater number of children. Even children from families who are legal residents can be traumatized by stories in the news and rumors in the community that spread misinformation and waves of panic that all families are at risk of deportation, at any time and any place. For example, there was talk—later proved false—of raids on trains going to the Bronx and Queens, and checkpoints

in Long Island (Seelye & Bidgood, 2017). Children's fears about their parents'—
and, at times, their own—legal status, reinforces a sense of themselves as being
marginal, criminal, disposable, and deportable.

This mounting fear, hypervigilance, and anxiety of imminent separation from
their parents has been a cause of declining performance in school and has led to
increasing numbers of students being kept home from school (Dreby, 2012). This
is particularly the case for immigrant parents who are deeply aware of the threat
of deportation, but not as familiar with their rights or social benefits in the child
welfare, health, and education systems.

However, even school efforts to support and inform parents of their legal
rights are now more challenging than before due to the panic that heightened police surveillance and deportation has created in immigrant communities. Even
though schools with large immigrant populations are holding "know your rights"
workshops for students and their parents, principals are reporting that many parents are staying away. Word apparently is spreading that such gatherings are dangerous to attend because they might attract ICE agents.

Perla describes how her mother kept her brother home from school and the
doctor because of the pervasive fear of being deported:

> When my brother and my mom came here, they didn't know anything. That
> my brother could go to school. That my brother could get insurance until
> a certain age. Things like that. My mom was afraid of getting deported.
> That's something like every person who comes to the United States thinks.
> . . . When he first came, he was 11 years old. And since that time, until like
> 4 years after, he never went to school. He never went like to the doctor.
> Because my mom thought he was gonna get deported. She was gonna get
> deported. (personal communication, December 22, 2015)

The fragmentation of the family and forced single-parent home that results
from the deportation of a parent suddenly places children in the hands of their
older siblings to raise. Deprived of the time, attention, social–emotional support,
and academic guidance that one or both parents can give, students' emotional
well-being and academic success suffers. In effect, when their family has been
so dramatically disrupted, immigrant students are forced to parent themselves.
This often leads to feelings of isolation and abandonment. Luis talks about his
experience:

> I rarely see my family, neither my brother or mother. My mom works
> ironing clothes and she also works as a cook. My brother and my mom
> have to work extra hours to be able to pay the rent. The moments that I see
> them are when they tell me, "Luis, wake up, it's time to go to school." My life
> changed since the moment my dad was deported to Mexico. It caused the
> separation of my parents. Everything changed. Before, I would get home and
> the food was ready. My mom was there waiting for me and she would ask
> me, "How was school?" "What do you have to tell me?" Things like that. Or,

"Are you hungry? Are you thirsty? Leave your stuff over there." "Come sit, let's talk." Things like that. Or, "Let's watch TV." But now I get home and no one is there. (Educational Video Center, 2015a)

"I WAS EMPOWERING MY PEOPLE": STUDENT IMMIGRANT RIGHTS

Luis, Mohamed, Perla, and the countless other immigrant students across the country struggle not only to survive the emotional trauma they experience from the loss of one or both parents from deportation and exploitation at work, but to go on and succeed in school. Just when they need the guidance and healing from their parents the most, they are forced to fend for themselves in a state of self-parentification. Just when they need schools that can provide culturally sustaining curricula with individualized bilingual linguistic, social, and emotional supports, and nurturing relationships, they most often live in low-income racially and ethnically segregated communities with underfunded, racially and ethnically segregated schools. Their high needs require schools with ample student health and social services, strong connections with students' families, and ongoing professional development support for teachers.

Instead, newcomer students too often have negative school experiences and social conditions, all of which put them at greater risk for falling into a downward academic spiral of declining self-worth and performance in school. Their school problems are further magnified as they struggle to survive the violence of the local gang and underground drug economy prevalent in poor immigrant communities, with insufficient support for access to college and well-paying jobs (Suárez-Orozco, Bang, et al., 2010).

As we know, however, immigrant students such as Luis, Mohamed, and Perla endure great hardships making the trip to America and have a great capacity for resilience and healing. Overcoming these traumas depends on a broad range of factors. We have seen time and again that negative school climates lead to decreased engagement, lowered expectations, and limited academic success for students from low-income communities, particularly newcomer students, as opposed to students from more privileged communities.

The opposite holds true just as well. For those who somehow beat the odds and achieve success in school, particularly those newcomer students in their early adolescence, it turns out it's not about grit or endurance in practicing new skills. Research shows that most often, it is the quality of the relationships that the students develop in school that makes a difference. The kinds of formal and informal relationships outside the family that students make with their peers, teachers, principals, counselors, coaches, or other supportive adults provide them with much needed social and emotional support, sustenance, and sense of belonging that is critical for the students' academic self-efficacy. We help foster such relationship building when we offer our students safe and inclusive spaces such as advisory classes, restorative justice, and after-school arts and civic engagement programs that tap into the strengths of their home language and culture. These nurturing relationships help newcomers build their resilience and develop their belief in their own competence and control of their own learning and language, all of which they need to bridge the gap between home and school cultures and to navigate the complicated transition into a new country (Suárez-Orozco, Rhodes, & Milburn, 2009).

At EVC, we created a safe, welcoming, and bilingual space for Mohamed, Luis, Perla, and other new immigrant students to share their private and often painful immigration stories with the larger group. We also created a nurturing environment that attends to the social–emotional needs of all students, and where peers celebrate one another (including celebrating one another's birthdays). Through their process of making their documentary, they visited and conducted interviews in one another's schools, communities, and homes, and even met one another's family members. We tapped into the strengths of their culture and home language and supported them in developing new relationships with their EVC video teacher, their fellow student video producers, and grassroots community activists. So, in addition to building their social capital through these new relationships, they are also building political capital. This is a critical step toward self-empowerment for vulnerable new immigrant students as their academic self-efficacy becomes intertwined with empowerment and political self-efficacy.

In this clip from *Growing Apart: The Politics of Family Separation* (Educational Video Center, 2015a), Perla encourages Luis (as he finishes his birthday cake) to join Make the Road, an immigrant rights organization, and invites him to attend a meeting there. This casual peer-to-peer conversation (translated from Spanish) signals an important turning point for Luis. Though he resists at first, he decides to join and take action for the well-being of his mother and himself.

Luis Decides to Become a Member

 View the clip online: www.tcpress.com/goodman-chapter-three#v3.5

Perla: I was talking to the organizers about you in the organization I go to. And they told me if you want to join the organization. That's why I asked you, if you would like to . . .

Luis: It's just that I am a busy person.

Perla: You're a busy person?

Luis: Yes, I would like to, but I don't have the time.

Perla: You don't have the time?

Luis: Because right now, I have this [internship at EVC] and I'm thinking of working after. As I'm telling you, I don't want my mom to be working anymore.

Perla: But it would be a way to help your mom.

Luis: I know, but, how can I tell you? The easiest way to help my mom is by her working less.

Perla: So you're thinking of working?

Luis: Yes.

The students narrate what happens next: "Eventually, though, Luis changes his mind. Perla takes Luis to an immigrant rights information session at Make the Road New York. Luis decides to become a member . . . Sí Se Puede!" (Educational Video Center, 2015a).

Perla and Luis's participation in organizing efforts for immigrant rights was inspiring to see. However, it wasn't the end of the story. The following year, Luis found work in a restaurant and missed a lot of school. As he mentions in this brief exchange with Perla, earning money to help his mother was a priority for him. He ended up failing many of his classes and never graduated, in spite of his principal's repeated efforts to keep him in school or help him transfer to another high school.

Luis's decision to place work over school is becoming a more frequent calculation for newcomer students. It can be seen as an example not so much of irresponsibility, but rather as Gross (2017) describes it, as "a deep sense of responsibility—just not to their schoolwork. If anything, they are hyperresponsible . . . [where] students have had to handle outsized responsibility in their homes and communities" (p. 54). In addition to the urgent need to support their family here, the increased targeting of immigrant communities for overpolicing and deportation is forcing them to plan for their financial needs back in their home country in the event that they are deported. As a principal recounted:

> Last year, one of our top students, a Salvadoran boy, decided to drop out in the 11th grade. He said, "Look, if they send me back to El Salvador, I can't show up empty-handed, without money." The whole point he was sent here was to work and earn money. So he quit to work in construction full-time. Imagine, a 17-year-old kid has that weight on him! That's a life-changing decision. (personal communication, October 17, 2017)

We all hope our students will make the most of their time in high school and go on to be successful in college and promising careers. But helping our students make postsecondary plans takes on new meaning when deportation becomes an ever-present fact of life for them. Such planning now may mean we need to connect them and their family members with social and legal support services. It may also include providing them with alternative educational options that they can attend while working, such as night school or GED programs.

Perla did graduate high school and go on to college. She also continued her work as a youth organizer. Reflecting on her own personal and political empowerment through the immigrant social justice organization and EVC, Perla said, "Before, I used to be afraid that my family be separated again. Because my family, all of my family was undocumented. . . . And when I got social justice, it was like, I was empowered. I was empowering my people that they're passing through the same thing as me" (personal communication, December 22, 2015).

In a screening of her documentary for teachers, however, Perla recalled how she struggled in school when she first came to the United States. She spoke of how humiliating and dehumanizing it felt when some of her teachers in middle school called her and other undocumented students "alien" and "illegal." She urged all of us in her audience to never use those words and to be mindful of the implicit biases we may bring to our teaching. She asked us to work harder to build positive relationships with immigrant students in our classes, and to take time to listen to their stories and learn about what they have experienced.

If we can bring a bilingual approach that taps into students' home language and culture, we as teachers, school leaders, counselors, and school social work staff can more effectively partner with our students' families to bridge the gap between school and family and community. In some cases, schools have reached out to affected families after a raid, explaining that the school is a safe haven and encouraging them to send their children back to school. Luis's school offers legal services for students and their families.

A principal in a high school serving undocumented students describes an incident:

> We had a student's stepfather who was deported. The kids were hiding out. The mother was also in hiding, but the kids didn't know where she was. We connected her to legal advice. It happened early in the morning and they had no idea why he was taken. We were able to reach out to get support to find him and to reconnect the kids with their mother. (personal communication, October 17, 2017)

Providing these kinds of services and building these positive supportive relationships plays an important role in meeting students' most pressing social and emotional needs and improving their academic performance in school (Capps, Hooker, et al., 2015; Suárez-Orozco, Bang, et al., 2010).

Offering these services as not only educators, but allies and advocates for their students, we create what Weiss and Fine (2004) call "sites of possibility," or "small safe spaces, fractures in the hegemonic armor" (p. xxiv). Like EVC, such school-based sites provide students with integrated support that furthers their academic growth, helps them heal from social and emotional trauma, and empowers them as youth leaders engaged in social justice work.

One such example in Luis's school is the DREAMers club, the first of its kind in New York State. DREAMers refers to undocumented students who came to the United States as children and were protected under the DACA program (Deferred Action for Childhood Arrivals), which was created by President Obama after Congress failed to pass the Development, Relief and Education for Alien Minors (DREAM) Act. This club engages students in advocacy work in the school and community, including writing letters and attending protests and rallies. Through the process, it develops their self-confidence and leadership skills as they learn to do political organizing with undocumented college students in the New York State Leadership Council.

Educators and administrators are creating sites of possibility in their school and developing a range of strategies for being culturally responsive to the social emotional and political issues their immigrant students and family members struggle with, whether they are facilitating advisory classes or integrating antibias activities and other immigrant-related subject matter into the curriculum during the day, coordinating DREAMers clubs after school, or holding "know your rights" workshops and offering legal or social service resources to students and their families in the evening. They are not only listening to and validating their students' stories but also building strong relationships that engage them in their education and empower them to defend their rights

Perla explains how making her documentary not only helped her overcome her own fears, but empowered her as a youth leader in her own community:

> None of my siblings were born here. I used to think being deported was, was something I was really afraid of. . . . You know, I was not afraid any longer. [With my documentary] I was able to teach other youth that were passing through the same thing about not being afraid. About empowering themselves and empowering other people. (personal communication, December 22, 2015)

In this way, as emergent bilinguals like Perla work past their fear and traumatic experiences, they experience what it's like to speak up and speak out in school, in after-school programs, and in the community. Telling their stories, and developing their voice and sense of agency, they become role models for their fellow students. Providing them with welcoming, bilingual, and culturally inclusive classes, clubs, and programs, we support our immigrant students in building closer relationships with their peers, teachers, and other adults in the community. With transformative teaching, we can help them bridge the gap between their home and school environments and open up more opportunities for their academic self-efficacy and resilience. Sites of possibility beget new sites of possibility.

CHAPTER 4

"People Are Strong When They Stand Together"

Gender and Identity

"Don't use that pink crayon."

It started in 3rd grade. Muzik was picked on and bullied throughout the entire year, for being "different." By the 6th grade when Muzik came out, school became a far more dangerous place: Homophobic verbal abuse turned to brutal violence. Irene also suffered from abuse in school about her sexual orientation, but teachers and administrators didn't take her complaints seriously and so she left her high school.

For Andrea, the verbal abuse and threats of violence were not about her sexual orientation or choice of lifestyle. It was simply because she was a young woman walking out on the streets in her neighborhood, to and from school. On a daily basis, men and boys reduced her to being a sexual object, just a body.

Friends and boyfriends shamed Nang and Samantha about their looks and body size, leading Nang to stop eating to reach the ideal of female thinness that she saw in the media. With such an intense focus on their own bodies, they began to see themselves as objects for the pleasure of others.

None of these students was left unscathed by the emotional and physical abuses they endured. It is no surprise that as their sense of safety and well-being declined, so did their participation and performance in school. No one can perform their best academically when they are weak from fasting, or fear for their physical safety going to their locker or walking home that day.

Although they were students in New York City schools over a span of nearly 20 years, they all participated in EVC after-school workshops and created documentaries that tell powerful stories about their struggles in the face of virulent homophobia, transphobia, objectification, and misogyny to maintain their identity and their dignity. *Moving Without Direction* (Educational Video Center, 2017) portrays a student's struggles with homophobic bullying and decision to join a gang to gain protection. In *Out Youth in Schools* (Educational Video Center, 1998), the crew interview students who express their fears of coming out and admit to hiding their identity by acting homophobic in school, just to fit in. The crew also report on the Genders & Sexualities Alliance that was established in one of the schools they attended to advocate in support for LGBTQ students. In *Losing Ground: The New Face of Homelessness* (Educational Video Center, 2007), students explain how they were forced to leave their homes because of their sexual orientation and now live in a homeless shelter. In *Gender Power* (2014a), students explore the spectrum of street harassment of girls from catcalls to being stalked on the way home from school, and in *What's Your Beautiful?* (2014c), objectification becomes self-objectification when girls use social media as a tool to create more sexualized selfie images in order to gain followers on Instagram, and internalize the male culture's caricature of the thin-ideal female body to the point of starving themselves.

What's clear is that these students' gender and sexual identity profoundly shape the daily experiences they have whether they're at home, in school, on the streets, or on the Internet. Through no fault of their own, in a culture that vilifies those with a nondominant identity and sexual orientation and objectifies the body image of girls and women, they must endure catcalls and put downs, threats of sexual harassment and violence, and learn to measure their self-worth by weight and dress size.

As school leaders, teachers, and counselors, we have a critical role to play not only in protecting our students from verbal and physical violence, but also in creating inclusive communities of compassion that promote their healing and well-being. Unfortunately, instead of being a safe refuge from such abuse, too many schools have become just one more space where students must run the gauntlet of daily indignities, harassment, and assaults. This is not only the fault of individual educators but also the fallout of unenforced or even discriminatory school policies that foster climates of fear and abuse.

There has been great progress in women's rights and in LGBTQ rights over the past 20 years since EVC students created *Out Youth in Schools*. But there are also powerful currents of discrimination, reaction, and regression, rolling back hard-won civil rights and human rights. This chapter gives voice to students struggling with poor body image, abuse, and trauma, and explores the broader legal, social, and cultural forces at play that shape how students view, interact with, and treat each other in school. Unfortunately, some teachers and administrators are indifferent and choose to look the other way when abuses occur. Some even express misogynistic, homophobic, and transphobic comments themselves, allowing a poisonous school culture and climate to grow that normalizes the verbal and physical harassment of female, queer, and transgender students.

Others are bringing a social justice consciousness to the problem and working as mentors, allies, and advocates for students to take action in their schools and communities. With transformative teaching, they have a consciousness of the systemic nature of heterosexist and homophobic oppression, as being larger than an individual's problem while also being subject to change with personal agency and collective action. Knowing how closely interwoven student learning, self-empowerment, and action really are, educators are coordinating girls' support groups, Genders & Sexualities Alliances, and other safe spaces of resistance, empowerment, and community in their schools

Some students form and participate in these groups at personal risk. And teachers have faced professional risk standing up for and with their students who are marginalized and unfairly targeted in school and in society at large. This all takes grit and perseverance, but not the academic skill-building kind. It takes a moral courage and commitment to the well-being of the entire school community. Program interventions and strong support from teachers and school leaders will go a long way toward building a more inclusive and humane school culture that will not only benefit the most vulnerable students, but also promote greater empathy and mutual understanding among *all* students. In some cases, being a compassionate, dependable, and supportive adult may save lives. But in every case, they are helping transform them.

"I NEVER WENT BACK": BULLYING AND ANTI-LGBTQ VIOLENCE

Muzik joined EVC's documentary workshop after the semester had already started. But it wasn't too late to help choose the subject the group would make their film about. Muzik's charisma and compelling pitch soon won the others over. Muzik's story was about being bullied and beaten up in school and then joining a gang, the Bloods, as the only way to gain protection and a sense of belonging.

Muzik's mother explains, "Muzik was growing up rough. Being mistreated. Being bullied, teased. It was hard. But she kept a lot of it to herself. So she learned to develop this wall. Even toward me." And Muzik said, "I got bullied for liking girls. I got bullied for, for being Black. I got bullied for not wanting to be down. I got bullied for wanting to be down. No matter what it was, people—they saw me as a target" (Educational Video Center, 2017).

I Got Bullied

 View the clip online: www.tcpress.com/goodman-chapter-four#v4.1

Muzik explains when the bullying began: "I remember it going on through my whole 3rd-grade year. Then, once I came out of the closet in 6th grade, everything became worse. I was 11 then, and it moved from verbal to being physical. . . . They tried to lock me in a locker" (personal communication, September 28, 2017).

Muzik's is unfortunately not an isolated case. Schools are often an unwelcoming and even dangerous place for LGBTQ students. They are harassed, bullied, threatened, and assaulted because of their sexual orientation at far greater numbers than their heterosexual peers. According to a GLSEN National School Climate Survey (2016), over three-quarters of LGBTQ students experienced verbal harassment in school; over half felt unsafe because of their sexual orientation; and nearly a third had skipped at least 1 day of school in the past month because of safety concerns. Forty-nine percent experienced cyberbullying, and 13% were punched, kicked, injured with a weapon, or otherwise physically assaulted in the past year because of their sexual orientation.

A gay male student interviewed by EVC students in *Out Youth in Schools* said that the threat of physical and verbal abuse was so great in his high school that he admitted to pretending to be homophobic to avoid being outed by his peers. Now, 20 years after that interview, another EVC team is making their documentary about homophobia. One of the students in the crew told of the taunting and harassment his gay younger brother experienced at school and at home—and his role as one of the people who used to bully his brother:

> You don't want to go to the lunchroom. Everybody points at you. You become a topic. School is not good. . . . He [his brother] would come to each class late, because you want class to already have started and the hallways to be empty when you are walking there. Me, I was bad, too. You know, when your brother gets you mad. I would always—it was a string I would pull. I'd say, "Faggot! Where is your boyfriend?" He would go to school to get bullied, come home and he'd get bullied some more. . . . I didn't give him a break. Just thinking about that made me want to cry. (personal communication, October 23, 2017)

Anti-LGBTQ harassment and violence against queer students makes it exceedingly difficult for them to actively participate and learn in school. First is the problem of forced truancy. According to the 2015 report from the CDC, LGB students were 140% more likely than heterosexual students (12% versus 5%) to miss at least 1 day of school because of safety concerns during the month prior to the survey (Kann et al., 2016).

Muzik's forced absences from school increased as the violence they (Muzik's preferred gender pronoun) suffered became more brutal:

> In one school in particular there was a gang and they didn't like me. They beat me up and robbed me on three separate occasions. It was on the third time that they actually pistol whipped me. This was when I was in middle school. After that, I ended up skipping school for 3 months. I was scared.

I was too afraid to go back to school. I had just been pistol whipped! And the school never even contacted my mother about my absences. I didn't tell my mother about it, either. I never went back. (personal communication, September 28, 2017)

The trauma that results from such chronic and severe violence leaves students physically and emotionally damaged. As they become more consumed by fear and anxiety and become more detached from school, their absences accumulate and grades naturally suffer from all the lessons, tests, and homework assignments they miss. In addition, when fear of bullying causes LGBTQ students to miss school regularly, it weakens the social relationships they can develop with their peers and teachers. With weak or no such social relationships, they can't take advantage of school programs and resources that might help them recover and improve academically. Without these relationships, resources, and participation in school-related activities, student achievement suffers (Wimberly, Wilkinson, & Pearson, 2015).

We can give critical support to our students in trauma, such as Muzik, by letting them know that that we care for them, and if they ask for it, we will help connect them with the medical and psychological resources they need in the school and community. We can also develop plans with our students to catch up on missed schoolwork. This also presents opportunities for us to address the issue of homophobic bullying, not just an individual student's problem, but a problem for the larger school community to grapple with.

Most of us know how pervasive a problem bullying has become and have brought antibullying, including cyberbullying, programs into our school districts across the country. The problem is, often these programs don't address one of the most prevalent forms of bullying—against LGBTQ students. None of 23 comprehensive antibullying programs studied that were designed for middle and high school students covered issues of sexual orientation, homophobia, sexual harassment, or sexual violence beyond a cursory mention (Espelage, 2015). It is deeply troubling to see the resistance many schools put up against diversifying their bullying prevention programs to include sexual orientation and gender expression. It's not only morally wrong to allow a hostile school climate to grow while excluding a group of students from the protection that such programs can provide, but it's also an ineffective way to address the problem.

It's difficult enough for queer students to see no mention in their school's antibullying programs of the abuse they face. But the social–emotional and academic impact is made immeasurably worse when their teachers, counselors, and administrators are indifferent when they report it, or are blatantly homophobic. Nearly two-thirds of LGBTQ students who reported an incident of harassment or assault said that school staff did nothing or told them to ignore it. Fifty-six percent said their teachers or other school staff made homophobic remarks, and 63% said teachers or staff made biased comments about gender expression (Kosciw, Greytak, Giga, Villenas, & Danischewski, 2016).

Irene spoke about how her teachers' indifference to her complaints of being bullied convinced her to leave school: "I was followed. I was harassed. People

I Had to Leave

▶ *View the clip online*: www.tcpress.com/goodman-chapter-four#v4.2

spread rumors about me. Teachers wouldn't take me seriously about my complaints. About threats against my safety. I wasn't able to learn in my school. I had to leave" (Educational Video Center, 1998).

Reflecting back on the lack of support or protection she received from the school staff at the time, Irene said:

> I actually was harassed by the school nurse. Just because I didn't wear dresses and fought guys who bullied me. . . . They [the school staff] just ignored me. They acted like it's my fault. It's not my fault for who I am. It's your fault for not protecting me from racist, homophobic, bullying boys! (personal communication, October 4, 2017)

Irene eventually had to move out of her hometown in New Jersey to complete her high school education in New York City. Without a caring adult to turn to for understanding and support, victimized LGBTQ students are at much greater risk for bodily harm and academic failure. In fact, fear of safety in school from constant bullying and harassment from other students is reported as their main reason for dropping out of high school.

To make matters worse, LGBTQ students are often punished twice for their sexual orientation: once by the abusive students who bully and assault them, and then again by administrators who disproportionately discipline them—even when they are the victims and fighting back in self-defense.

Muzik also explained the lack of school support:

> I remember in 6th grade, they tried to beat me up going home. And I got suspended. Because I fought back. They had a zero-tolerance policy. Why did *I* have to be penalized for fighting back? When I did mention it to

teachers and administrators, it didn't go far. They always told me to let it go, and focus on my schoolwork. And if it was a problem, it was *my* problem. (personal communication, September 28, 2017)

Often, it's not just a problem of individual teachers or administrators who may be indifferent or unhelpful. It's a systemic problem of unfair and discriminatory school policy. LGBTQ students are up to three times more likely to receive harsh disciplinary treatment than their heterosexual peers (Hunt & Moodie-Mills, 2012). Eight in 10 students experienced discriminatory school disciplinary practices that enforce traditional gender norms and unfairly target LGBTQ students, including preventing students from wearing clothing that supports LGBTQ issues such as a rainbow flag, attending a school dance with someone of the same gender, or wearing clothing deemed gender-inappropriate. These factors contribute to high rates of absence when students who feel unsafe and unfairly targeted in a hostile school climate simply choose to stay away from school (GLSEN, 2016).

All of us who are teachers, counselors, and school leaders of conscience must act in the best interest of our LGBTQ students and the entire school community to advocate for the review and reform of such biased disciplinary policies. Although it may be an unpopular position to take in communities that include homophobic stakeholders, it's the right position. Our school climates will be further improved by working to diversify school antibullying programs and implement inclusive in-service professional development workshops for teaching staff that includes antibias programs.

"GET THE HELL OUT!":
FAMILY REJECTION AND LGBTQ HOMELESSNESS

Students whose parents or guardians will advocate for them when they are bullied or unfairly punished by their school administrators have a fighting chance of maintaining their mental health and their GPA. But the bottom can fall out psychologically and academically for those students who have no parental support they can count on at home. Conditions are worse still for those LGBTQ students who become homeless.[1]

Family rejection is the biggest cause of LGBTQ youth homelessness. These are students who run away or are evicted from their home even though they want to remain, because their parents or guardians rejected them for their sexual orientation or nonconforming gender identity and behaviors. Some family members blame the LGBTQ child in the family as the cause for problems in the home such as alcoholism, separation or divorce, or financial troubles (Rudacille, 2005). Often, they run away because they can no longer tolerate conditions living there. In some cases, youth who aren't comfortable disclosing their sexual identity while living at home, leave their family as a coping strategy for coming out, even at risk of becoming homeless (Keuroghlian, Shtasel, & Bassuk, 2014).

In the documentary *Losing Ground: The New Face of Homelessness* (Educational Video Center, 2007), EVC students interviewed Jenny Lynn and Raquel, a lesbian couple who live in Sylvia's Place, a homeless shelter for LGBTQ youth. Jenny Lynn tells of being thrown out of the house by her grandfather, and Raquel chose to leave:

> *Jenny Lynn:* When I lived with my grandparents we had a lot of fights and stuff. They didn't agree with my life. The way I lived it. They're like, "You're not gay. Don't go like that. You're not like that." The only way I had freedom is if I left. So I used to leave my house a lot. And then one day, on Thanksgiving, my grandfather told me straight up. He was like, "I don't want you here no more. Get the hell out!"
>
> *Raquel:* I used to live, I lived with my aunt. Until I was 15 and a half. Then after that, when I had told her I was gay, she made me—she was like, she was like, "Either you go to church and forget about that, or you can't stay here no more." So I said, "Forget that." I left. (Educational Video Center, 2007)

When EVC students made *Shadows of Ignorance: The Love That's Feared* (Educational Video Center, 2010b), another film about LGBTQ youth–related issues, they interviewed one of their male gay friends who was afraid to come out to his family. He talked about the fear he experienced growing up in an extremely homophobic family:

> My younger sister, her best friend came out to her as a lesbian. And her friend's mother called my mother and said she didn't want my little sister in her house, because she thought that they were girlfriends. When my little

Get the Hell Out!

 View the clip online: www.tcpress.com/goodman-chapter-four#v4.3

sister came home, my mother gave her a bag, and told her to go live with my aunt. My little sister was 14 at the time. I think it was at that point that I realized that—it was never going to happen. That I was never going to be able to come out to her, and have that family where oh, you come out and your family's still there for you. . . . I already know if I say I'm gay, I'm all on my own. Not just with my mother but with my whole family, basically. Because the only other place that I would have to turn would be my grandparents. And my grandparents—their first instinct would be to send me to a straight camp or a religious camp. (Educational Video Center, 2010b)

Although the exact numbers are not known, it's estimated that between 240,000 and 400,000 LGBT youth become homeless at least once each year.[2] Once they become homeless, their school attendance becomes all the more sporadic as their resources and options become more limited, daily struggles become more desperate, and connections with peers and teachers in school become more difficult to maintain. When homeless LGBTQ youth live on the streets, they are at greater risk of engaging in sex work, becoming HIV infected, being fined or arrested, and struggling with substance abuse. They also are at high risk of a major depression and other mental illness, even higher than homeless heterosexual youth. However, they often lack consistent access to medication and are also at risk of being over-medicated, based on the proposition at some shelters that it is easier "to change youths' brain chemistry than their living arrangements or their childhoods" (Ream & Forge, 2014, pp. 8, 15; see also Durso & Gates, 2012; Keuroghlian et al., 2014).

As a transgender teacher activist explained:

We have a record number of homeless students in New York City. A large percentage are LGBT youth. The biggest thing I would say is teachers should be careful, sensitive how they engage parents of homeless LGBT students. They shouldn't assume that parents know that their children are gay. A lot of times a student is not forthcoming about it. It has to be addressed on a whole-school level. Even recommending shelters to students is difficult since shelters are inconsistent. Some are violent. In some cases, the streets are preferable to the shelters. It's also sensitive to recommend social services and government systems that they get involved with—if they are undocumented you can get the student, or their whole family deported. So much of it really comes down to listening to the student. (personal communication, November 21, 2017)

"THE PLACE FOR ME!":
INCLUSIVE SCHOOL CULTURES AND LEGAL SILENCING

Whether our students are living in shelters, on friends' couches, in subways, or elsewhere, they are still more likely to stay in, or return to school if there are adults they can trust to support and not judge them, and if our school's culture is inclusive, welcoming, and responsive to them. We need to make sure that the social and emotional connection is there. However, this connection will be that much stronger when we reinforce it with academic curriculum that includes readings, whether in English or history classes or elsewhere, that speak to their lived experiences and creative, intellectual lives. Such readings can help counter stereotypes and build a greater sense of safety within the classroom. Without this, LGBTQ students can experience the contradiction in our schools where they are singled out for attention and targeted for abuse, at the same time as they are rendered invisible by the curriculum.

We can remedy this problem by developing LGBTQ-inclusive hallway environments with public displays and classroom environments with curricula that affirm and engage queer students including, for example, poets and writers such as Audre Lorde, James Baldwin, David Henry Hwang, Leslie Feinberg, Manuel Puig, and Tony Kushner. Other changes such as gender-neutral bathrooms communicate a message of inclusivity to the rest of the school body. In some schools, teachers and students wear red ribbons and "Out for Safe Schools" badges to create a safe environment and show their solidarity with LGBTQ students. Even though teachers may not know how many queer students they are teaching or how many of their students have LGBTQ family members, by tossing a stone in the pond this way, they can be sure the ripples will touch lives in important ways.

Irene never forgot her first visit to City-As-School, on her search for a safer and more welcoming school to attend: "One of the main reasons I ended up going to City-As-School was when I saw a bulletin board in the hall that was very large. And it was celebrating LGBT history. And nobody defaced it! I thought, that was the place for me!"

Twenty years later, a gay male student at EVC working on the LGBTQ documentary crew describes the homophobic bullying in his Catholic school that caused him to leave, and the climate that makes him feel welcome in City-As-School, the same school Irene attended:

> I didn't care about school. I didn't care about my grades. I didn't participate in anything after school. I didn't have any friends. I couldn't see myself going to that school another year. I didn't think I would graduate on time. I feel more accepted here. It's a very open school. Everyone is very respectful toward everyone's identity. A lot of the teachers ask us to name our gender pronouns. We have gender-neutral bathrooms. (personal communication, October 23, 2017)

Intentionally creating LGBTQ-inclusive curricula helps queer students feel safer, more connected, and more visible in our schools. Conversely, gaping holes in the curriculum with no LGBTQ inclusion or representation serve to silence and alienate them. These are often the product of discriminatory policies specifically designed to exclude and stigmatize queer people and representations of them from school curricula and programming. For example, at least seven states have "no promo homo" laws, which may ban positive mention, or promotion, of queerness in public schools. They also may require teachers to disparage nonheterosexual sex, and three states require public schools to teach that people who engage in same-sex sexual conduct are recognized as criminals. There are even some school districts that use filter software companies to block positive LGBTQ content on school computers, including antibullying information and resources for Genders & Sexualities Alliances. Students describe how these laws and policies censoring or restricting their discussion and access to LGBTQ information create a hostile school environment that exposes them to violence and discriminatory treatment by students and teachers, as myths, conflicting information, and stigmas proliferate (American Bar Association, 2016; American Civil Liberties Union, 2011; Human Rights Watch, 2016).

Harmful myths are particularly widespread about transgender students, such as that they are trying to trick or deceive others about their sexual identity, or that they are mentally ill and "conversion" therapy can change them. These and other such myths create hostile climates in schools of anti-transgender bias, stigmatization, and violence.

We should all be concerned by the alarming impact this anti-transgender bias has on our students: 75.8% of transgender students report that they feel unsafe in schools, 69% avoid school bathrooms, 64% are verbally harassed, 24.9% are physically harassed, and 12% are physically assaulted (Kosciw et al., 2016). In addition, the intersectionality of transphobia, sexism, and racism in the culture outside of schools has led to a crisis of homicides against transgender women of color. This is a multiyear trend where transgender and gender-nonconforming people of color are the overwhelming victims of hate violence, and even murder (National Coalition of Anti-Violence Programs, 2017).

The risks for our LGBTQ students further multiply when they don't have a trusted adult in school in whom they can confide, or from whom they can seek guidance, resources, or refuge. This is particularly true for those of our students who are in crisis and who may be homeless, or on the verge of being homeless. Without a teacher, coach, administrator, social worker, or counselor to talk with, some students are left without a critical lifeline just when they desperately need one the most.

We can make a difference in their lives. Transformative teaching involves creating LGBTQ inclusive spaces in our classes with a range of activities relating to our students' interests, experiences, and needs. That can include discussions about common assumptions and homophobic and transphobic stereotypes people may have (such as that LGBTs are obsessed with sex, or LGBT teachers are bad role models), and slurs they may say (such as *faggot*, *dyke*, or *that's so gay*), and how students can respond if they are being used. We can give our students positive LGBTQ role models, teaching them about the lives of queer artists, writers, political and business leaders, and others. We can also engage our students in researching the "no promo homo" laws and write to Lambda Legal, the American Civil Liberties Union, or another legal advocacy organization to learn more about student and community efforts to repeal them.

Although those of us of any gender or sexual orientation can give significant support to our LGBTQ students, it is invaluable for them to have other LGBTQ adults in school as role models who more fully understand what they are going through. However, in the current political and legal climate, queer educators choosing to become such a role model may do so at great personal risk. Yes, there have been many important legal advances since the start of the gay liberation movement of the late 1960s: In 1973, the American Psychiatric Association, which long pathologized homosexuality, voted to remove homosexuality as a mental illness from the Diagnostic and Statistical Manual of Mental Disorders (DSM) II, often referred to as the bible of psychiatry[3]; in the *Lawrence v. Texas* case of 2003, the Supreme Court decriminalized private same-sex sexual conduct and prohibited states from passing laws that targeted queers for harm; and in 2015, the Supreme Court struck down laws prohibiting same-sex marriage (Lugg & Adelman, 2015).

However, the legal system still works to keep queer educators in the closet. Eighteen states have not yet formally repealed statutes known as antisodomy laws. Even though they are constitutionally unenforceable, the fact that these statutes remain "on the books" makes LGBTQ teachers, administrators, and other school staff in those states vulnerable to police harassment, embarrassment, and stigma (American Bar Association, 2016). Rolling back LGBTQ civil rights, the Trump administration's Department of Justice removed any protection for transgender people from sex discrimination under the Civil Rights Act of 1964. As LGBTQ educators continue to be vulnerable to homophobic and transphobic discrimination from within the school and community, our LGBTQ students learn that positive discussion of queerness is unmentionable (Lugg & Adelman, 2015).

The absence and silencing of queer teachers and general lack of any adult support can have devastating outcomes for queer students. With no adult to turn to for help, the cumulative stress for many who experience anti-LGBT bullying, assaults, discriminatory school discipline, and isolation from their peers can help push them into deep, and even suicidal, depression. The high risk of suicide among this population is disturbing. LGB students (transgender youth were not in this study) seriously consider suicide at three times the rate of their heterosexual peers. Nearly half of transgender youth have seriously thought about taking their lives, and a quarter report having made an attempt. And LGB youth are nearly five times as likely to have attempted suicide compared to heterosexual youth[4] (Kann et al., 2016). These statistics are another disturbing reminder of the absolute urgent need for building a more LGBTQ-inclusive culture in our classrooms and schools.

As painful as it is to talk about, Muzik wanted others to learn from their story, and describes what happened:

> I actually attempted suicide when my depression got the best of me. I just gave up. I was depressed for a year. I didn't have an inspiration to graduate anymore. I sent an email what I was going to do to my counselor, who sent it to my therapist. They rushed to my house with the police. It was almost too late. Next thing I remember hearing my mom's voice and waking up. I stayed there in the hospital for 11 days. I came out blank, drugged up. Lifeless and hopeless. . . . Because of that, the school kicked me out. They had already felt I was causing problems when I came to school looking like a boy. (personal communication, September 28, 2017)

In February, 6 months after their suicide attempt, Muzik returned to school, attending a transfer high school in Manhattan's Lower East Side. Muzik immediately joined the Genders & Sexualities Alliance there. Muzik's school advisor recommended that they join EVC's documentary workshop after they had recovered from the trauma and felt safer in the new and more welcoming school. After a semester at EVC, Muzik premiered their documentary with the rest of the EVC crew for a standing-room-only audience at the Film Society of Lincoln Center. There is no one single factor that contributes to Muzik's resilience. Transferring to a small school with a GSA, and with teachers and counselors who knew Muzik well, was an important part, just as was being engaged in a loving and academically challenging learning community of peers in the after-school workshop at EVC, with a caring instructor who connected Muzik's life to their learning, and publicly celebrated Muzik's artistic documentary accomplishments.

"I NEVER TALKED WITH ANYBODY ABOUT THIS": SEXUAL HARASSMENT

Andrea is harassed on the streets of her neighborhood every day. She says men make comments to her when she goes to the store, to school, whether she's going out alone, or even walking with her brother. One time something more threatening happened. It was dark out, when she noticed a man was following her in his car. He was driving slowly alongside her. He actually followed her all the way until she was across the street from her house. There were no police. No one else was there to witness what was happening or to help. Terrified, she ran into the house and grabbed a knife. She now carries a knife to protect herself, because she is a girl and has to walk on the streets alone. After retelling this traumatic story for her documentary *Gender Power: Street Harassment in NYC* (Educational Video Center, 2014a), the EVC students shoot a reenactment of it.

Andrea Followed

▶ *View the clip online*: www.tcpress.com/goodman-chapter-four#v4.4

Street harassment and threatening action toward women and girls are a form of gender violence. It's so prevalent that most female students either have been harassed themselves or know someone who has. According to a Stop Street Harassment survey (Kearl, 2014), 65% of all women had experienced street harassment. Among all women, 23% had been sexually touched, 20% had been followed, and 9% had been forced to do something sexual. People of color, low-income women, and LGBTQ people were disproportionately affected.

Street harassers will say their words and actions are meant as harmless compliments. But the impact of these microaggressions on girls and young women—our students—is anything but harmless (Nadal, 2008). Girls and young women who experience such microaggressions and have been harassed this way on a daily basis develop habits of constant vigilance to their physical appearance and their safety in their most routine experiences in public. They may decide to alter their travel routes, walk with others, or even limit their time in public places. The cumulative impact of an almost continuous stream of anxiety-provoking and frightening experiences can take a serious toll on their psychological well-being and lead to significant mental health problems, including depression and trauma. Such debilitating problems can lead to increased sleep loss, absences from school, and declining academic achievement.

Andrea continues her story of being stalked by a man in a car while walking home alone from school (Educational Video Center, 2014a):

> Nobody was there. And nobody see it. And I decided I have to take care of myself. Because who would do it. There are no police. When I get to my home, I decide to wear a knife. And that's how I protect myself.

Though we'd like to view schools as a sanctuary for female students from sexual harassment and violence in the streets, for too many of our students this is not the case. The harassment and humiliation often continues in our schools unabated. An AAUW study (2011) found that 56% of girls in grades 7–12 experienced sexual harassment in a given school year, and 40% of the boys did. Nearly half of the harassment took place in person and 30% electronically. Thirteen percent of girls reported that they'd been touched in an "unwelcome sexual way" at school and 4% reported that they'd been forced to do something sexual.

Sexual harassment not only impacts our students' health and well-being, but also their participation and achievement in school, with our female students more likely to be negatively affected than our males. Those of our students who have been sexually harassed often feel diminished self-esteem, humiliation, anger, and anxiety, and tend to lose concentration on their schoolwork, participate less in class, skip class more frequently, and even leave school as a result. A third of students who were harassed reported feeling sick to their stomach, about a fifth had trouble sleeping, and a third had a hard time studying. Students of moderate and low-income families were significantly more likely to report feeling negatively impacted than those of higher socioeconomic status (AAUW, 2011).

Nobody Was There

View the clip online: www.tcpress.com/goodman-chapter-four#v4.5

But too often our students don't report these incidents of sexual harassment to adults in school. To compound this problem, many of our schools don't take any action when students do report these incidents. In fact, the AAUW (Prangley, 2016) found that two-thirds of school districts nationally reported a total of zero allegations of sexual harassment during the 2013–2014 school year, even though Title IX mandates that a staff member in every school be responsible for coordinating compliance. Although it's dubious that zeros reflect the actual number of incidents, they do give an accounting of just how many of our school districts still need to make the bureaucratic and moral commitment to accurately record and report sexual harassment in their schools.

As is the case with those educators who fail to reliably stand behind LGBTQ victims of bullying, ignoring claims of sexual harassment or viewing them as typical adolescent behavior just makes for a more hostile and sexist school environment. The message for our female students, then, is that they can't necessarily count on us to protect them in school, and that, without consequences for the perpetrators, their harassment may just continue to get worse. As school leaders and teachers, we must be sure to send a strong counter message—that we will create a class and school culture that promotes norms of respectful behavior and that claims of bullying and sexual harassment will be taken seriously and acted upon.

Many schools view the problem of sexual harassment as part of their antibullying programs. However, in addition to the fact that different laws regulate them, there is a distinct gendered quality to sexual harassment. Boys tend to experience more bullying, and by other boys. But girls are far more often the targets of sexual harassment, and boys are the perpetrators. Sexual harassment in the form of homophobic slurs by boys against boys is the main exception. Studies show that sexual harassment—including requests for sexual favors or other sexually related verbal or physical conduct—can be even more harmful to our students than bullying, especially for girls. This is due in part because sexual harassment is targeted at a specific category of person, and anchored in unequal, culturally sanctioned, male-dominant power relations and gender stereotypes (Gruber & Fineran, 2016).

Because of this gendered power imbalance, negative stereotypes about girls, and their internalized feelings of shame about their experiences of harassment, many of our students remain silent and never report it. If they push back against traditional stereotypes of passivity, girls risk getting a "bad" reputation and teasing from both male and female peers. But Andrea and the team of EVC students producing their documentary decided to break their silence and speak out. They believed that telling their stories was one way to take action and make a change. Andrea said,

> I feel a lot of emotions. Because, the people think this is normal. I never talked with anybody about this. And I never spoke to someone because nobody cares about it. And I'm trying to do this because we can make a change. And I hope all the people who see this will have a reaction. Because this is not okay. (Educational Video Center, 2014a)

Make a Change

And I'm trying to do this because we can make a change.

 View the clip online: www.tcpress.com/goodman-chapter-four#v4.6

It is critically important to create safe spaces in classes and extracurricular clubs and programs where our students, especially girls, can feel empowered to speak out against sexual harassment. As Andrea said, doing this can make a change. Starting a meaningful dialogue that informs, educates, and sensitizes our broader student community can help address the social, emotional, and academic impact that harassment has on students and develop a school culture where everyone feels safe, respected, and empowered. Giving our female students structured opportunities to share stories of the harassment and microaggressions they have experienced in school and on the streets, and how they have felt as a result, will sensitize the boys and be empowering for girls.

"BEING THE SEXY GIRL": BODY IMAGE AND SELF-OBJECTIFICATION

Sexual objectification of girls and women is a serious problem. And for EVC students Samantha and Nang and many other teen girls, they are not only objectified by others, but objectify themselves. Described as objectification theory (Fredrickson & Roberts, 1997), this phenomenon involves internalizing the observers' perspective of the female as an object, with the Anglo-European impossibly thin-ideal with its aura of female beauty and success and its stigma of fatness that saturate the media images of our popular culture. With the onset of puberty and their changing bodies, adolescent girls are particularly vulnerable to measuring their own self-worth by these cultural standards of the idealized body. When they feel they can't measure up, their self-esteem can decline as their body dissatisfaction with their weight and physical appearance rises. They experience shame of their supposed failure to meet the mythic ideal. This can have damaging consequences for their physical and mental well-being and their academic achievement in school.

Girls' body image is shaped by many factors, including the media. Misogynistic images that depict women as sexual objects for men to possess are prevalent throughout American consumerist society, with increasingly explicit images in music videos. Though videos across music genres have long exhibited sexualized messages of women, hip-hop music videos have become notorious for doing so. The industry is filled with videos that portray mainly women of color placed in demeaning, sometimes violent, and sexually provocative positions wearing skimpy outfits or next to no clothing, and referred to as "bitches" and "hoes."

The sexual objectification of women can be found across media forms and industries. In print media, men tend to be portrayed as a full person with an emphasis on the head and face. In contrast, the focus of women is on their body, with blemishes and curves airbrushed and Photoshopped out to meet the standard of Anglo-European thin perfect. Some photographs represent women as a collection of body parts, as if they are dismembered, without a head. In a content review of women's fashion and fitness magazines, researchers found that 95% of the models were characterized as lean, and only 6% had rounder, softer body types (Wasylkiw,

Emms, Meuse, & Poirier, 2009). Turning the media's objectification of women into a learning opportunity, teachers can have students critically analyze how girls and women are represented in a range of media—including magazine advertisements, teen fashion magazines, movies, hip-hop music videos, video games—as compared to boys and men.

The socialization of girls to this objectified way of life starts young, not only with magazines, television, movies, video games, and the Internet, but also with toys and dolls. Feminist cultural critics often point to the iconic, but impossibly proportioned, Barbie doll as the popular embodiment of the norms of beauty and objectification that young girls learn to aspire to (Rehabs.com, 2012).

So it's not surprising that children as young as 5 years old are already anxious about their bodies and want to be thinner, and more than 80% of girls over 10 are afraid of becoming fat (Andrist, 2003). Internalizing these media appearance ideals, many girls who develop body dissatisfaction are socialized into a constant state of self-scanning and appraising their body. As they grow older, this is accompanied by ongoing efforts to change their bodies through exercise, beauty products, clothes that flatten or add curves, and chronic dieting. Dissatisfaction and a sense of shame can be influenced by peer pressure, when male or female peers make disparaging, and sometimes bullying, comments, negatively comparing them to the media saturated thin-ideal for women.

Samantha was both an EVC youth producer and one of the students profiled in her group's documentary on beauty and female body image called *What's Your Beautiful?* (Educational Video Center, 2014c). Samantha talked about how her boyfriend would constantly put her down and make demeaning comments to her about her physical appearance. She was 15 years old, and felt she couldn't

He Put Me Down

 View the clip online: www.tcpress.com/goodman-chapter-four#v4.7

please him no matter how hard she tried to change her looks. Her sense of self-esteem and her image of herself both declined. She began to hate seeing pictures of herself:

> The reason the way I act now has a lot to do with my past relationship. The guy I used to date 4 years ago, was—I don't know—like, a horrible person. He always tried to put me down. Like, I would feel like I look my best. And I'd go see him, and he's like, "Ew! Why you look like that?" I was like, "What you mean? Like, I tried!" I didn't say I tried, but I'd say, "How you gonna put me down like that?" And I don't know. I just looked at myself differently. (Educational Video Center, 2014c)

Later, Samantha found that she could gain control over how she wanted to present her own image through selfies. She began posing in sexualized ways and gained more than 10,000 followers on Instagram. She calls herself an "Instagram junkie:"

> I love makeup. It hides what I don't want. Eyeliner. I think it brings more attention to my eyes. I'm a Instagram junkie. I love Instagram. I have a lot of followers. 10K. Everyone says, "Oh my God! You're famous!" I strive for those 10,000 followers on Instagram! When I finally got my 10K followers, Oh my God! I felt like nobody could tell me anything. I was the thing! I'm like, you don't wanna be my friend? That's your problem! I enjoy taking selfies like, a lot. Whenever I have my phone, I'm like, click, click, click. The fame, the attention that I get. From the comments, to the hearts, to you know, the emojis. It's just so much. (Educational Video Center, 2014c)

I Love Instagram

 View the clip online: www.tcpress.com/goodman-chapter-four#v4.8

Samantha's Instagram addiction is part of a broader tendency for girls who find their sense of self-worth in a sexualized identity they create online. Beauty app companies are fueling this addiction, selling girls a growing arsenal of digital make-overs to edit their Instagram selfie images. With these virtual beauty products, they can give themselves digital plastic surgery with smaller noses, higher cheekbones, longer eyelashes, and even whiter skin (Hess & O'Neill, 2017), reinforcing the message that it's not who they are as a person that counts in their postings, but how they look as a body—their sex appeal. Their worth is then measured by the popularity it brings them from their followers, affirming the dominant male cultural message that women's physical beauty can bring them power (Fredrickson & Roberts, 1997).

However, studies show that self-objectification and internalized messages of sexualization for girls are associated with decreased academic achievement. Integrating the need to be sexually attractive into their identity can overshadow or exclude the development of other characteristics. Some female students who identify as "sexy girls" often see their identity as incompatible with the identity as the "smart girl." So they tend to opt out of more difficult academic courses, which can then lead to lower academic aspirations and outcomes. They also tend to avoid participating in athletics, which are activities that can actually lead to improved body satisfaction. Internalizing the notion that women should be sexual objects for men, they are more likely to associate with boys who share that view. Such peer relationships then reinforce the existing problems of low self-esteem and poor body image (C. S. Brown & Stone, 2016; McKenney & Bigler, 2016).

It is a complicated process, particularly for our female students, to shift their identity from being defined by their physical appearance to who they are as a whole person. We need to support this process of development by inviting students to share their questions and concerns about how comfortable they feel about their body. It's important that we don't deny or invalidate their feelings but rather facilitate a process of reflection and critical inquiry into the issue, collaboratively generating questions that might, for example, ask what kinds of messages they receive about their body images, where they receive them from and who benefits, how different people may respond to those messages, and, finally, who gets to define their sense of worth.

Through the process of exploring the issue of self objectification and body image in her documentary, Samantha came to reflect more deeply on her own identity:

> I think I do objectify myself. 'Cause like, basically what I put out on Instagram, dressing sexy. And being the sexy girl that everybody want to talk to. I think I put myself out there as that. But that's not really how I am. . . . I feel like a pretty princess in my pictures versus how I really see myself. In the mirror, it's crazy, like. Do I really look like that? Like who is this monster? Glasses. No makeup on. Big—big, big! Just nasty! Horrible! (Educational Video Center, 2014c)

Not Really How I Am

View the clip online: www.tcpress.com/goodman-chapter-four#v4.9

During the making of her documentary, Samantha continued to struggle with these contradictions, viewing herself negatively, whether in the mirror or in the video interviews, and positively in the sexualized selfies she produced and posted. However, a year later, she was able to screen her documentary and analyze the process of self-objectification for a class of teachers attending an EVC professional development course at NYU.

"I LOOK FAT": BODY IMAGE AND EATING DISORDERS

Girls respond in a range of ways to their struggles with negative self-judgment and poor body image. Sometimes they act in self-destructive ways as they strive to change their bodies to fit the thin-ideal. They may try to change their bodies by taking more drastic measures such as starving, binging, and purging themselves.

These eating disorders are a serious and potentially fatal public health problem for middle school and high school students, affecting approximately 3.8% of females aged 13 to 18 years, a rate that is two and a half times higher than for boys. There is a spectrum to consider, spanning from mild dieting to a relentless pursuit of thinness, intense fear of gaining weight, and other symptoms that constitute full-scale eating disorders. The CDC reports that almost two-thirds of high school girls, or 61.2%, try to lose weight, and 17.4% fast for a day or more to lose weight. The good news is that a significant number of students are in touch with mental health and school service providers about a range of issues. The bad news is that only a minority of them actually talk about their eating disorder. Most don't receive treatment for their condition (Eaton et al., 2012; Merikangas et al., 2010).

Multiple biological and psychological factors influence the development of eating disorders, as well as social and cultural elements such as bullying and harassment from peers in school. Nang was another member of the *What's Your Beautiful?* (Educational Video Center, 2014c) EVC youth crew and had her story featured in the documentary along with Samantha's. In Nang's case, her female friends also told her that she was too fat. She wanted to be thin like the Burmese and Chinese singers, models, and celebrities that she and her friends admired. So she began working out in the school gym every day. She also began starving herself to look better to her friends and on her Instagram photos.

Nang explains how she started to see her body differently:

> I go to the gym like 5 days a week on my school day. Because I have a gym in school. Sometimes I feel I look good, but sometimes I feel that I look like really fat. I don't know. It started since I was, I was 16. I started to think that I'm fat. At the time, because I cut my hair very short, like a boy. And then, people start to say I look fat with that hairstyle. And then even my hair grown back, they still say I look fat. So, and then I just realize that like, maybe I really get fat. So, also I think I'm getting fat more. (Educational Video Center, 2014c)

I Look Fat

 View the clip online: www.tcpress.com/goodman-chapter-four#v4.10

It is a significant and potentially dangerous step when our students go from having the perception that they are overweight to actually engaging in disordered eating. Here, Nang tells the story of when she decided to stop eating to lose weight:

> One day, one day I decided like to, not to eat. And to get on diet like because I want to lose weight. So I don't, I try not to eat lunch and dinner. Like, if dinnertime, my dad would come and say it's dinnertime and I say that I'm not hungry. As I keep like, skipping my meals a lot like that, about a week or something like that. One night I got my stomach ache. I couldn't even walk properly. I have to crawl, something like that. And then I found that there was nothing left. Only rice. Even though from that experience that I had, I feel bad about it. But I still want to lose weight and to be healthy. Yes, I still want to be healthy and lose weight. (Educational Video Center, 2014c)

Students can experience serious medical complications over time as a result of eating disorders and low body weight, such as muscle loss and fatigue, tooth decay, ulcers, low blood pressure, and even heart and brain damage (National Institute of Mental Health, 2014). Along with these physical health problems, students with a distorted body image and disordered eating behavior often experience declining mental health and academic performance in school. Because there is a range of eating disorders, students may exhibit a range of psychological symptoms, including mood swings, depression, irritability, and hypersensitivity to what others may be saying or thinking about them. Feeling listless and tired all the time, they

[handwritten marginalia: X Missed two months of senior year]

Skipping My Meals

 View the clip online: www.tcpress.com/goodman-chapter-four#v4.11

can have difficulty participating in class. They may lose concentration and focus during their reading and other assignments, and they may withdraw from school and extracurricular activities.

We need to be aware of these symptoms and be compassionate and patient with those of our students who may be at risk. Simply telling them to eat more is usually not an effective strategy because these students are often in denial about their condition. Creating safe spaces in classes, girls clubs, and after-school programs will lead to more trusting environments where frank conversations are possible between students and adults in the school. This will help open dialogue between the students and school physical and mental health professionals, and students' parents or guardians.

"SAVE A KID'S EDUCATION": GIRLS SUPPORT GROUPS AND GENDERS & SEXUALITIES ALLIANCES

Nang, Samantha, Andrea, Muzik, Irene, and the other students whose stories are shared in this chapter all expressed the need for a trusted adult in their school who they could talk with about their problems. We need to take that to heart and consider how we can be that trusted adult in school for our students, and how other staff can be informed and get involved.

All students, and particularly LGBTQ students and girls who are systemically silenced, need safe spaces in schools to talk openly with teachers or other staff about their experiences of being bullied and assaulted because of their sexual orientation and identity, being sexually harassed in person or electronically shamed about their bodies, or having eating disorders. And it makes a difference for them to have opportunities to talk about the positive things happening in their lives as well, to socialize with their peers and share interests, resources, and plans after high school.

Some schools offer girls' support and empowerment groups where girls can share their stories, help one another cope and heal, educate their peers, and fight back against harassment in their schools. They are safe spaces where girls can feel free to speak their minds on any number of issues. As a coordinator of a high school girls group described it:

> This is a space where they can be themselves. I will often start groups [by] asking, "What's on your mind and what's in your heart for today?" That opens it up. If they had a rough day, they can talk about it and get it off their chest. . . . I also stay on top of things that are going on in students' life. Topics that are trending on social media that I know they are talking about. Like the "#MeToo" hashtag about sexual harassment. And connecting them with political themes going on in the world. Sometimes the activity can be as simple as a video on catcalling or street harassment. Or on healthy and unhealthy relationships. With that we draw a figure and inside we write what

makes up a healthy relationship. On the outside are unhealthy characteristics and traits. I'll ask the group questions like, "What does this topic bring up for you?" "Have you ever experienced anything like this?" We're giving them the space to talk about these things. What's said here, stays here. (personal communication, October 17, 2017)

Guest

Guest presenters can also be invited to give antidiscrimination workshops about harassment and everyday verbal and behavioral microaggressions against females, as well as LGBTQ students, and students of color. Community and youth-serving programs, such as Girls Incorporated, Planned Parenthood, and Project Reach, can provide curriculum resources for staff and students to complement school-based activities and programs. Some groups offer critical media literacy activities deconstructing magazine fashion ads or music videos to show how women's body images are constructed and messages are conveyed. Such groups can help female students develop greater appreciation for their health, personal talents, and creative abilities rather than only their personal appearance or sex appeal. Through these groups, students develop new relationships with their peers, benefit from adult guidance, and learn that they are not alone experiencing these problems, and not alone in trying to do something about them.

Similarly, safe spaces for education, support, and advocacy for LGBTQ students are Genders & Sexualities Alliances (GSAs).[5] They are extracurricular, student-led clubs that serve as sites of support, community building, and activism for LGBTQ students and are open to all students regardless of their sexual orientation or gender identity (Bidell, 2007). They contribute to a more inclusive and supportive school climate, stronger student relationships, increased student trust in teachers, and more willingness on the part of teachers to intervene in anti-LGBTQ bullying or other harassment. These factors all correlate with fewer discipline problems and improved LGBTQ student attendance and GPAs when queer students feel safer and more connected to their school. GSAs have been found to increase the visibility of LGBTQ teachers and awareness of LGBTQ issues for all students, including those who do not participate in the GSA (Espelage, 2015; Fisher & Kennedy, 2012; Walls, Kane, & Wisneski, 2010; Wimberly, Wilkinson, & Pearson, 2015).

A transgender teacher in New York City described the GSA in her small high school:

We felt there was a kind of a pressing need for it [a GSA]—a forum for discussing their issues. Making them more visible, less taboo. I was really, really happy with the reception that we had. Our first meetings we were pulling in 15 to 20 students. Which for a school of our size, is a lot of students. . . . I let the students come up with their own topics. And the students facilitate the discussion. They are really big on talking about healthy relationships. It's a space for students to listen to each other and to unpack assumptions. It's important that these kinds of discussions have a home in our school. (personal communication, November 21, 2017)

GSAs can be powerful spaces for LGBTQ students where peers will listen with empathy and without judgment in a way that normalizes their experiences. Twenty years before Muzik joined a GSA in their school on the Lower East Side, Irene and her fellow student Lailah were active in forming a GSA at City-As-School across town in Manhattan's West Village. EVC students interviewed Lailah about it in their 1998 documentary, *Out Youth in Schools* (Educational Video Center, 1998):

> The political implications of having a Gay-Straight Alliance basically means the school, or some faction of the school, is taking a stance against homophobia. And that is such an important message to be sent—that young people are all different. We're very diverse and there's going to be tolerance. People are strong when they stand together. That's why you want to have things like Gay-Straight Alliances. . . . A GSA, and knowing that there's a GSA at City-As [-School], I would go so far as to say it can save a kid's life. Definitely save a kid's education if they need it. If they were fleeing their old school. (Educational Video Center, 1998)

Irene reflected on the broader impact the GSA had on the school:

> I think the GSA was good for students in my time, for students who were still figuring out their sexuality. I assumed all the gay teachers in the school were out and comfortable. But when students started coming out as LGBT students, it also encouraged the staff. It made it more of a community. I remember then one English teacher started having the students read *Stone Butch Blues*, by Leslie Feinberg, an early transgender activist. (personal communication, October 4, 2017)

Save a Kid's Life

 View the clip online: www.tcpress.com/goodman-chapter-four#v4.12

Whether in classes, extracurricular clubs, or school–community programs, creating spaces of trust, learning, and advocacy is vitally important for girls, LGBTQ students, and their straight allies. Giving spaces for marginalized and silenced voices in the school helps move students from a place of fear and victimization to empowerment. As places of healing and solidarity, they also help improve the health and well-being of the school culture and are a benefit to all the students who learn there. They give students a means to tell their stories, know their rights, take back control of their lives, and support their peers in taking back control of theirs.

CHAPTER 5

"Some Place to Call Home"
Foster Care and Child Welfare

When EVC students first met Makeba, she was a teenager living in foster care. They interviewed her and included her story in their documentary *Some Place to Call Home: Surviving the Foster Care System* (Educational Video Center, 1994). She was eager not only to make her voice heard but also to advocate for the rights of other teens, particularly young mothers like herself who were struggling in the child welfare system. This was in the early 1990s, at the height of the War on Drugs and the mass incarceration it produced, when the numbers of children and youth living in foster care in New York City were reaching an all-time high of nearly 50,000.

Makeba was 9 years old when she was forcibly removed from her grandmother's home, and then was placed in a startling number of different foster homes, maternity shelters, and schools. A decade later, EVC students interviewed Makeba again in *Not Me, Not Mine: Adult Survivors of Foster Care* (Educational Video Center, 2003). While Makeba tells us about her particular family and her life growing up and "aging out" of foster care, she is also shining a spotlight on a much broader systemic problem—one that is decidedly tilted against low-income women of color, particularly Black mothers and their children. In Makeba's case, it was arrayed against her, her mother, and her grandmother.

Often conditions of poverty are confused with conditions of neglect, which may mean that their children are going hungry and are malnourished, and living in an unhealthy or unsafe mold- and rat-infested building. Unemployment and poverty weigh down on both the mind and the body. The chronic stress they experience, coupled with systemic racism, sexism, and the inequitable access to high-quality housing, jobs, and health care heightens the crisis for low-income parents struggling with mental illness and drug abuse. Gaining insight into those struggles also provides insight into the well-being of their children—our students.

The problem must be viewed through the lens of gender, along with race and class. Instead of ameliorating these underlying social and economic conditions, too often the system punishes the mothers by removing their children and destroying their family. The result is that youth of color are disproportionately removed from their homes and placed in foster care for longer periods of time, with multiple changes in placement, and lower rates of reunification with their parents. Consequently, students in foster care change schools and are absent more frequently, fall behind in their schoolwork, have behavior problems, and have lower grades and literacy levels as they struggle to cope with the traumatic loss of their parents. That is in addition to the losses they may suffer of relationships with their siblings and extended family members, friends, and neighbors. The problems multiply and then become passed down across generations (Courtney, Roderick, Smithgall, Gladden, & Nagaoka, 2004; Mastin, Metzger, & Golden, 2013; Tobis, 2013).

This chapter will follow Makeba's story through adolescence and adulthood, weaving in other students' experiences in foster care now some 25 years after Makeba, as well as a mother and daughter's perspective from *High on Perceptions* (Educational Video Center, 2014b) on the impact that mental health and opioid addiction has on the family. We will explore the institutional factors contributing to the racial, class, and gendered inequities in the child welfare system, and the negative impact they have on our students' schooling. We will also discuss strategies for teaching and advocating for those of our students caught in the "system" and how some youth are developing their skills for self-advocacy. Listening to their stories of trauma and resilience surviving the foster care system will give us a deeper empathy and understanding for our students struggling to succeed in our schools.

"THEY STOLE 10 YEARS FROM ME": THE TRAUMA OF FAMILY SEPARATION

It may be late in the evening, or it may take place early in the morning. A caseworker knocks on the door unannounced. She enters, inspecting rooms, looking for dirty and unsafe conditions. She opens cupboards and closets. She asks the children to take off their clothes, and examines them for marks or bruises on their body. She interviews them separately from their mother. She talks with neighbors and teachers, all part of the investigation to determine whether there has been abuse or neglect and whether the mother has put them in imminent danger. If the finding is for removal, they may immediately be placed, spending the night in a complete stranger's home or in an emergency shelter. They may also be prevented from calling their mother, or possibly grandmother, at a time they most need her reassurance, her explanation of what is happening and why. They are frightened and confused and traumatized by the experience (MacFarquhar, 2017).

As Makeba described it, there was an epidemic of heroin use in the community at the time, and either you were a dealer or an addict. Her mother became an addict, and asked her grandmother to adopt Makeba and her two brothers. But after a couple of years, the Child Welfare Administration[1] forcibly removed her from her grandmother's home and placed her in foster care. Thinking back on that traumatic day, she said:

> I didn't know they were coming to get us. All I know is, I had to get in the car. . . . I didn't want to go. When we got to a red light, I jumped out of the car and ran back to my grandmother's. . . . That night they placed me with

this woman. She had nine boys there. They told me she is now my mother. (personal communication, September 16, 2017)

It was my brother who was 15, I was 9, and my little brother was 8. And I remember when they took us from the house. You know, I'm asking them, "Why?" And they're telling me 'cause my grandmother was gonna die. 'Cause she old. And I was 9. And my grandmother died when I was 19. So I felt like, I was—they stole 10 years from me. (Educational Video Center, 2003)

Makeba had a loving relationship with her grandmother, who could have helped raise her and provide more stable emotional and academic support through her critical early adolescence and teenage years. When she was taken away first from her mother, and then from her grandmother, family bonds were severed that would never be repaired. Repeatedly placed in special education classes, Makeba struggled against the low expectations in her schools, which consistently failed to meet her academic potential or feed her intellectual curiosity. She never understood why she was separated from her family and put in a stranger's home.

Since that time, it's become commonly accepted that whenever possible, maintaining the preservation of intact families is best for the long-term stability and well-being of children. In most cases, families are the best resources for children. Instead of improving conditions, removing children from their biological family often traumatizes them, leading to feelings of guilt and self-blame for breaking family bonds. Parent advocates point out that in most cases in which children are removed from their parents, the children can be safely returned to extended family or the family itself if they are provided preventative social services such as housing assistance, mental health treatment, or substance abuse counseling (Tobis, 2013). This is unfortunately not done enough. And so families

I'm Asking Them Why

 View the clip online: www.tcpress.com/goodman-chapter-five#v5.1

are pulled apart and destroyed in what the state deems to be in the child's or young adult's best interest.

And as it turns out, in Makeba's case, she actually had a large kinship network of extended family that could have supported her. Showing her adoption papers and then her family tree, she explains:

> This is the paper that my mother, when she relinquished her rights as a mom to free us for adoption in 1982. It's really, you know, a shame. . . . I went through the system all my life, and I had so much family I didn't know. And it's like people that you ask, Why? Why did this happen? My grandmother, or my mother, or my father. They're all dead, so. It's like I get no answers. (Educational Video Center, 2003)

"THE SYSTEM FAILED ME": THE DISPROPORTIONATE ACADEMIC IMPACT OF FOSTER CARE

On any given day, there are more than 437,000 children in the foster care system across the country, and the numbers continue to grow (U.S. Department of Health and Human Services, Administration on Children, Youth and Families, Children's Bureau, 2017). In New York City, fewer than 10,000 children and youth in foster care are managed by a more than $1.3 billion industry of often poorly coordinated government organizations and private religious and secular agencies providing protective, preventative, placement, and adoptive services. It is a system with what seem to be contradictory goals: on the one hand, to protect children from abuse and neglect; and on the other, to strengthen families so parents can better care for their children. As child welfare sociologist and activist David Tobis (2013) explains, courts and caseworkers must balance the risk of decisions that might

I Had So Much Family I Didn't Know

 View the clip online: www.tcpress.com/goodman-chapter-five#v5.2

contribute to the destruction of the family, or to the neglect, abuse, or even death of a child who is not removed from the home. Protecting the child has historically been the predominant goal, and removing the children from their families the prevailing practice meant to achieve it.

All too frequently, highly publicized stories of child abuse or death in the news have been followed by political pressure and an increase in children being removed from their homes and placed in foster care, rather than keeping their family intact. They live without what we take for granted as part of childhood: their families, physical safety, their own bed and personal possessions, and a consistently decent education. In some cases, when youth feel hungry, they have to ask foster parents' permission to get food from the refrigerator. The outcome of these forced removals is often a profound sense of powerlessness for the children and youth put into the system. As foster youth advocates Betsy Krebs and Paul Pitcoff (2006) describe it, being "put in one strange placement after another is terrifying and disorienting. Once they settle in, if they do, the system still makes hundreds of decisions about them that they have little or no control over" (p. 52).

In the 2010s the pendulum began to swing more in the direction of kinship placement or keeping children with their families and providing parents with drug treatment, parenting classes, and other social services, rather than placing them in foster care. Parents are more empowered now with legal representation. The number of children in foster care in New York City has dropped from more than 21,000 children in March 2003 to fewer than 10,000 children as of February 2016.[2]

Yet even with these and many other hard-fought reforms in the 30 years since Makeba was removed from her family, New York City's is still considered "one of the most dangerous foster care systems in the country." As documented in the New York City public advocate's 2015 civil class action complaint:

> The emotional damage—and, far too often, abuse—suffered by these children at the hands of a system designed to keep them safe is unacceptable. . . . New York City's child welfare system is causing devastating, ongoing and long-lasting harm to New York City children in its care. . . . Children who cannot be safely returned to their parents languish in foster care, many moving from place to place, growing older and more damaged by their experiences, not knowing to which adults to form attachments, or trusting no adults at all. Children traumatized by the disruptions in their young lives do not know where they will be living from one month to the next. . . (*Elisa W. v. City of New York*, 2015, pp. 1, 3)

Thirty percent of youth in foster care have had eight or more placements with foster families or group homes, and 65% experienced seven or more school changes between elementary and high school. Between the ages of 9 and 11, Makeba was placed in seven different foster homes, and five schools. As she put it, "When we go to a new house, foster care kids don't unpack our bags. 'Cause we are so used to moving all the time" (personal communication, September 27, 2017).

Makeba explains these constant changes in homes as punishment for the strong connection she had with her grandmother. She says:

> I had a lot of problems in the foster homes I was in. I was around 10 or 11 and there was a foster father who would get drunk and want to get in bed with me. Every Sunday, it was like clockwork. He would look for me and I would hide underneath the bed. I would hide in the closet. And his wife knew what he would do and was mad and took it out on me. . . . So, once I found public transportation, I would always run away and find a way to go back to my grandmother's house. I was a "runner." That's what they called me. I would run away a lot. They called me a high risk. (personal communication, September 15, 2017; September 27, 2017)

The trauma and upheaval foster youth experienced in care was compounded by the multiple placements in homes and the constant disruption and gaps in their schooling that they experienced as a result of their mobility. These changes are stressful and anxiety-provoking for any children, and particularly so for foster kids making the transition through the upper elementary and middle school grades.

With each change of school, they have to make new friends and adjust to new teachers and new curricula. Falling further behind in homework and assignments, they are at least twice as likely as nonfoster students to be at least a year older for their grade, and by high school, to have fallen three or more grades below standardized reading and math levels. The social and emotional stress of this up-heaval makes it far more likely for foster care students than nonfoster students to be placed in special education for some kind of disability and to be suspended or expelled from school. Fewer than 50% graduate high school by the time they have aged out of the system. What's more, those who don't finish high school are less likely than their peers to obtain a GED (Child Trends Databank, 2015; Mastin et al., 2013; Smithgall, Gladden, Howard, Goerge, & Courtney, 2004).

In Makeba's case, she was a bright student but was placed in special education from ages 11 to 16. As she described it:

> They automatically wanted to put me in special education. Because I was in care, because I was in a residential treatment center, and then when I was pregnant in a maternity shelter, the only educational opportunity I had was special education. They had a teacher come in to teach us. I just had to do the same work over and over. I got good grades but that was the only thing I had available to me. I later found out I was identified as gifted and talented. (personal communication, September 27, 2017)

She was suspended from her comprehensive high school after cursing out a teacher who made a racially derogatory comment to her. Her foster mother was drinking heavily at this time and never came to the school to advocate for her. So she left, and then enrolled in an alternative high school designed to serve teen mothers and overage, undercredited students. She struggled to heal from the emotional wounds caused by the double loss of her mother and then her grandmother, and the breakup of her family, in addition to the trauma of sexual harassment by her foster parent. From this perspective, her frequent attempts to run away from foster homes and shelters were a strategy for survival.

In this brief narrative, Makeba highlights a range of deeply troubling problems with the education and child welfare systems. She was subjected to the low expectations, repeated misdiagnosis, labeling, and negative stereotypes that teachers too often have of students of color, particularly pregnant teen girls. This was worsened by racially biased microaggressions that she experienced in the classroom, and the school's use of suspension as a zero-tolerance means of discipline rather than mediation as a strategy for resolving conflict. Makeba's caseworker provided inadequate oversight of her neglectful and abusive foster parents, who did little to help her navigate through these broken systems. As an adult reflecting back on her life then, she says:

> I used to call myself an angry Black woman. Because, because I just had so
> much hate in me. I had self-hate. I had hatred for my family. Things that
> I didn't understand. . . . None of my foster parents loved me. I was told I
> was I was just a check to them. (Educational Video Center, 2003; personal
> communication, September 16, 2017)

After all the academic, social, and emotional harm that Makeba experienced as a child and young adult under what passed for "care" in these systems, she had more than enough reason to be angry. Outrage would even be an appropriate response. But she explained that at that age, at that time, she internalized a lot of her feelings; her anger, profound sense of loss and abandonment, and distrust of adults were turned inward as self-hatred and self-blame for the breakup of her family.

Elena attends a New York City high school serving students in foster care, juvenile justice, and transitional housing, some of whom participate in EVC video workshops. Though she is a generation younger than Makeba, she also tells of the deep emotional scars, as well as physical ones, that her experiences at home, in school, and foster homes left on her:

> I ended up going to 21 foster homes between the ages of when I was 6 to
> 8. They didn't want me 'cause I had scars on me. Because of what I went
> through, and because of the way I responded to it. I was acting up. . . . At the
> age of 8, I had to be a mother to my siblings. I have 4 younger siblings. I had
> to cook for them, clean them, and bring them to school. After that point,
> I never went to school myself. When I went to school, I would get bullied.
> Because of the scars. The other students would always bully me. 'Cause I
> had scars. And because I didn't go to school before, I was in a low level of
> reading and writing. I never learned to read. They thought I was retarded.

Now, I always be a person who stays by myself. I smile and keep it to myself. (personal communication, September 29, 2017)

Tears streak her face as she finishes telling her story. Visibly moved, fellow high school student Ray sitting next to her in the focus group hands her a tissue and says, "Damn. I never knew this about you. We only 16, 17, 18. But we are strong. We cannot let it break us" (personal communication, September 29, 2017).

Elena and Makeba certainly do not lack in determination and grit. But it's not Duckworth's grit of practice and academic skill building. It's the grit of survival, keeping oneself whole in the face of all oppressions—institutional, interpersonal, and internal. As they both report, their learning and literacy levels were misunderstood and misdiagnosed, their intellectual potential was underestimated, and their trauma was compounded by the adults who were charged to teach and care for them. Elena's and Makeba's stories speak to the urgent need for adults in school—whether school leaders, teachers, counselors, or social workers—to closely attend to, care for, and advocate for the most vulnerable of our students.

As the American Academy of Pediatrics (2017) affirms, "Mental and behavioral health is the largest unmet health need for children and teens in foster care." Whether our students externalize and act out their pain and trauma or try to keep it hidden, we need to develop trusting relationships with our students in foster care. Our students need to know we are listening to them, and that their voices will be heard. We need multiple strategies that provide them the safe space and creative outlets to share their stories. This might take the form of journal entries, poems, spoken word performances, dramatic dialogue, video blogs, photo essays, murals, and even comic books and graphic novels. To help them get started, it may be useful to have students read models of other books and articles written by and about youth in foster care, such as in the magazine *Represent: The Voice of Youth in Care* (www.representmag.org). They may be inspired to create their own foster youth magazine, website, or podcast. The point is that storytelling and other forms of creative expression can help our students give voice to the trauma they have experienced and develop closer connections with their peers and with us as their teachers, school leaders, and counselors. It can also open a window into their inner life, giving us an insight into their academic, social, and emotional strengths and needs and how we can help.

When we fail to tap into their strengths and talents and connect with our students on a deeper level than just their attendance and grades, the ongoing trauma and instability that foster youth experience at home and in school can spiral into a range of deeper problems. Foster youth are at risk of higher rates of pregnancy, poor health, drug use, dating violence, and homelessness. They are also at higher risk to be arrested at a younger age, arrested more frequently, and placed in juvenile detention facilities (Mastin et al., 2013; Reilly, 2003).

Too often, our students are making their way through these difficult changes with little active involvement from their foster parent, guardians, or caseworkers. This is not to say foster care workers are not well-meaning individuals. The lack of educational advocacy and support for foster youth is endemic to the system. Work in foster care is an exceedingly difficult job. With large caseloads and high turnover, caseworkers face numerous challenges finding an appropriate school for a particular child, securing the special services they might need, or placing them on a college-prep track where they can choose among postsecondary education options (Courtney, Roderick, et al., 2004). Those child-care staff in group homes with most contact with teens are typically the lowest paid in the agency, have little or no training in youth development, and are not given the role of actively supporting a child's education (Krebs & Pitcoff, 2006).

As Krebs and Pitcoff (2006) explain:

> When parents become a missing link in the process of education, the children suffer. Reports and studies confirm that foster care students fare poorly in school, they often receive low grades and do not advance to their full academic potential. Children in foster care are the most educationally at-risk population. The foster care system for the most part neglects this problem. It does not provide adequate coordination, case management, and assistance in regard to the education of children in care. (p. 34)

It's not that foster kids don't have high hopes and aspirations for their educational success, because they do. But the system too often throws obstacles that slow or block their path to academic success. Makeba described herself as an avid reader:

> I was always reading books. I would put myself in the story to avoid my reality. . . . Because a lot of kids bounce around from home to home and school to school, they lose your school records. When I was 16, I had to start from 9th grade because they couldn't find my records. I was ready to drop out and take a GED. All of my friends were graduating. I wanted to graduate with them, and wanted to be part of the senior class. It wasn't until I was in an alternative high school, and my homeroom teacher found the 48 credits that I had had! I was the last person added to the graduation list. I missed everything that year. The senior trip. All the senior activities. But it was okay. I just wanted to graduate. (personal communication, September 16, 2017)

And thus do our students struggle to succeed in school, while caught up in a child welfare system that stacks the odds against them with educational outcomes that are indeed bleak.

But these poor outcomes do not affect all students equally. Although middle-class White students may also experience abuse and neglect, and also have parents who struggle with depression or with alcohol or drug abuse, their parents are rarely reported for these practices. Middle-class White children represent only a small fraction of the students who are forcibly removed from their homes by the state.[3] They therefore enjoy a great advantage over low-income students of color as compared with the rates at which these populations experience trauma, school disruption and dropout, court involvement, and other negative life outcomes.

African American children are disproportionately represented in foster care at nearly twice their percentage in the general population, far greater than other races and ethnicities. In some states, the disparity is much greater, such as in California, Illinois, New York, and Texas where the proportion of Black children in the foster care system ranged from three to more than 10 times that of White children. In fact, African American children are "disproportionately represented at every stage in the child welfare process [and] the disproportionality increases the further into the child welfare pipeline the children go" (Tobis, 2013, p. 183).

There are complex and diverse factors that lead to this systemic bias, including budget cuts that unfairly fall on struggling families, lack of essential preventative services for them, and a continued culture and mindset of frontline caseworkers who devalue and blame poor Black parents for their problems of poverty (Tobis, 2013). They are more likely than any other racial or ethnic group to be forcibly removed from their homes; placed in foster care for longer periods of time; have less placement stability, lower adoption rates, and lower reunification rates with their parents; and receive fewer services from the child welfare system (Child Welfare Information Gateway, 2016; Courtney, Barth, et al., 1996).

Then there are those who are called dual-status, dually involved, or crossover youth, who are involved concurrently in both the child welfare and juvenile justice systems.[4] The youth who fall into this category are disproportionately girls and students of color, and they are at even greater risk of out-of-home placement rates, frequent placement changes, more detention stays, and overall higher offending rates (Sickmund & Puzzanchera, 2014). Unfortunately, school zero-tolerance policies are doing more to push them out of school into the justice system, rather than to nurture, retain, and teach them. Too often, a racialized and gendered school culture labels girls of color as "loud," "defiant," "sassy," and "disruptive," and so they end up being suspended, as Makeba was, for speaking up or questioning authority (Morris, 2016; Sherman & Balck, 2015).

"WELFARE QUEENS":
THE CRIMINALIZATION OF POOR BLACK MOTHERS

Makeba's separation from her grandmother and placement with a strange family in foster care is an all-too-common story for children in Black families living in marginalized communities. However, the disproportionate number of Black families broken up by the foster care system is not a flaw in the design of federal and state child welfare policy. It has historically been the design.

Dating back to the trope of the "welfare queen"[5] introduced in 1976 and tirelessly repeated by Ronald Reagan (Levin, 2013) up through Bill Clinton's pledge to end "welfare as we know it" in 1996, political leaders and the mass media have succeeded in publicly denigrating poor Black mothers as the undeserving, criminal poor. Sensational news stories publicizing the most tragic, but statistically rare, incidents of child abuse served to vilify low-income Black mothers in the popular imagination. Branding them as abusive criminals the public loved to hate made it politically and morally acceptable to create punitive welfare policies that devalued the bonds of Black families and promoted foster care as the solution rather than antipoverty programs (Tobis, 2013).

These negative stereotypes on a macrolevel of policy also impacted how social workers view and make decisions about their clients on an individual basis. As a study of Michigan's child welfare system showed, many social workers frequently described African American parents in case files with terms such as *hostile, aggressive, angry, loud, incorrigible,* and *cognitively delayed* without acknowledging the context or providing any justification for these labels. Even when Black women are the victims of domestic violence and sexual assault, some laws and child welfare services have blamed and punished these women for their own abuse. In these cases, mothers lost custody of their children on the grounds that they allowed their children to witness the violence or reside in the house where it occurred (Roberts, 2012). However, in New York State, such cases no longer constitute neglect since they were legally prohibited by the New York Court of Appeals (NYCLU, n.d.).[6] The problem is further complicated when many frontline workers are not trained social workers and lack proper supervision.

In addition to demeaning portrayals of Black mothers, negative portrayals of their children in the media and popular culture have labeled them over the years as crack babies, and teens as super predators, delinquents, and thugs. Studies show that people often see Black children as older than they actually are (Goff, Jackson, Culotta, Di Leone, & DiTomasso, 2014).[7] They are perceived to be less innocent and needing less nurturing, support, or protection than their White peers. Noguera (2008) shows how teachers' embedded stereotypes of Black males as behavior problems and less intelligent undermine their academic success in school, just as Morris (2016) describes how teachers' perceptions of Black girls as "defiant" and "disrespectful" diminishes their educational outcomes. These dehumanizing stereotypes and misperceptions contribute to policies that render Black children disproportionately overmedicated, overpoliced, and underprotected. Such narratives and policies have well-documented and pernicious consequences through frequent microaggressions that target Black students for discipline and punishment as the only response to their behavior, and move them along the pipeline out of school and into prison, detention facilities, and other institutions of exclusion and control.

It's important to acknowledge that we all carry our own assumptions about the students we teach. As educators committed to teaching and supporting our students, we owe to them and to ourselves to reflect on our assumptions and unconscious embedded stereotypes about race, gender, poverty, and youth in foster care or in the justice system. There may be ways, small and big, that our teaching impacts our students' self-esteem and academic achievement. For example, our implicit bias may cause some of us to consistently ignore girls and students of color when their hands are raised, assume they aren't interested in rigorous science or math classes and program their classes on this basis, steer them to noncollege postsecondary options when that is their choice, or discipline them more harshly than other students for minor infractions of rules. The point is not whether we have these attitudes, but for us to have the hard conversations and work to change them in our classes and in the school at large. Developing ways to constructively incorporate student perspectives and experiences with teacher bias will inform the process.

Historically, negative stereotypes and misrepresentations in the media of Black and Brown families in poverty correlate with our government's public welfare policies that punish them by removing public supports for struggling parents and children living in communities most depleted of resources and most vulnerable to the inequities. Dorothy Roberts (2012) describes welfare reform in the Clinton years this way: "The main mission of child welfare departments became protecting children not from social disadvantages stemming from poverty and racial discrimination but from maltreatment inflicted by their mothers" (p. 1485). This punitive approach to social policy brings to mind Nina Bernstein's observation in *The Lost Children of Wilder: The Epic Struggle to Change Foster Care* (2001): "There has long been an iron rule in American social welfare policy: conditions must be worse for the dependent poor than for anyone who works" (p. xiii).

The family's conditions of poverty remain an overwhelming cause or factor in the breakup and regulation of these families by the New York City Administration for Children's Services.[8] According to Brooklyn Defender Services (2015), over 90% of the child protective cases filed are based on allegations of neglect, not abuse. And most of these cases are caused or exacerbated by parents' conditions of poverty beyond their control, such as not providing their children with enough food to eat or with clean and safe housing to live in.

In one case reminiscent of Millie's East Harlem apartment in Chapter 1, a single mother who lived in a rat-infested apartment sought to protect her children from being bitten by the rats at night by having them sleep in a closet bundled in blankets from neck to toe. The rats made it impossible for her to keep fresh food in the apartment, and despite her struggles to maintain her younger son's weight, he become undernourished. Rather than providing the nutrition, housing, and financial services she and her children so urgently needed, the city charged her with parental neglect and took her children away from her. She struggled with depression and turned to alcohol after she lost her children (Ketteringham, 2017).

This is just one example cited by the legal aid organization the Bronx Defenders, of thousands of their child protection cases where the state takes children away from impoverished mothers rather than providing them with the food and housing support for their children, and mental health and substance abuse services they themselves need. Teachers and school counselors are then left to teach students damaged by the consequences of these policies—students living in extreme poverty and with parents struggling with mental health and substance abuse problems, or separated from their parents altogether.

Helping our students in these situations is both a complicated and simple thing for teachers to do. It can be complicated because our students' family may be struggling with a number of interconnected problems at once, including food insecurity, mental illness, and substance abuse, all of which need urgent attention. But as a point of departure, help can be as simple as being a compassionate listener to our students and creating openings for conversation and relationship building with them. After agreeing to ground rules for having a safe and respectful group discussion, we can talk about why it can be hard to talk about issues of family poverty and mental health, the stigma and shame that students may feel, and how we can counter that in our classes by telling our own stories. We can engage students in critically analyzing the content, representation, and misrepresentation of low-income families of color in the television and print news, focusing separately on depictions of teens, mothers, and fathers. Students will be sure to come up with their own topics, and may want to start their own ongoing discussion group.

As our students consistently tell us, if they come to school angry, or agitated, or unable to sit still and focus on the lesson, they want teachers to be caring and take time to really get to know them and the problems they are struggling with. Attending the same high school as Elena, Ant had lived with his mother in a homeless shelter, with his grandmother, and was now in foster care. He had this to say:

> I'm currently in foster care, living with somebody who don't care. I'm just a check to them. I was in 6 homes since 14. Being in foster care, you never know who you are going to be with. You never know what's coming next. In foster care, you watching shit go down and there is nothing you can do about it. You just have to deal with what you have. They control what they want you to do. You have no voice. . . . My mother died 5 months ago. I don't want other people to know. This shit is not easy. . . . Everything I did was for my mother. To make her feel proud of me. Just the thought you'd never been able to see her again. I'll never hear her voice again. Now there is nobody for me. And I'm only 16. I think, what did I do to deserve this? Since my mother died, I walk around like I'm good. But I'm not good. (personal communication, September 29, 2017)

Listening to Ant tell his story, fellow student Keisha added: "I think they [teachers] should sit down and hear what you have to say. 'I notice you're not smiling. You don't look happy. What's wrong?'" (personal communication, September 29, 2017).

Ant's feelings of lack of control and lack of voice are understandable given the instability and mobility in his life in homeless shelters and multiple foster homes. Certainly, the "You don't look happy" check-in is important for us to do, all the more so when students like him may try to show a tough exterior that they are "good" when they are actually "not good," and are feeling great pain and loss. This is especially important for adults in schools to recognize when students like Ant, and also like Makeba, feel so disconnected from their foster parents, and feel the only value they have is as a source of income—the check they as a foster child bring into the home. In addition to the check-in and being available to listen, we should be prepared to connect students with school counselors and social workers who can provide therapy and help them access additional resources.

"SHE COULD NOT TAKE CARE OF HERSELF":
PARENTAL SUBSTANCE ABUSE

Most parents feel to some degree the social and economic stress of feeding, clothing, and providing safe housing for their children. Parents with families near or below the poverty line experiencing food insecurity endure heightened psychological stress. This is particularly the case for mothers whose children are taken from them, or who experience the physical and emotional trauma of sexual assault and domestic violence. They are more likely to suffer increased rates of depression and other forms of mental illness, and physically and emotionally traumatized people are also at high risk of self-medicating their trauma through alcohol and drug abuse, both with illegal and legal prescription drugs.

Substance abuse and mental illness are strongly associated. In fact, the U.S. Department of Health and Human Services advocates treating drug addiction as a mental illness because it changes the brain in fundamental ways. As many as 50% to 70% of people struggling with substance abuse problems also suffer from depression, posttraumatic stress, and other psychiatric disorders (Editorial Board, 2017; U.S. Department of Health and Human Services, National Institutes of Health, 2010). So it's no surprise that students' foster care stories often involve parental struggles with the co-occurring problems of substance abuse and mental health. Parental substance abuse is increasing as the opioid crisis grows nationally (U.S. Department of Health and Human Services, 2017). And the physical and mental well-being of parents can't help but have a deep impact on the social, emotional, and academic well-being of their children.

A decade after *Not Me, Not Mine* (Educational Video Center, 2003), EVC students explored the stigma of both illegal and prescription drug use and its impact on teens and their parents in *High on Perceptions* (Educational Video Center, 2014b). In the film, EVC student Adina interviews her mother, who is addicted to painkillers. As a survivor of rape, her mother tells of her long-term struggles with opioid addiction and depression, including a suicide attempt. It is almost incidental to the story that she was in foster care as a child, perhaps about the same time as Makeba was. And now as a mother, she fears she is at risk of losing Adina and her younger sister to foster care. She says the only thing keeping her going is her children.

Getting to really know our students well is crucial to teaching them well. That includes knowing their family. Even though this a different family and a different generation, Adina's account of how her mother's struggles with addiction affects her day-to-day life at home and in school can shed some light on what Makeba's childhood experience may have been when the drugs "take over":

Living with a family member who is addicted to prescription pills isn't easy. You have to check on them. And constantly worry if they're all right. Things like waking up on time for school get harder than they need to be. And with me being a high school senior, I can't afford to worry. A lot of the responsibility of my little sister falls on me. And whenever I can't help, I feel guilty. Which puts me in a bad mood. My mother's taken pills for as long as I can remember. But it's at the point where the medication has taken over. She's almost always irritable and she can bring a lot of negativity to our house. It makes me sad to think about how she used to be back when she was happier. She had a lot of energy. She made plans, threw barbecues. Like she did things. My sister may never get to see that or remember it. And I think that part hurts me the most. (Educational Video Center, 2014b)

And here is the story from Adina's mother's perspective as she opens up about her day-to-day struggles with opioid addiction and depression:

Sometimes I really thought I overcame it. A few times. And—excuse me. . . . It's terrible. Sorry. I lost my teeth. I almost lost my daughter earlier this year to protective services. Just for not being involved in her life like I should. Not taking her to school. And just not wanting to get out of bed. Sorry. And um, those are just. Okay, all right. Um, those are things that—I fight with every day. Um, the only reason why I think I'm still here to this day is because of my children. (Educational Video Center, 2014b)

Adina's mother shared these painful personal stories with Adina for the first time because she trusted the purposes of her student documentary project and the teacher facilitating it, and also because Adina asked her. Such conversations are not easy to have, but Adina developed a deeper and more empathetic understanding of her mother's struggles as a result. The students knew the negative stereotypes of the drug-addicted mothers in low-income communities of color who were so often vilified in the mainstream media and wanted their video to give a

It Makes Me Sad

 View the clip online: www.tcpress.com/goodman-chapter-five#v5.3

counter-narrative. By giving voice to one such parent, they were able to challenge the stereotype, humanize the drug problem as a mental health problem, and call for more public health services in the community.

As teachers we can also learn about our students' families from our students, and about our students from their families. We don't necessarily need to create student documentaries, but we do need to create supportive nonjudgmental spaces and creative activities in their classes that prompt them to think, talk, and write about family, foster care, and community-related subjects. For example, students might want to write a letter to Makeba, or half the class might choose to have an imaginary dialogue with Adina and the other half with her mother. Or they might want to create a Bill of Rights for students in foster care, or a letter explaining what every teacher should know about kids in foster care.

Makeba didn't know that much about her mother except that when she became addicted to drugs she gave Makeba to her grandmother for adoption—and also, that she died young. With the benefit of hindsight as a mother herself, Makeba reflects back on her own mother's addiction and how she felt at the time when she was a student like Adina:

> My mother was addicted to drugs. And I used to think that the drug was more important than her children. Growing up I thought that. But it was the drug. She could not take care of herself. So she could not take care of me. (Educational Video Center, 2003)

> One thing I learned—she was really, really smart. She was always at the top of the class. How am I so resilient? How am I still standing? My mother was strong. She didn't know it. People didn't tell her what they told me. (personal communication, September 16, 2017)

Things That I Fight with Every Day

 View the clip online: www.tcpress.com/goodman-chapter-five#v5.4

Makeba wanted to ask her mother and father how and why she ended up in foster care but they were not alive to give her any answers. Perhaps Makeba's mother might have talked about her struggles with addiction in a similar way as Adina's mother—except that Makeba's mother *did* lose her children, and then her life. "I later found out that my mom was murdered," Makeba said.

> That day, my mother got into a fight with my baby brother's father. He got her high. And he beat her. He beat her so bad, he hemorrhaged her to death. . . . They forced me to go to the wake and I saw her in the casket. (personal communication, September 15, 2017)

Struggling with poverty, Makeba's and Adina's mothers were also victims of rape, domestic violence, and even murder. Oppression and violence against women, and particularly Black women and girls, is a recurring theme throughout the stories of foster care students and their families. Yet, when their mothers self-medicate their physical and emotional pain, they are demonized as objects of scorn and punished with social policy that stigmatizes mental illness and treats addiction as a crime rather than a disease. And when their sons and daughters— our students—also suffering from the trauma of this brutality against their mothers then become angry, exhausted, anxious, or absent, or do not participate, or act out in class, they are suspended or expelled. Consider how differently they might be treated if these students with emotional and behavior problems in class didn't have the stigma associated with foster care, poverty, or parental drug addiction, but were in intact White middle-class families with a parent with cancer. Yet in both situations, they are kids acting out in school due to the stress of having an ill parent. Regardless of their race, class, or the cause of their trauma, all students deserve to be taught with compassion.

"NOT ME, NOT MINE": AGING OUT AND YOUTH ADVOCACY

The largest group of children in foster care is made up of older youth. They stay in care longer and are more likely to age out without being reunited with their custodial parent or being adopted. This is the case for nearly 15% of the 14- to 17-year-olds and over 70% of those ages 18 and over (Mastin et al., 2013). Each year in New York City, nearly 1,000 of these older foster youth age out of the system (Office of the NYC Public Advocate Letitia James, 2014). Leaving the system is often a traumatic experience for foster youth who are unprepared to live on their own. As a foster youth advocate interviewed in *Not Me, Not Mine* (Educational Video Center, 2003) explained:

> Who on this earth at 21[9] is ready for their parents to kick them out and say, "Don't call me! Don't come back. And don't ask me for no money in case you need it. Or don't ask me for anything!" . . . When I aged out, I heard

the four walls talking to me, I swear I was losing my mind. I was so lonely. (Educational Video Center, 2003)

Sadly, the child welfare and school systems are doing these young people a disservice by so poorly preparing them to graduate from high school and make the transition to college, work, and independent life on the outside. Although focused on their safety and protection, the child welfare system has failed to make education a priority for the youth in its charge. Narratives of low expectations, as shown in Makeba and Elena's stories of lost credits and misdiagnosed assessments, can then go on to erase college as a possibility for foster care students. We need to ensure that our struggling students are given the same all-hands-on-deck support, guidance, and resources for high school graduation and college readiness as their more privileged, nonfoster care peers enjoy. This will likely require an extra investment of time partnering with our students, their foster parents, and caseworkers to plan and coordinate college visits and job applications, and set goals for life after high school. In addition, it would be helpful to connect these students with mentors who were formerly in foster care, someone who really understands what they are going through and has successfully transitioned to independent life.

More than in previous generations, transitioning from school to work or college requires a range of social, emotional, and material support from teachers, parents, and other family members. Students in out-of-home care are at a great disadvantage without the benefit of all the time, money, and other resources that parents must invest in their children's schooling and out-of-school enrichment. Bringing transformative teaching to our classes can begin to address this gap.

With this unmet need, the ongoing trauma and instability that foster youth experience at home and in school can lead to a range of problems, including higher rates of pregnancy, poor health, drug use, dating violence, and homelessness. They are also at higher risk to be arrested at a younger age, arrested more frequently, and pushed out of school and into juvenile detention facilities (Mastin et al., 2013; Reilly, 2003).

Though these statistics give a demographic picture of the sweeping inequitable trends of foster involvement across race, class, and gender, they do not determine individual destiny. Each individual student carries his or her own aspirations to struggle against the odds and emerge from the system with an intact sense of agency and possibility. Now in her 40s, Makeba has an associate's degree and is an educator working at a Head Start program and at an organization that serves intellectually challenged adults. All of her children have graduated high school and one has a master's degree. As Makeba puts it:

My life is not supposed to be this way. Statistically speaking. . . . But I broke the chain, you know. I said, "Not me, not mine." . . . Because I was denied an adequate education, one thing I want to do is make sure my kids had one. (Educational Video Center, 2003)

There are many factors contributing to Makeba's resilience and determination to break the chain, but one stands out: a close relationship with a supportive adult whom she could count on. Research on resilience supports how critically important it is for youth to have a strong, stable adult relationship in the face of adversity (National Scientific Council on the Developing Child, 2015). Makeba had the consistent support of lawyer Betsy Krebs, who not only advocated on behalf of the rights of foster care youth, but also engaged them to advocate for themselves. In self-advocacy seminars, Makeba and other foster youth learned to advocate for a better education in high school as well as in college, developing goal-setting, research, and information analysis skills in preparation for life on the "other side." With a strengths-based approach, Krebs's Youth Advocacy Center program challenged the low expectations of the foster care system and offered foster care youth training in goal setting, self-empowerment, and knowing how to advocate for their rights (Krebs & Pitcoff, 2004, 2006).

Makeba reflects on that experience:

> When I was graduating high school, I wanted to go to college. The counselor was very discouraging about me going to college. She told me maybe I should take a trade. If the guidance counselor couldn't help me, I decided to ask the principal for help, and then a social worker. And I finally got myself into college. . . . Because I was a teenage mother I had a passion for helping other young mothers in foster care. And I had credibility with them. . . . We don't see a lot of people who are like us in the system. We see lawyers, judges, caseworkers, social workers, counselors, but none of those people really are able to identify with us. So having advocates in care, it gave me a different type of credibility than a judge or a lawyer. Because we were their peers. . . . Everything I had gone through I would share with the young people. The advocacy agenda was "know your rights." A lot of people don't know their rights. When you have mothers who are temporarily separated from your kids, in group homes, residential treatment centers. I encouraged young people to sit at the table where decisions were being made about their education and about their children. 'Cause I had sat at the table and advocated for myself. I didn't have parents to advocate for me. My parents were dead. I had to advocate for Makeba. If I didn't advocate for myself, I don't know where I'd be. I don't know where I'd be. (personal communication, September 16, 2017; September 27, 2017)

As Makeba put it, students in foster care are so used to being beat down, they believe they don't deserve more. We need to assure them that they do, and assure them that we are there to listen if they want to open up about their experiences in the system. This means creating inclusive and trauma-sensitive classrooms and being committed to building relationships with the most vulnerable students, even when large class size makes this a challenge. With time and trust, the students will feel empowered to break their silence. They may want to talk about their anxiety being new to the school, or their anger at having to eat off a separate set of plates[10] and being treated as a stranger in their own foster home. Of having to endure the regular interrogation and monitoring by foster parents, case workers, lawyers, judges, and others in the system. They are looking for a caring adult who will listen, someone who will be on their side, who can share resources and help them learn to advocate for themselves.

In New York City, the Office of Postsecondary Readiness transfer high school model creates small schools where teachers do develop close relationships with overage and undercredited students through advisory classes and partnerships between the schools and community-based social service organizations. It includes Edward Reynolds West Side High School, where Makeba graduated in the 1990s, and Cascades High School, where Adina graduated some 20 years later. The high school where Elena, Ant, Ray, and Keisha are students offers a closely related model. The principal explains:

> In some way, shape, or form our students are struggling. Even though they are kids, they are dealing with very grown-up issues. As a school, we are building an understanding of the students we are teaching. You have to know the student. Not just on paper. Really know them. As a new principal, I went on home visits to learn who they are, where they've been, how they think, and learn. I want to not only give them fish, but teach them how to fish, how to advocate for themselves. We even role-play how to effectively advocate and ask a teacher for change. . . . We are giving them the tools for survival, connecting them with their peers, and developing their sense that, I am not alone in this. You went through this? I went through this too. Our teachers can say, "I built a relationship with this student. I will listen to their problems and what they are saying. I may not have all the solutions, but I'll keep listening." It may be the difference between life and death. (personal communication, September 29, 2017)

The school culture that the principal describes is one that honors the strength and resilience in students such as Makeba, Adina, Elena, Ray, Keisha, and Ant. And as an essential part of resilience, students need strong relationships with adults who can be culturally sustaining educators, mentors, and advocates. This means all of us who can see the big picture—the systemic and institutional roadblocks our students face every day—while also supporting them individually in the specific areas they need to grow, keeping them on track, and nurturing their sense of hope and possibility.

Makeba found such teachers at EVC when she joined the youth video team there the semester after EVC students interviewed her for their documentary on surviving the foster care system. As part of the first cohort of AmeriCorps, she was mentored to produce a public service documentary on domestic violence that brought healing to the youth producers and the audiences who watched it.

These are examples of transformative teaching in school and after school, where we take the time to really know our students well and develop close relationships with them, and where we create spaces and strategies that inspire our students to tell their own stories and build school and community audiences who will listen and have greater empathy for them as a result. Supporting them to take action to teach and advocate for others takes it a step further. In the spirit of Makeba's statement "Not me, not mine," it is empowering for our foster care students to take back their own narrative and see that change is possible and needed on both individual and structural levels. It is empowering for them to see us, their teachers, social workers, and other adults who reject the deficit discourse and debilitating racialized, gendered stereotypes about them, their parents, and marginalized communities, to see us as educators and allies who will teach them, as Makeba's lawyer and Elena's principal did, to advocate for themselves and stand up for their rights. And then, as Makeba showed, they will go on and teach other students in the system to stand up for theirs.

"I've Got Your Back"

Moving from Trauma and Resilience Toward Student Activism

The capacity to listen to, learn from, and care for our students is essential to what makes transformative teaching so powerful. Listening to the personal stories of trauma, inequity, resilience, and activism of EVC students throughout this book, we can see how unjust and oppressive social systems and institutions are impacting their lives at home and their achievement in school. This is the case whether they developed asthma from mold in public housing; are harassed by police on the street corner or in the classroom; are detained by ICE agents on the way to school; are bullied in school for gender, body size, or sexual orientation; or are torn from their family by a caseworker. These are all parts of systemic injustices that make up our students' reality and negatively impact their health, well-being, and educational achievement. And they most assuredly occupy their thoughts across their day in school.

But it's not about grit. The students we have met are brimming with determination, passion, and perseverance. They have struggled repeatedly to resist and overcome the systemic barriers in their way. So, we must join Alim and Paris (2017) in reframing the object of critique from our students to the systems that oppress them. Understanding how systems of power and inequity have developed over history, and how they work today to constrain our students' opportunities individually, gives us the pedagogical tools to teach our students to question and take action to disrupt those systems. Using those pedagogical tools so students can develop their critical skills and make their voices heard in our classes, schools, and communities will spread the student-centered and community-based power of transformative teaching.

Seeing the spectrum of oppressions in our students' lives—the institutional, interpersonal, and internal—makes visible and gets at the root of why students like Raelene, Rob, Luis, Muzik, or Makeba may be too fearful or exhausted to come to school, or silent, anxious, angry, aggressive, or unable to sit still when they do attend. The hunger, anxiety, depression, hypervigilance, and trauma that so many of our students carry within them into our classes, hallways, and schoolyards are responses to witnessing or being on the receiving end of some form of chronic violence. That includes the day-to-day violence of poverty, whether from living in apartment buildings where the landlord won't turn on the heat or exterminate the rats; from suffering from lack of proper mental, physical, and dental care; or from being hungry and sleep deprived. Then there is the interpersonal violence at home and in the streets, and state violence at the hands of some branch of law enforcement.

Our students are victimized by these conditions three times over: First, they suffer from the physical or emotional wounds of the assault or condition. Second, they experience psychological trauma that continues on as a result. Third, schools punish and track them for their inattention, poor behavior, absences, and poor grades when their social and emotional health declines.

The physical and emotional wounds run deep for children and teenagers, whether they are victims or witnesses, or sometimes also perpetrators of violence. And in the aftermath, they may be summonsed, transported, remanded, or in some way pass time in the myriad offices and wards invisible to most on the outside, but familiar destinations for the poor, immigrant, and marginalized among us. So the sights, sounds, and smells of juvenile detention centers, homeless shelters, immigration detention facilities, child welfare and family courts, emergency trauma clinics, or psychiatric hospitals may well be a recurring presence in our students' minds, competing for their attention while they sit in our classes.

Suspending and expelling those Black, Brown, and poor students or allowing them to slip through the cracks and leave school on their own won't make these unjust conditions go away, nor will improving their grit or mindset toward learning. Making meaningful improvement in their test scores, attendance, and graduation rates won't happen without making radical changes in the violent social systems that impoverish those students' communities and traumatize the students in them.

Listening to our students' stories makes clear not only the many ways they have been victimized and abused, but also the many ways they have struggled and are resilient, full of intelligence, determination, and creativity. And so we must be compassionate listeners, good at attending to, and learning from and with our students. One can't help but be more empathetic to students after hearing their stories of struggle and of resilience—after feeling what it's like to walk in their shoes. Listening, we get to know and connect with them on a deeper level, knowing that those who act out and are the most troubled are usually the most in trouble and in need of our support. We see through the trouble to the inner strength, intelligence, and talent each student possesses.

Although they have been stigmatized and pathologized in the past as dropouts, thugs, and illegal aliens, they consistently say that these labels do not define them. They say they are tired of repeatedly being told that they aren't going to make it. We need to listen to them.

Teaching from a strengths-based approach, we know how to build on students' positive assets, their knowledge, and their talents rather than their weaknesses. We know how to listen closely, get to know students well, and build strong relationships with them, their parents, and others in their students' communities. These are absolutely essential and necessary, but not sufficient conditions for transformative teaching.

More is needed and more must be done to attend to the needs of individual students and the structures that block them from reaching their full potential. To nurture students' healing from trauma into resilience and self-determination, we need to call upon a range of strategies, activities, projects, and school structures that create more welcoming, inclusive, trauma-sensitive, and culturally sustaining classes and schools. There is no one solution; and although they vary in the intensity, skills, and resources required, they all take time to grow roots and take hold.

Though the primary audience of this book is educators, the content and video clips from the preceding chapters are also meant to be used with our students as engaging and relevant resources for scaffolding class discussion, research, creative expression, and action on the critical issues in their lives. It is essential that our students can connect their lives to their learning across the school day. Seeing and hearing from other students who may look like them and have experiences similar to theirs inspire our students to reflect on their lives and tell their own stories. The clips can also be used to create a more inclusive school culture by prompting discussions about common assumptions, microaggressions, and stereotypes others in the school may have about students who may be homeless, court involved or with incarcerated parents, undocumented, LGBTQ, suffering from an eating disorder, or living in foster care.

Finally, there is a range of collaborative youth participatory action research projects that not only develop students' skills as critical readers and researchers, but also activate them as change agents examining and proposing solutions to urgent social justice problems in their school and community. These may involve any number of different forms of art, music, drama, journalism, and social investigation. One such EVC action project on students and policing can serve as a blueprint for projects on any range of other social issues.

"SITES OF POSSIBILITY"

Participating in what Weiss and Fine (2004) call "sites of possibility," or "small safe spaces, fractures in the hegemonic armor" (p. xxiv) often produces important shifts in students' identity toward resilience and empowerment. This was evident in the students who mediated restorative justice circles as a strategy for disrupting the school-to-prison pipeline. Inclusive groups such as Genders & Sexualities Alliances, girls support groups, and DREAMers clubs build healing and solidarity as students see they are not alone, and educate and support one another and the larger community to stand up against nativist discrimination, sexual harassment, and homophobia. They also contribute to a more inclusive school culture with more empathy and understanding among all students.

Through discussion, debate, and community projects where students investigate their lived experiences, the systemic context of their oppression comes into focus, and they begin to believe in their own capacity for making change. Growing to assume the role and see themselves as youth leaders or advocates, they feel a greater sense of purpose and efficacy and a greater control over their lives. Learning takes on a bigger meaning than credits and grades. They are making a difference in the world, however small—whether in their classroom, school, or neighborhood—and they have an adult mentor and ally working alongside them.

When we as educators work in these spaces, placing our students' questions, ideas, experiences, and stories at the center, we also experience shifts in our identity. As we build closer relationships with our students outside their academic classes and get to know their personal history, we stretch in new ways to become advocates, activists, and allies. This may involve using our place of privilege to help our students navigate various systems, whether they involve public housing, hospitals, the courts, or child welfare. With time and trust, students welcome this closer relationship and identity shift. As Julian, a student who is actively involved in restorative justice circles in his school put it, "We want our teachers to tell us, 'I've got your back'" (personal communication, October 13, 2017).

Through participation in these sites of possibility, students' belief that change is indeed possible, both personally and politically, grows over time with each experience and each small victory. EVC's philosophy of education is based on this approach. With intensive support and scaffolding from instructors, as our students learn to create documentaries that shine a spotlight on injustice in their lives, they also learn that it is possible for them to raise their voices to resist those injustices.

The personal development and political changes are interwoven and intergenerational, as students and teachers are learners and advocates together. And the impact can be lasting. Part of a safe and supportive community of social documentary filmmakers, they learn that the art and new knowledge that they create has value as a tool for dialogue in their schools and in the broader community. And they learn that they as the researcher/filmmaker/storyteller/activist have great value, too.

Students' self-esteem and resilience increases when they feel at home in a safe space with close, caring, and supportive relationships with fellow students and with teachers who have "got their back." This is particularly important for students who may experience being stigmatized, or internalize the stigma because of their status, whether they are homeless, undocumented, LGBTQ, have incarcerated or deported parents, or are living in foster care. As Jean, who had witnessed his father's arrest by ICE, reflected on his experience at EVC's Documentary Workshop, "At EVC, we meet as strangers, and leave as a family" (personal communication, October 6, 2017). With these networks of compassionate support, graduation from high school and making postgraduation plans become that much more within their reach.

"A KNOCK ON THE DOOR": A SIGN OF THE TIMES

It's a sign of the times that a knock on the door can bring terror to a family, not in some far-off totalitarian country, but here in the United States. A New York City principal tells of the two students, both cousins who are actively involved in her school's restorative justice program and political discussion group. One cousin's family was just evicted due to gentrification in his community. His family was forced to move in with their cousins who were born in Mexico. This family is living in fear of deportation. Now, when they hear a knock on the door, the cousins say they're not sure if the knock is the police, whom the landlord called to evict them, or ICE coming to deport them.

The systems of justice, immigration, and housing all intersect in this story, and in the real lives of our students. It's encouraging that the students had developed the political consciousness to make these kinds of systemic connections, and also want to make a film that tells the story of their predicament. It's profoundly discouraging that these are the lessons we have to teach our students.

These times bring to mind Antonio Gramsci's (1971) aphorism that opens this book—*pessimism of the intellect, optimism of the will*. As educators we need to take a hard look at the conditions of our times, and particularly the conditions in which our students struggle. This requires a sober social analysis—pessimistic and without any illusions—of the intersecting structures shaping their (and all of our) lives, while also being attentive on an individual level to each student's experiences outside our schools.

No question these are dark times for our students, their families, and the communities in which they live. Fifty years after the Kerner Commission report of 1968 famously warned, "Our nation is moving towards two societies, one black, one white—separate and unequal" (Jones, Schmitt, & Wilson, 2018), ours remains a profoundly segregated and inequitable society. The income gap between White and Black Americans is as wide as it was 50 years ago, and the median White household has about 13 times the wealth of the median Black household, much of it transferred between generations. Black applicants for low-wage jobs receive callback interviews or jobs at half the rate of equally qualified White applicants. Structural racism remains such a pernicious force in limiting intergenerational economic mobility that, according to a comprehensive study covering 20 million children and their parents, even Black boys who grow up in affluent families and communities still earn less as adults than White boys with similar backgrounds. Black boys from affluent families are also more likely than their White counterparts to become poor as adults, rather than remaining wealthy (Chetty, Hendren, Jones, & Porter, 2018). In 1968, African Americans were 5.4 times as likely to be incarcerated as Whites, and today they are 6.4 times as likely. In fact, on any given day, an astonishing 21% of Black men from the poorest families are now incarcerated (Chetty, Hendren, Jones, & Porter, 2018). More than 60 years after the landmark *Brown v. Board of Education* decision, many Black students attend schools that are as segregated as they were in the 1960s (Campos, 2017; Jones et al., 2018).

Five years after the most diverse electorate in history elected the nation's first African American president, the Supreme Court struck down a key provision of the Voting Rights Act (1965), disenfranchising millions of student, elderly, and minority voters. Poor and working people, Muslims, women, the disabled, LGBTQ, and Latino and African American communities are all under attack. Our democracy is indeed in a precarious state.

And now here is where the second part of Gramsci's dictum comes in: *optimism of the will*. This is cautioning us not to become disillusioned by the pessimism of our social analysis, or allow it to cloud over our hope and possibility for a better world. In this case, it's holding onto a belief in the students we teach, and in the transformative power of education coupled with social action. It's also making sure that when students conduct critical investigations of their current and historical social conditions, there is an attendant optimism in their power as change agents and a hope in the possibilities of their collective research and collective action.

Hope and optimism of the will in this sense is not just a utopian belief but is rooted in experience and in history. We have the experience of seeing our students grow more confident, more consciously aware or "wide-awake," as Maxine Greene (1995) calls it, of inequitable and unjust conditions in their lives and their capacity to do something to change them through student "spaces of action" such as GSAs, DREAMers clubs, girls groups, restorative justice circles, and social documentary teams. These steps are the first rungs of a ladder toward self-empowerment and youth leadership. These students develop further as morally and socially responsible youth leaders when their clubs and programs extend their activity outside the school, bringing their education and justice work into the community.

Historically, we know that student engagement in grassroots education and grassroots community organizing have been successful even in conditions more oppressive and violent than today. The Student Nonviolent Coordinating Committee's (SNCC's) Freedom Schools and the Highlander Folk School's Citizenship Schools led by Septima Clark were inspiring examples of radical popular education experiments on a grand scale in the 1950s and 1960s. The power of these projects lay in the interweaving of literacy education, personal empowerment, and active participation in the voter registration civil rights movement. In both cases, activist educators grounded their pedagogy in their African American high school and adult students' direct experiences of oppression, and in their students' need to read and understand the political documents and the structures of power in their local communities in order to open pathways to their full citizenship. This innovative combination of learning, research, and civic action lay the groundwork that eventually dismantled the racist voting laws in the Jim Crow South (Charron, 2009; Clark, 1964; Cobb, 1963; Horton, 1990).

"WHERE WE WANT TO BE": YOUTH PARTICIPATORY ACTION RESEARCH

Although the times that characterized the student and freedom movements of the 1960s are different from today (though many critical problems such as inequitable schools, police brutality, and voter suppression remain with us 60 years later), the boldness of their vision and depth of their practices have left a rich legacy that contemporary popular education practitioners and culturally relevant and responsive educators continue to build upon. Strategies for collective student civic engagement and research on social problems are informed by those radical experiments in social justice education.

Participatory action research (PAR), still practiced at Highlander, is among the most well-known of such strategies. Influenced by Freire, PAR brings together action and reflection as a critical pedagogy with oppressed people, not for them (Charles & Ward, 2007). Practiced internationally, it is based on the notion that problems can best be solved by bringing together the very people from the community who experience them. In this case, students are, in fact, the best people to do the research because they understand the problems from their own everyday experience, and so the research is done with, by, and for them, in partnership with the larger community. The new knowledge they have created through their collective inquiry will then be applied to solve a problem of injustice. Cammarota and Fine (2008) describes this new knowledge as

> active and NOT passive (i.e., mere facts and figures organized for storage). Research findings become launching pads for ideas, actions, plans, and strategies to initiate social change. . . . [PAR] redefines knowledge as actions in pursuit of social justice. . . . Through participatory action research, youth learn how to study problems and find solutions to them. More importantly, they study problems and derive solutions to obstacles preventing their own well-being and progress. (p. 6)

Participatory action research and youth participatory action research (YPAR) projects are about the democratization of research and knowledge creation. And as such, they look different across the wide variety of schools, communities, and countries in which they take place. They have a lot in common with EVC's youth documentary projects because both reject the supposed neutrality of the researcher, and the monopoly that experts and academics typically have on knowledge production. They don't necessarily have to involve video production as with EVC's work, but can include student research papers, surveys, creative writing, music, or drama.

Researching problems of systemic injustice can seem overwhelming and sometimes pessimistic for students. But an optimism and sense of hope grows as they become immersed in the flow of their creative work and the possibility of change emerges. Whether through collective art, writing, spoken word, drama, journalism, mapping, websites, photography, graphic novels, podcasts, or documentary, students will surely engage in some form of sharing local knowledge, asking questions, gathering data, speaking out, and telling stories about their lives and experiences. As they go about "naming the world," as Freire described it, identifying and describing the conditions, problems, and obstacles that they encounter in their schools and communities, they sketch a collective picture of "where we are," as Clark (1964) put it. Then, as they "learn to be action research minded," they pose questions about how things can be different and what needs to be changed to get there, they set their sights on "where we want to be" (p. 122).

There are extraordinary examples of YPAR work with students across the county. Several are collaborative intergenerational projects where community organizations and academics engaged students in action research on the educational problems they face in their schools:

- Over six summers, Morrell (2008) conducted YPAR seminars engaging low-income youth in a range of inquiries, including research on equity and access in public schools, how hip-hop culture can transform school literacy curricula, how youth research can support legal advocacy, and the creation of an educational Bill of Rights for California's public school students.

- Torre, Fine, et al. (2008) worked with a diverse PAR collective of close to 50 high school students, college students, faculty, and artists from urban and suburban districts in New York and New Jersey to investigate the "unfulfilled promises of *Brown v. Board of Education*," conditions of educational injustice in the opportunity gap both locally and in cross-site research camps.
- Duncan-Andrade (2006) led a summer seminar for high school students in Los Angeles where students conducted a qualitative research study of local youth civic participation and created a documentary that incorporated their findings.
- Ginwright (2008) and Cammarota convened six youth and adult PAR teams in Arizona and California, where they explored the question of what rights young people have in a democratic society. The teams documented school and community problems and developed what constitutes a Youth Bill of Rights and a youth rights handbook.
- The Lawrence Youth Council led a 3-year student-driven "What is Education? Liberation Through Education" campaign in Lawrence, Massachusetts, to increase educational equity and raise awareness about what students want from their education. With deep involvement of Andover Bread Loaf and Elevated Thought in a youth and community collective, the students produced videos, conducted surveys, presented at the Department of Education in Washington, D.C., and convened the first-ever citywide town hall forum, where students questioned school committee candidates on their vision for youth and education (McKenna, 2016; L. Bernieri, personal communication, November 21, 2017).
- Inspired by Kozol's *Savage Inequalities* (1991), Goodman (1994) and Murdock facilitated a team of recent EVC graduates to chronicle a year in the life of two 7th-grade students to investigate the race- and class-based disparities in resources provided in their two Bronx schools, one located in a predominantly White middle-class neighborhood and the other in a working-class Black and Latino community. Their documentary *Unequal Education: Failing Our Children* (Educational Video Center, 1992) was broadcast by Bill Moyers on PBS and used by parents as an organizing tool.

Though only briefly described in summary here, whether in New York, New Jersey, Arizona, Los Angeles, or Lawrence, MA, each project represents transformative teaching driven by students' stories, questions, observations, and findings. Students' inquiries and social critiques of the educational inequities in their own communities challenge conventional notions of who is an expert, who gets to conduct research on whom, and what are the questions that get asked in that research.

The following description gives a blueprint of a collaborative EVC youth participatory action research project that used video documentary as a tool for student research, presentation of their findings, and public conversation. But the same basic principles apply to youth participatory action research in other settings and contexts, regardless of whether video was used. This project sought to spark dialogue and change among the youth participants, teachers, police, schools, and the broader community. In partnership with the New York City Department of Education's Office of Postsecondary Readiness (OPSR), in the Division of Teaching and Learning, EVC developed a semester-long YPAR project on police violence and misconduct in schools and communities with 70 students in three high school classes in two high schools serving overage and undercredited students and English language learners.

As noted in Chapter 2, even after learning about their rights and civil liberties from viewing the EVC documentary *Policing the Times* (Educational Video Center, 2015b), many students still had little faith that it would protect them from harm the next time they were stopped by the police. Their doubts were not unfounded as the list of police shootings of unarmed Black men grew, followed by their successive acquittals of any wrongdoing—even with shocking footage of the shootings taken from cell phone, dashboard, or body camera recordings.

This project, called "Youth Powered Change," gave students the opportunity to create video documentaries on problems they collectively chose to explore and propose actions that youth and community members can take to address the problem. One class chose to research the impact of policing on gentrification in their communities, particularly in Harlem where many students lived. Another class explored how police abuse of students in communities and in schools contributes to the school-to-prison pipeline. The third class, with a large number of Dominican students, investigated how the police department's "broken windows" tactics—arresting residents, particularly youth of color, for minor infractions such as jumping a subway turnstile or writing graffiti—might lead to increased deportations and prevent New York from being a sanctuary city for unauthorized immigrants.

This was an experimental project in two key ways. First, it was designed to implement YPAR pedagogical philosophy and practices within the structure of the school day, rather than in alternative settings outside of school. This then required intensive professional development and curriculum development support for the participating teachers in learner-centered, inquiry- and project-based strategies in addition to documentary production techniques. Second, it was designed to not only engage the teachers and students in these two schools but also to be scaled up by other principals in transfer schools systemwide as a model that privileges student voice and the collective study and problem solving of social injustices in their lives. This then required the documentation to be disseminated of the process and projects produced including the students' documentaries, a "making of" video capturing teachers and students in action, and the teacher curriculum and unit plans.

Integrating this work into the classroom brought the excitement and student engagement that "real-world" project-based work almost always produces.

It also brought a number of challenges, mostly involving time and technology. These challenges included scheduling time within the school day for students to interview their peers as well as scholars, advocates, police officers, and other guest presenters in the building. They also included planning trips outside of school to conduct research and interviews with community advocates, public officials, and residents on the streets throughout the city. Given these constraints, EVC developed a timeline to guide the process (see Figure 6.1). Although video is not the only way to engage students in action research, because it was central to this project, we used the following milestones to support the intersecting processes of student research and engagement, civic engagement, and documentary production.

These milestones served as an important guide pedagogically as well as a timeline to help everyone stay on track. Though the diagram is presented as a one-way linear arrow for the purposes of scheduling deadlines, its steps of research, action, and reflection are in fact iterative, overlapping, and sometimes circular. With the hard work of committed students, teachers, principals, EVC coaches, and technical consultants, along with the support of the OPSR, it all came together in time for the end-of-year Transfer School Conference.

Following EVC's motto of "real work for real audiences," the students presented their final projects and answered teacher and principal questions at a citywide education conference at the end of the school year. They aired and streamed their documentaries on the cable access Youth Channel. The day following the conference screening, the students and teachers presented the other two films at a schoolwide town hall meeting for students, teachers, and community leaders. The deputy Manhattan borough president attended, as did School Safety Agents.

Students received grades and credits for their work on the final project. But in this case, indicators of success were measured on a deeper level of changes taking place for students, teachers, community, and school culture.

One principal described it this way:

> The town hall was quite magical. To be able to bring all the stakeholders into the same room and engage in authentic dialogue and problem-solving session is no easy task. . . . Both of my teachers said this has been a highlight of their careers. This has all been for a cause, which has allowed us to take student voice to a new level. This is the work. To create spaces in our classes, where the classroom becomes a laboratory to understand and deconstruct complex issues, and to take action with the hope of creating change. It changes our mindset around the role students play in owning the learning: Are they students taking an ELA class one assignment at a time? Or are they citizen journalists solving complex problems? (personal communication, June 19, 2017; June 20, 2017)

The project was transformative for the teachers who participated for the same reason it was for their students. They were part of something bigger than the usual requirements of testing and grades. They were standing with their students and their families, supporting them to ask critical questions of people in power, create

Figure 6.1. Student Participatory Action Research Project Milestones

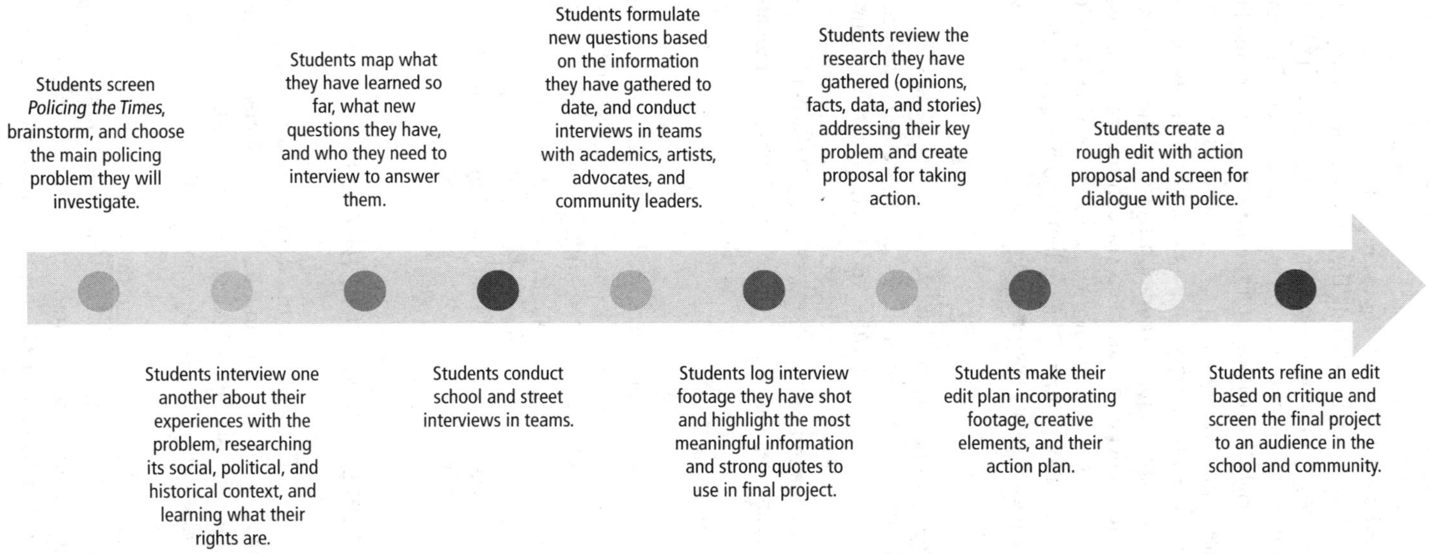

Students screen *Policing the Times*, brainstorm, and choose the main policing problem they will investigate.

Students map what they have learned so far, what new questions they have, and who they need to interview to answer them.

Students formulate new questions based on the information they have gathered to date, and conduct interviews in teams with academics, artists, advocates, and community leaders.

Students review the research they have gathered (opinions, facts, data, and stories) addressing their key problem and create proposal for taking action.

Students create a rough edit with action proposal and screen for dialogue with police.

Students refine an edit based on critique and screen the final project to an audience in the school and community.

Students interview one another about their experiences with the problem, researching its social, political, and historical context, and learning what their rights are.

Students conduct school and street interviews in teams.

Students log interview footage they have shot and highlight the most meaningful information and strong quotes to use in final project.

Students make their edit plan incorporating footage, creative elements, and their action plan.

new knowledge, and prompt public dialogue about making a positive change in the world.

The principal and teachers of the other school are partnering with immigration rights organizations in their neighborhood. The students' clear bilingual explanation in English and Spanish of what to do and what rights they have when ICE agents come knocking on their door make their action research video an invaluable tool in "know your rights" workshops for the students' parents and families, as well as for immigrant families citywide.

The principal acknowledged the positive impact that her students' project is having on her school and local community. In addition, she gave evidence that creating spaces in school for her students to make their voices heard on critical issues in their lives can have a profound impact on their individual social–emotional development. She then spoke about Hector, the student who had conducted the main interviews with immigrant rights lawyers and presented on the panel with his teacher at the conference:

> One of the biggest changes in a student that I've seen in my life was the transformation of Hector. He was a clinically depressed student. I remember one Saturday at a community school forum. And Hector's mother, she broke down crying talking about how much he changed. This was amazing. He had been an in-patient in an institution. . . . He wouldn't talk. He would always look down. He didn't care about anything. This changed him. He graduated this June . . . and he told me he wants to go to college, into criminal justice. (personal communication, July 27, 2017)

The remarkable changes that Hector experienced speak to the power of this transformative pedagogy, and in some ways to its simplicity. It makes a difference when teachers can have the time to listen to their students and develop trusting, supportive relationships with them. It makes a difference when students can feel they connect their learning to their lives, and their lives to their worlds. As with other students, as Hector's sense of purpose and belonging grew, so did his sense of stature and possibility.

AT THE SCREENING: PARTING THOUGHTS

There are no more seats left in the theater. It's the second week in June at EVC's annual student documentary premiere screening at the Film Society of Lincoln Center. People are sitting in the aisles and standing along the back wall. Parents and other family members, students, teachers, principals, EVC staff, and board members are all there.

Hector and his teacher make their way onto the stage. This is now the evening of the same day that they presented at the Transfer School Conference. They should be exhausted, but somehow they summon the energy to introduce and give an award to an internationally renowned journalist whom EVC is honoring.

Hector is a pro up there in front of 300 people, like he has been introducing celebrities all his life. It's hard to believe this is the same student who couldn't even pick his head up to look you in the eye.

Muzik's documentary *Moving Without Direction* (Educational Video Center, 2017) is now ending. The last of the credits roll up the screen and the lights come up. Muzik and the rest of the crew of youth producers take to the stage, awkwardly standing in line, squinting into the lights, ready for Q&A. The audience erupts in applause. The film is a powerful but difficult documentary to watch about why youth join gangs.

Watching Muzik up there on the stage is pure joy. The violence and trauma Muzik has endured in their young life is unimaginable: being bullied and beaten because of their sexual identity; joining a gang for protection; living in a shelter; the suicide attempt and the mental hospital; and then leaving the gang after almost getting shot and watching a best friend die. Now Muzik's hands tremble a little. But Muzik calls their mother up on stage to share the applause. She gives Muzik one of the biggest hugs ever. People are tearing up.

Muzik and their mother step down off the stage and get lost in the crowded reception. Perla is there near the information table, smiling broadly. She is back from her first year in college, volunteering to hand out programs to the guests. She is still working as a youth organizer and had been in Washington to testify for immigrant rights.

And then Raelene walks in. Dressed in a cap and gown, she is coming straight from her college graduation in Brooklyn. She is positively beaming. And so is her mother, and her former teacher (now an English professor) who has asked her to speak at a conference. Still involved in housing rights organizing, Raelene taught our documentary workshops for court-involved youth in Harlem in the spring, and will teach for EVC again in the coming year. Lots of hugs and pictures all around.

These are a few of the extraordinary stories of inspiring young people who have struggled all their lives, and continue to struggle. But they are full of grit and tenacity, moving through trauma, resilience, resistance, and activism. They will go on to be amazing adults and do spectacular things in this world. We as transformative educators can claim modest credit for listening well and learning from our students, for addressing their needs and honoring their strengths, and always teaching with compassion. Knowing the oppressive systems arrayed against our students and their communities, we remain committed as their advocates, keeping one eye on their personal and intellectual growth and the other on the fight for a more just world for them to grow up in. Drawing from whatever the right mix may be of Gramsci's revolutionary pessimism and optimism, we insist on making our classes and schools culturally responsive spaces of healing, learning, and action— and making sure our students always know we've got their back.

Guide for Using Videos

Overview

The video clips discussed in this book, and the full documentaries from which they are selected, are intended to be used by both teachers and students. These clips can be used to scaffold student discussion, reflection, inquiry, and action. This guide provides tools for facilitating active viewing of the videos and safe, supportive, and dynamic conversations that, when facilitated well, will make discussions rich and engaging. Incorporating these videos in the classroom lends meaning to teaching and learning:

- For teachers, they provide critical insight into their students' lives at home and in their communities outside of the school, so they can be more culturally sustaining and responsive to their students' family experiences.

- For students, they bring student voices into the classroom from culturally diverse families and communities, addressing relevant social issues that connect with their lives.

Student age, gender, grade, demographic, subject area, and context of video screening all play a role in shaping the kind of conversations and activities that will flow in and around these screenings. The policy analysis and statistical evidence provided in this book and endnotes of each chapter can be used to give students important historical and structural context to the personal and family stories they will hear in the video clips. This information can be summarized and otherwise adapted for the students in your class to supplement the screenings. Using articles and other readings from your local area would keep these lessons current and locally relevant.

Note that if a video or online access isn't available for screening during class, you can download transcripts of the video clips ahead of time from the Teachers College Press website (www.tcpress.com/goodman-video-clips) for students to read and discuss. The transcripts are excellent prompts for a range of letter, journal, essay, and creative writing activities and can also be useful for students with undeveloped note-taking skills as parallel texts to reinforce the visual/oral dialogue in the videos. You might also ask students to take turns reading a line aloud that they like the best from the transcript on the issue you are discussing. As they randomly choose lines to read aloud, it can create a feeling of being in a theater or spoken word performance.

GENERAL PRACTICES AND PRINCIPLES TO CONSIDER BEFORE VIEWING

EVC documentaries are powerful and often deal with sensitive social and emotional issues. For this reason, I recommend that you preview the clips or the complete documentary before using them in the classroom. If any of the activities are not useful to you, feel free to modify them and design your own. Before using these materials, consider the following questions:

- How similar/different are your students and their experiences from the students who made this video?
- How does this video relate to the subject you are teaching or are discussing in your advisory class or club?
- What concerns do you have about your students' responses to the issues raised in this video?
- What information from the book can you use to provide context on the issue before and as a follow-up after they view the video clips?
- What additional articles, statistics, or other background information will your students need to better understand the issue, update the information presented, or make it more relevant to your local school or community?
- What results do you hope to see from using this video?

Assumed in this guide are the following beliefs about teaching and learning:

- All learning starts from the students' own experiences, and learning from one another's experiences is powerful.
- Students can make a difference in the world, particularly in their school and local community.
- Students learn best through experiences that incorporate a variety of methods.
- Diversity of opinion is useful in a classroom and must be respected.
- Social and cultural issues and community problems are an integral part of the school curriculum and students' lives; however, students are not defined by those problems.

A core component of EVC's approach to teaching is a belief in *active viewing*, whereby students reflect critically on what they are watching and discuss it with their peers. For many teachers, having students write or take notes while viewing is not something new. For others, this aspect of active viewing is a bit controversial. Some feel it gets in the way of their viewing experience, while others feel it enhances it. EVC believes that writing deepens thinking and is one of the best ways to explore sensitive issues, even before discussion. Therefore, you may want to show the video twice: the first time to view it, and the second time to complete the viewing exercise. You may want to model an active viewing approach first for your students by playing a video clip, jotting notes in response to a prompt while you watch, and then sharing your reflections with them.

INTEGRATING COMMON CORE STATE STANDARDS

The activities outlined below meet several Common Core State Standards (CCSS). Selected standards are listed; however, these video clips and suggested activities meet more standards, depending on how extensively you decide to use them as springboards for student viewing, discussion, writing, and reading on the issues explored (see the full list of standards at www.corestandards.org/ELA-Literacy/).

CCSS English Language Arts Standards for Writing: Text Types and Purposes, Grade 11–12 (www.corestandards.org/ELA-Literacy/W/11-12/)

1. Write arguments to support claims in an analysis of substantive topics or texts, using valid reasoning and relevant and sufficient evidence.
1.B. Develop claim(s) and counter claims fairly and thoroughly, supplying the most relevant evidence for each while pointing out the limitations of both in a manner that anticipates the audience's knowledge level, concerns, values and possible biases.

CCSS College and Career Readiness Anchor Standards for Speaking and Listening: Comprehension and Collaboration (www.corestandards.org/ELA-Literacy/CCRA/SL/)

1. Prepare for and participate effectively in a range of conversations and collaborations with diverse partners, building on others' ideas and expressing their own clearly and persuasively.
2. Integrate and evaluate information presented in diverse media formats, including visually, quantitatively, and orally.
3. Evaluate a speaker's point of view, reasoning, and use of evidence and rhetoric.

CCSS English Language Arts Standards for Speaking and Listening: Comprehension and Collaboration, Grade 9–10 (www.corestandards.org/ELA-Literacy/SL/9-10/)

1. Initiate and participate effectively in a range of collaborative discussions (one-on-one, in groups, and teacher-led) with diverse partners on grades 9–10 topics, texts, and issues, building on others' ideas and expressing their own clearly and persuasively.
1.D. Respond thoughtfully to diverse perspectives; summarize points of agreement and disagreement, and, when warranted, qualify or justify their own views and understanding and make new connections in light of the evidence and reasoning presented.

CCSS College and Career Readiness Anchor Standards for Reading: Range of Reading and Level of Complexity Informational (www.corestandards.org/ELA-Literacy/CCRA/R/)

10. Read and comprehend literary nonfiction independently and proficiently.

CCSS College and Career Readiness Anchor Standards for Writing, Range of Writing (www.corestandards.org/ELA-Literacy/CCRA/W/)

10. Students will write routinely over extended time frames (time for research, reflection, and revision) and shorter time frames (a single sitting or a day or two) for a range of tasks, purposes, and audiences.

CREATING A SAFER SPACE

It is important to make sure students feel as comfortable as possible discussing sensitive and potentially triggering issues. The following steps can be taken to create a safer space:

- Write the name of a school counselor or social worker on the board and let students know s/he is available for anyone who wants more immediate and professional counseling, referrals, or other support services.
- Write contact information for local and national resources on the board, such as hotlines, local agencies and programs, and so on.
- Create group ground rules at the start of the class.
- Lead an opening activity to begin to establish trust and a level of comfort among students and facilitators.

Group Ground Rules

Group ground rules first need to be established for students to feel safe, respected, and listened to while they share their ideas, opinions, questions, and often personal stories. This is particularly important because the class discussion will focus on sensitive social, emotional, and cultural issues. At EVC, we involve the students in generating the list of ground rules. Based on our experience, the following steps will help make it a successful and inclusive process:

- Arrange the chairs (without desks) in a semicircle so everyone can see one another's faces (instead of being seated in rows where students may only see the back of one another's heads).
- Ask for one volunteer to take a marker and draw the outline of a body to represent the group, or a house to represent the safe space, on a large sheet of poster paper.
- Ask the class to brainstorm a list of positive behaviors that they want to ensure a safe, inclusive group discussion about controversial issues. They write the positive rules inside the body or house, and the negative behaviors on the outside.
- If they need help getting started, here are possible suggestions: Only one person talks at a time (one mic), respect all opinions even if you don't agree with them, speak from your own experience (use "I" statements), equity of voice (be aware of how much you are speaking so as to participate, but not dominate discussion), listen actively (let others know that you hear them, try to relate what you say to comments others have made), avoid negative labels (such as saying that comment was stupid, wrong, or bad), and avoid body language (such as eye rolls and finger pointing).
- After the group has no more rules to add, invite all students to sign their name in agreement to the group's ground rules that they just generated. This agreement should be publicly displayed in the class during the discussion, and for as long as needed.
- While facilitating the discussion, it may be necessary to refer back to the ground rules to ensure that girls, English language learners, and quiet or shy students have opportunities to actively participate and are not overshadowed by boys, native English speakers, and more vocal students.

Group Openings

For classes or groups that meet regularly, open the discussion with a check-in that builds community and allows them to be more present and focused on the discussion to come. A check-in can gauge students' feelings, provide an opportunity for them to clear their thoughts or share what's on their mind, or celebrate successes. The following are examples of check-ins that we use at EVC:

- "Highs and Lows" or "Roses and Thorns." Sit in a circle and have students take turns to briefly share one thing that was good or positive that they experienced in the time since they last met, and one thing that was not good. If they don't feel comfortable sharing, they can pass.
- "Heart and Mind." Ask students to share one at a time in the circle something they are thinking about (What is on your mind?) and something they are feeling (What is in your heart?).
- "What's the Weather?" Students take turns describing their feelings that day using a weather report format. For example, "The morning was cloudy with light rain, but the afternoon cleared and there was some sunshine." This provides a low-risk, fun method for understanding each student's current state of mind.

PLANNING THE VIEWING EXPERIENCE

Before Viewing the Video Clip or Complete Documentary

- Consider asking students to brainstorm some common stereotypes they may have heard about people experiencing the issue explored in the video. This might include people who are homeless, living in transitional housing, or living in unhealthy buildings, tenements, or public housing; students who have been suspended; people with incarcerated parents or family members; new immigrant or undocumented students; students who identify as LGBTQ; students with eating disorders; and students living in foster care.
- If students are too shy or uncomfortable to generate their own list of stereotypes, consider creating an "anticipation guide" that will give students biased and stereotypical statements to respond to and help them to launch safely right into a discussion of relevant topics. Anticipation guides can also help you prepare the key ideas or take-aways you might want to highlight in the video. Examples of such statements:
  » "People are homeless because they are too lazy to find work."
  » "Police stop Blacks and Latinos on the streets more than Whites because they can tell they are dealers or gang members."
  » "Our country will be better off if undocumented people go back to where they came from."
  » "Gays just choose to be attracted to people of the same sex and can change if they want to."

» "Women like it when men catcall them on the streets, because they are being complimented."
» "Watch out for kids in foster care, because they will steal your things."

- Discuss some of the problems that they believe students and other people experiencing the issue explored in the video may face in school and out of school.
- Be sure to note the running time of the video clips or complete documentary in order to leave ample time for post-viewing discussion.

While Viewing the Video Clip or Complete Documentary

Critical Viewing Activity: It is important that students actively observe and listen to the video, looking for information and taking notes during their viewing. Here are some suggested focal points students may note and discuss after viewing:

- Lines or phrases that they strongly agree or disagree with and statements that surprise them, remind them of something, or cause a strong reaction
- Ways the students and other people in the video contradict the stereotypes
- Ways the issue discussed in the video creates problems for the students and other people in the video to succeed in school and out of school
- Ways the students connect or identify with the students and other people in the video
- A particular viewpoint or perspective—for example, comments from a student or adult perspective and opinions that are pro or anti
- Evidence that students or other people in the video give to support their viewpoint
- One character that they either relate to or find interesting, especially if viewing the full documentary

After Viewing the Video Clip or Complete Documentary

Discussion: As the students refer to the notes they took or the video transcript, lead a discussion about important points in the video. The following questions might be useful:

- What problems did the students and other people in the video have?
- How might those problems have hurt their opportunities to succeed in school and outside of school?
- Which systemic or interpersonal forms of oppression did the people in the video describe as causing problems in their lives?
- If you were interviewed for this video, what opinions would you express about how to help the students and other people in the video?
- What individuals or groups in school or in the community might you think of contacting to help students in your school or local community experiencing similar problems?

- How do the problems discussed in the video relate to issues in your school or local community, and what questions do you have about them?
- How might your class, club, or community organization find more information about those local issues, and take action to address them?
- Which common stereotypes were contradicted by the students and other people in the video?
- Which person in this video do you connect to or identify with the most?
- Which person in this video would you most like to have a conversation with, and what would you hope to discuss?
- What opinions do you think your parents, younger siblings, police, storekeepers, and/or public officials would have about this issue?

If viewing the full EVC documentary, you might use the following questions to discuss how it was made:

- What point of view do you feel the students who made this documentary have?
- What evidence did they give to support their point of view?
- What do you feel is missing?
- How did the presence of the camera influence the words/actions of the people in this video?
- How fairly do you think the students who made the video dealt with this issue?
- What would you have done differently if you had been involved in making this documentary?

Writing Activity: Ask the students to think about a comment that someone made in the video clip they just watched, and think about what they would like to ask or say to that person in response. Then ask the students to write an imaginary dialogue between themselves and the person in the video who made the comment. Allow 5 to 10 minutes for writing. Tell the students not to worry about where the dialogue is going, just to let the words flow. Divide the students into pairs or small groups to read one another's dialogues.

Bring the whole class back together; you might use the following questions to lead a discussion about their writing:

- What surprised you in what you wrote or what you heard?
- What discoveries did you make?
- What difficulties did you experience while writing, and how did you overcome them?

Alternatively, after students write and read one another's dialogues, ask them to write a response to one another's writing. Or ask them to write a dialogue with one pretending to be the person in the video.

In-Class or Homework Assignment: Ask students to respond to one or two of the following questions. Feel free to add your own questions to the list, specific to the video clip viewed.

- Did watching this video clip change your opinion of _____ (the topic of the video)? Give evidence of what made you change.
- Write an essay or letter to the editor of your local paper describing a problem, with supporting evidence, that the student or people in the video spoke about and how you would change things to improve that problem.
- How does it make you feel knowing that students produced this documentary? Why?

DOING ACTIVITIES WITH TOPICS RELATED TO THE VIDEOS

Listed below are two to four topics related to each of the videos, organized by chapter, to generate more extended student research and expression. This list is just a start. As you watch the clips or the complete documentary, you can futher develop this list or invite your students to brainstorm their own related topics. Following these lists are guidelines for a range of writing, arts, analysis, and action research activities designed to engage students in learning, expressing themselves, and making their voices heard about these issues.

Suggested Related Topics

Chapter 1: Health and Housing

Suggested related topics for *2371 Second Avenue: An East Harlem Story*:
- Poverty
- Landlord neglect
- Housing rights and violations
- Health and school

Suggested related topics for *Breathing Easy: Environmental Hazards in Public Housing*:
- Environmental justice
- Public housing
- Childhood lead poisoning
- Asthma in low-income communities

Suggested related topics for *As the Sun Comes Up, the Bricks Fall Down*:
- Gentrification
- Landlord abandonment
- Increased rent and housing value
- Affordable housing

Suggested related topics for *Mortgage Mayhem: Living Inside Fraud*:
- Housing foreclosure
- Family stress

- Homeless shelters
- Race-based predatory lending

Chapter 2: Police and Juvenile Justice

Suggested related topics for *Policing the Times: Youth Perspectives on Police Brutality*:
- Broken windows
- Race and school to prison pipeline
- Zero-tolerance
- Black Lives Matter

Suggested related topics for *Life Under Suspicion: Youth Perspectives on the NYPD's Stop and Frisk Policy*:
- Stop-and-frisk
- Police training
- Know your rights
- Racial profiling

Suggested related topics for *Growing Apart: The Politics of Family Separation*:
- Incarcerated parents
- Extended family

Suggested related topics for *Another Part of Me: Youth Views on Drugs and Incarceration in Our Community*:
- Mass incarceration
- War on drugs
- Juvenile incarceration
- Reentry from prison

Chapter 3: Immigration

Suggested related topics for *Growing Apart: The Politics of Family Separation*:
- Immigration journeys
- Reunifying with and separating from parents
- Deportation
- Parent involvement in school

Suggested related topics for *New Visions: A Deeper Look at the American Dream*:
- Media and immigrant perceptions of America
- Reunifying with parents

Chapter 4: Gender and Identity

Suggested related topics for *Moving Without Direction*:
- Homophobic bullying and leaving school
- Gangs and protection

Suggested related topics for *Out Youth in Schools*:
- Gender identity
- Homophobic bullying and leaving school
- Genders & Sexualities Alliances
- Inclusive school culture

Suggested related topics for *Losing Ground: The New Face of Homelessness*:
- Family rejection of LGBTQ youth
- Homelessness

Suggested related topics for *Gender Power: Street Harassment in NYC*:
- Street harassment/sexual harassment
- Gender roles/power dynamics
- Objectification
- Trauma

Suggested related topics for *What's Your Beautiful?*:
- Self-image
- Influence of media
- Low self-esteem
- Eating disorders

Chapter 5: Foster Care

Suggested related topics for *Not Me, Not Mine: Adult Survivors of Foster Care*:
- Race and family separation
- Foster homes
- Aging out of foster care
- Changing schools

Suggested related topics for *High on Perceptions*:
- Parental opioid addiction
- Depression and mental health
- Raising siblings
- Addiction as a crime or health problem

Suggested Activities

Survey: Having your students formulate a survey and calculate the results is an effective approach for infusing math into the curriculum. Ask your students to construct a survey that compares the attitudes and/or behaviors of different age, gender, or ethnic groups about one of the items from the related topics list. The students should be aware that responses to the survey must be easy to code. The survey can be distributed in the school or the community. Small groups can tabulate the data and bring their results back to the large group for comparison and discussion. Have your students make charts and graphs of their results and display them on a bulletin board in school.

Brainstorm to Essay: This series of short activities can be used to help your students do some thinking and writing around an issue. Put the related topic on the board or poster paper. Have your students brainstorm all the words that come to mind when they think about this topic. Fill the board or paper with their words and then help your students create categories based on their words. Ask your students to choose one category each about which they would like to write. The students could share these first drafts in small groups in order to get feedback on the piece. Encourage them to revise their writing and publish their pieces on a bulletin board, school website, or blog.

Role-Play: Many students love the chance to be someone else for a short time. Role-plays are a fun way to bring a group closer together, while also examining important issues. In order to get some ideas for the role-plays, ask the students to choose one of the following open-ended sentences about a specific related topic and complete it anonymously. You might distribute index cards or post-it notes for the writing. Fill in the selected related topics where the blank is:

- Something I worry about often concerning _____ is . . .
- Something I want to change concerning _____ is . . .
- Something I'm still unsure about concerning _____ is . . .

Collect and mix the cards or notes. Divide the class into groups of four. Give each group four completed index cards. Ask each group to prepare a role-play that deals with the concerns, fears, and/or questions on the index cards. They might choose to deal with all or one of the cards. Have each group present its role-play. Discuss how each role-play dealt with your chosen issue.

Creative Expression: If you are interested in having your students express their thoughts and feelings artistically about one of the related topics, use the video clips or transcripts as a scaffold for one of the following art forms:

- Spoken word
- Written poem
- Comic book
- Children's book
- Bulletin board display
- Class collage
- Illustrations for a collection of class writings
- Murals
- Posters
- Sculpture
- Slogan
- T-shirt or button design

Critical Media Literacy: Have students read news articles or watch and/or listen to news reports from different sources—independent, mainstream, local, regional, national, and international—that cover the same issue or event. Then direct the students to write a critical essay on the report, using the following questions as a guide:

- What is the main message being conveyed in the story?
- How accurate is the story and what evidence is there to support its claims?

- What information is missing in one source or included or reported differently in another?
- How are the subjects of the stories—youth in public housing, incarcerated youth, immigrants, females, LGBTQ youth, foster youth, people of color, and others—represented in each of the sources?
- How are the photos, video, narration, or text used to represent people in the different stories?
- Whose story is being told or whose perspective is included? Whose is left out?
- How would you change the story?

Instead of writing a critical essay about the news report, students can interview fellow students, family members, or people in the community to learn their opinions about the issue or event. Another option would be for them to write a letter to the editor or record their own editorial about the news issue or event.

Video: With as little as a cell phone or tablet, your students can produce interesting videos about one of the related topics. Different kinds of video projects include the following:

- A "take action" video
- A public service announcement
- An investigative report
- A talk show
- An instructional or "how-to" video
- Recording of a class role-play or skit
- A segment for a younger audience
- A survey of students' opinions in the school or person-in-the-street opinions
- A news story

Youth Participatory Action Research: Use the video clips or the full documentary to spark discussion of how students experience the social justice problem in their school or local community. Have students do the following:

- Brainstorm and identify the problem they want to research and take action on. They should consider what they think the causes might be, how they would like to see the problem solved or improved, and to whom in the school or community they would like to present their final action.
- Identify partners in the school or community who might have knowledge and resources to help carry out the project.
- Decide what kind of research they will need to investigate the problem and the resources they will need to conduct it. They will need to generate questions and potential sources, including people in the school and community, to provide information.

- Develop an action plan and carry it out to solve or improve the problem.
- Reflect on the participatory action research process and the outcome of the students' action.

Interviewing: Interviewing is an essential tool for youth participatory action research and many other student journalism and community-inquiry projects. Here are a few prompts and activities we use at EVC that can help support your students to become engaged in the process.

Ask students to brainstorm what they already know and what they want to know and learn about the subject they are researching. Then ask them to brainstorm the people and organizations they would like to talk with to find answers to their questions. Ask them who is the audience or audiences they would like to present their project to and influence with their findings.

Encourage the students to access their own "funds of knowledge" in their own school, family, and community and reassure them that they can conduct interviews in their home language, and "translanguage" as needed. In addition, you should also encourage them to stretch beyond their comfort zone, and seek out diverse perspectives. The class should share, discuss, and narrow down what they have brainstormed:

- Ask students to think about any reporter, sports, music, or talk show host they like and to share their opinion of what makes their interviews good. Have them share what they notice about the person's interview style. This might include how the interviewer makes the interviewee feel comfortable, how they know their subject, and how they ask follow-up questions and probe for information.
- Ask if anyone knows the difference between "open" and "closed" questions. If necessary, explain that "closed" questions are questions that can be answered with yes/no answers. Explain that "open-ended" questions are questions that get people talking. Key words and phases in open-ended questions are: "How", "Why", "Can you explain . . . ", "Can you tell me more. . .", "Can you describe . . ."
- Divide students in small groups and ask each to develop at least three "open" interview questions related to the main issue or problem students are investigating. They should incorporate into their questions some specific facts and history on the topic from their research, and be able to cite the sources to ensure that their interview is based in evidence.
- Have students list their questions on the board, combining similar questions together and ordering them. The goal is to try to create a natural flow in the interview so that it feels as much like a conversation as possible.

To start their interview, students should introduce themselves and give a brief, clear description of who they are, what their project is about, who their intended audience will be for the video, and why they want to interview the person. You may want to have them conduct practice interviews with one another before they actually interview a stranger. Then they should ask the following types of questions:

- General questions first, more specific and detailed questions later.
- Questions about problems first, questions about solutions later.
- Questions about society or general opinions first, questions about the interviewee's personal experiences later.
- Probing, paraphrasing, and clarifying questions to guide the interview.

If your students are using cameras to record their interview, here are some "Do's" and "Don'ts" to review:

DO make eye contact	DON'T look away from interviewee
DO listen carefully	DON'T read mechanically from list
DO ask follow-up questions	DON'T interrupt
DO ask open-ended questions	DON'T ask "yes" or "no" questions
DO speak clearly	DON'T chew gum
DO be respectful and build trust	DON'T hold the mic too close or too far away
DO help clarify information for the interviewee	DON'T let the interviewee take control of the mic
DO thank the interviewee for their time and permisson to use the interview in their project	DON'T walk away without thanking the interviewee and getting their consent

Notes

Introduction

1. The problem of inequity has only gotten worse over the past decades. The top 10% saw their wealth increase fivefold over the past 53 years (between 1963 and 2016), while wealth grew sevenfold during that time for those at the top 1%. Families near the bottom of wealth distribution went from no wealth to being about $1,000 in debt (Urban Institute, 2017).

2. African American youth are three times more likely to be victims of robbery and five times more likely to be victims of homicide than their White peers. One quarter of low-income urban youth have witnessed a murder (National Center for Victims of Crime, 2012).

3. Children of color are disproportionately separated from their birth parents and placed in foster care and in the child welfare system in general, and "experience poorer outcomes and receive fewer services than their [White] counterparts" (Courtney, Barth, et al., 1996, p. 99). A class action suit alleges that children in foster care spent more than twice as much time in the New York City system waiting, to be reunited with their parents or adopted, than in the rest of the country (Yee, 2015).

4. Black students are three times more likely to be suspended than White students. Sixty percent of students involved in school-related arrests or referred to law enforcement were Black or Hispanic (U.S. Department of Education, Office for Civil Rights, 2014). Children eligible for Medicaid are given powerful antipsychotic medication four times as often as middle-class children and for less severe conditions (D. Wilson, 2009).

Chapter 1

1. Studies show that people who suffer from asthma in childhood may be more than twice as likely to develop obstructive sleep apnea later in life (Hagen, Peppard, Barnet, Young, Finn, & Teodorescu, 2013).

2. Established at the height of the Depression to make homeownership widely accessible, the Home Owners Loan Corporation (HOLC) in 1933 and the Federal Housing Administration (FHA) in 1934 also institutionalized the discriminatory practice of *redlining*. This was the policy of rating neighborhoods in central cities based on their perceived stability or risk, designed to steer investment away from those rated as risky. And racially mixed or predominantly minority populations were considered too risky to be financed or insured (Fullilove & Wallace, 2011; Massey & Denton, 1993). Segregation in public housing simply reflected the prevailing patterns of residential segregation in the United States and can be traced to decisions made by the local housing authorities, who built some of the earliest public developments in New York City in the 1930s (Marcuse, 1986; Massey & Denton, 1993; Stoloff, 2004).

3. Since 2000, the number of people in extreme poverty rose from 7.2 million to 13.8 million. More than one in four of the Black poor and nearly one in six of the Hispanic poor lives in a neighborhood of extreme poverty, compared to one in 13 of the White poor (Jargowsky, 2015).

4. Fifty-seven percent of students facing foreclosure were Black, as compared to just 33% of public school students in New York City as a whole (Been, Ellen, Schwartz, Stiefel, & Weinstein, 2010).

5. See Charbonneau (2011) for an in-depth critical analysis of this film.

6. In 2015, *2371 Second Avenue: An East Harlem Story* was screened in the *Wohnungsfrage* exhibition (The Housing Question) at the *Haus der Kulturen der Welt* in Berlin, and in the exhibition *Not Yet. On the Reinvention of Documentary and the Critique of Modernism* at the Museo Nacional Centro de Arte Reina Sofia in Madrid.

Chapter 2

1. In 1994, President Nixon's aide John Ehrlichman admitted the real reason for the War on Drugs:

> The Nixon campaign in 1968, and the Nixon White House after that, had two enemies: the antiwar left and Black people. You understand what I'm saying? We knew we couldn't make it illegal to be either against the war or Black, but by getting the public to associate the hippies with marijuana and Blacks with heroin, and then criminalizing both heavily, we could disrupt those communities. We could arrest their leaders, raid their homes, break up their meetings, and vilify them night after night on the evening news. Did we know we were lying about the drugs? Of course we did. (Baum, 2016)

2. In the 1980s, President Reagan greatly expanded the War on Drugs budget so that between 1980 and 1984, FBI antidrug funding increased from $8 million to $95 million. President Clinton expanded Reagan's funding even further, signing the largest crime bill in U.S. history—the 1994 Violent Crime Control and Law Enforcement Act—allocating $30.2 billion more for huge increases in police officers and prison building, which led to an explosion of mass incarceration of mostly poor Blacks and Latinos to fill them.

3. New York State's total prison population grew more than five times its size from 13,400 in 1973, when the Rockefeller drug laws were enacted, to a peak of 71,538 in 1999. The number of people behind bars for drug offenses increased 15 times in that time from 1,488 to 22,266 (New York State Division of Criminal Justice Services, 2010, p. 6).

4. The top 10 schools with the highest suspension rates of students with special needs issued 98 suspensions per 100 students with Individualized Education Programs (IEPs). In New York City, Black students made up only 30% of all students from 1999 to 2009 but accounted for 50% of the suspensions; and in the 2014–2015 school year comprised 28% of student enrolled and 61% of arrests. Low-income students eligible for free and reduced-price lunch were given three-quarters of the total suspensions, but were two-thirds of the student population (City of New York, 2015; New York Civil Liberties Union, 2016).

5. According to the U.S. Department of Education's Office for Civil Rights (2014), Black children represent 18% of preschool enrollment, but 48% of preschool children receiving more than one out-of-school suspension; in comparison, White students represent 43% of preschool enrollment but 26% of preschool children receiving more than one out-of-school suspension. On average, 16% of Black students are suspended and expelled compared to 5% of White students. Although boys receive more than two out of three suspensions, Black girls are suspended at higher rates (12%) than girls of any other race or ethnicity and most boys. Students with disabilities are more than twice as likely to receive an out-of-school suspension (13%) than students without disabilities (6%). Although Black students represent 16% of student enrollment, they represent 27% of students referred to law enforcement

and 31% of students subjected to a school-related arrest. In comparison, White students represent 51% of enrollment, 41% of students referred to law enforcement, and 39% of those arrested.

6. The youth incarceration rate in the United States is five times higher than the next highest rate in a developed country, in South Africa. Because New York is just one of two states that still prosecutes 16- and 17-year-olds as adults (North Carolina is the other), Rikers Island is the destination for such high school–age youth.

Chapter 3

1. The U.S. immigrant population numbered more than 43.7 million, or 13.5% of the total U.S. population, according to the U.S. Census Bureau's American Community Survey data in 2016, and about 86.4 million people when their U.S.-born children are included. In 2014, an estimated 11 million unauthorized immigrants resided in the United States (Zong, Batalova, & Hallock, 2018).

2. Although dropout rates have decreased over the years, in 2014 the Hispanic status dropout rate (10.7%) remained higher than the White (4.4%) and Black (7.9%) status dropout rates. The dropout rate for Hispanics born outside of the United States was twice as high, at 21% (U.S. Department of Education, National Center for Education Statistics, 2018).

3. Forty percent of the entire U.S. child population lives in families below the poverty line (Capps, Fix, & Zong, 2016).

4. On a typical day, more than 34,000 immigrants are imprisoned in the world's largest immigration detention system (Morgenthau, 2014). According to the U.S. Department of Homeland Security, Office of Immigration Statistics. (2016), an all-time high of nearly 415,000 immigrants were deported in 2014, of which nearly 276,000 were Mexican. More than 3 million immigrants have been deported between 2007 and 2014. There is a long and shameful history of mistreatment of immigrant populations in our country conflating a fear of terrorists and criminal elements with foreign-born people who are perceived as a threat to national security. This has included 19th- and 20th-century nativist discrimination against new immigrants in education, work, and housing, and the forced confinement in internment camps of the Japanese during World War II. In the modern era, ICE is the main federal agency which attacks immigration, crime, and terrorism as inseparable problems of national security through its powers of surveillance, mass detention, and deportation.

Chapter 4

1. The mean age of becoming homeless the first time for LGB youth is 14 years (Rosario, Schrimshaw, & Hunter, 2012).

2. Housing discrimination against LGBTQ youth makes it even harder for them to get off the streets and find permanent housing (Ream & Forge, 2014).

3. Although homosexuality was removed from the 1974 edition of DSM II, it was replaced in the DSM-III in 1980 with the diagnosis of ego-dystonic homosexuality, a mental disorder with anxiety caused by a conflict between the sexual orientation they possess and the orientation they want to have. This was removed by the APA in 1987, but continues to be listed as a mental health disorder by the World Health Organization.

4. The prevalence of having made a suicide plan during the 12 months prior to the survey was higher among gay, lesbian, and bisexual students (38.2%) than heterosexual students (11.9%). Nationwide, 8.6% of all students; 6.4% of heterosexual students; 29.4% of gay, lesbian, and bisexual students; and 13.7% of not-sure students had attempted suicide one or more times during the 12 months before the survey (Kann et al., 2016).

5. GSAs have been controversial since their inception back in the late 1980s. There have been several attempts by school districts to ban them, although these anti-GSA lawsuits have repeatedly lost in federal courts. Students often have difficulty finding a GSA teacher advisor, due to an anti-LGBTQ climate in many schools.

Chapter 5

1. The Child Welfare Administration was renamed the Administration for Children's Services (ACS) in 1996.

2. This drop in numbers is due in part to federal legislation and the New York *Nicholson v. Scoppetta* decision in 2004 (Lifting the Veil, 2016).

3. According to the NYC Administration for Children's Services, as of December 31, 2016, Black children accounted for 54% of the kids in foster care in New York City; the city's population is 25% Black. Just over 32% of the children were Hispanic, and only 6% were White (New York City Administration for Children's Services, 2016).

4. The juvenile justice system and child welfare system are closely intertwined, and students involved with one often become involved with the other. This dual involvement is also intergenerational as low-income children of color with incarcerated parents have a high risk of ending up in foster care.

5. For the background of this trope, see the investigative article by J. Levin (2013) on Linda Taylor, the actual person from whom Reagan drew his Welfare Queen story.

6. In 2004, the New York Court of Appeals held in the *Nichols v. Williams* case that a mother's inability to protect a child from witnessing domestic violence does not constitute neglect and can't be used as sole justification for removing her children, and must be weighed against the potential psychological harm to the child caused by the removal itself (NYCLU, n.d.).

7. Studies also show that people view Black men as larger and more threatening than same-sized White men (J. P. Wilson, Rule, & Hugenberg, 2017).

8. Nearly a quarter of children in New York State live with families who struggle each day to put food on the table (Mastin, Metzger, & Golden, 2013).

9. In New York City, young adults in the foster care system are permitted to opt out of the system at the age of 18 but may consent to remain within the system until they are 21.

10. This was an actual story that a foster care student wrote about in New Youth Connections and was included in *Someplace to Call Home: Surviving the Foster Care System* (Educational Video Center, 1994) and in *Not Me, Not Mine* (Educational Video Center, 2003).

References

AAUW. (2011). *Crossing the line: Sexual harassment in school*. Washington, DC: Author.

Abramo, A., Hogan, G., & Smith, G. B. (2014, December 14). Exclusive: Mold still a growing problem for hundreds of NYCHA tenants a year after promise of fixes. *New York Daily News*. Retrieved from www.nydailynews.com/new-york/exclusive-mold-growing -problem-nycha-tenants-article-1.2044723

Acevedo-Garcia, D., & Osypuk, T. (2008). Impacts of housing and neighborhoods on health: Pathways, racial/ethnic disparities, and policy directions. In J. H. Carr & N. K. Kutty (Eds.), *Segregation: The rising costs for America* (pp. 197–236). New York, NY: Routledge.

Aizer, A., & Doyle, J. J., Jr. (2015, May 1). Juvenile incarceration, human capital, and future crime: Evidence from randomly assigned judges. *The Quarterly Journal of Economics, 130*(2), 759–803.

Alexander, M. (2012). *The new Jim Crow: Mass incarceration in the age of colorblindness*. New York, NY: The New Press.

Alim, H. S., & Paris, D. (2017). What is a culturally sustaining pedagogy and why does it matter? In D. Paris & H. S. Alim (Eds.), *Culturally sustaining pedagogies: Teaching and learning for justice in a changing world* (pp. 1–21). New York, NY: Teachers College Press.

American Academy of Pediatrics. (2017). Mental and behavioral health. *Healthy Foster Care America*. Retrieved from www.aap.org/en-us/advocacy-and-policy/aap-health-initiatives /healthy-foster-care-america/Pages/Mental-and-Behavioral-Health.aspx

American Bar Association. (2016, February 8). *Report no. 102*. Retrieved from www .americanbar.org%2Fcontent%2Fdam%2Faba%2Fdirectories%2Fpolicy%2F2016_hod _midyear_102.authcheckdam.docx

American Civil Liberties Union. (2011, August 15). ACLU asks court to stop Missouri school district from illegally censoring LGBT websites [Press release]. Retrieved from www.aclu.org /news/aclu-asks-court-stop-missouri-school-district-illegally-censoring-lgbt-websites

Andrist, L. S. (2003, March–April). Media images, body dissatisfaction, and disordered eating in adolescent women. *The American Journal of Maternal/Child Nursing, 28*(2), 119–123.

Associated Press. (2015, May 18). Traumatized students sue California district for support. *San Diego Union-Tribune*. Retrieved from www.sandiegouniontribune.com/sdut -traumatized-students-sue-compton-unified-school-2015may18-story.html

Attendance Works, & Healthy Schools Campaign. (2015, September). *Mapping the early attendance gap: Charting a course for school success*. Chicago, IL: Author. Retrieved from www. attendanceworks.org/mapping-the-early-attendance-gap/

The Babel Project. (2016, July 5). *The price of nuestros sueños* [Video file]. Retrieved from vimeo.com/173534870

Barnam, M. (2016, April 1). Exclusive—Data shows 3 of the 5 biggest school districts hire more security officers than counselors. *The 74*. Retrieved from www.the74million.org/article /exclusive-data-shows-3-of-the-5-biggest-school-districts-hire-more-security-officers -than-counselors

Baudenbacher, G., & Goodman, S. (2006). *Youth-powered video: A hands-on curriculum for teaching documentary.* New York, NY: Educational Video Center.

Baum, D. (2016, April). Legalize it all: How to win the war on drugs. *Harper's Magazine.* Retrieved from harpers.org/archive/2016/04/legalize-it-all/

Beaumont, E. (2011, January). Promoting political agency, addressing political inequality: A multilevel model of internal political efficacy. *The Journal of Politics, 73*(1), 216–231.

Been, V., Ellen, I. G., Schwartz, A. E., Stiefel, L., & Weinstein, M. (2010, September). *Kids and foreclosures.* New York, NY: New York City Institute for Education and Social Policy and NYU Furman Center for Real Estate and Urban Policy.

Bernhardt, A., Milkman, R., Theodore, N., Heckathorn, D., Auer, M., DeFilippis, J., . . . Spiller, M. (2009). *Broken laws, unprotected workers: Violations of employment and labor laws in America's cities.* New York, NY: National Employment Law Project.

Bernstein, N. (2001). *The lost children of* Wilder: *The epic struggle to change foster care.* New York, NY: Vintage Books.

Bidell, M. P. (2007). Gay-Straight Alliance Network. In G. L. Anderson, & K. G. Her (Eds.), *Encyclopedia of activism and social justice, Vol. II* (p. 607). Thousand Oaks, CA: Sage.

Blad, E. (2017, January 24). She recorded her classmate's arrest, then got arrested, too. *Education Week.* Retrieved from www.edweek.org/ew/articles/2017/01/25/she-recorded-her-classmates-arrest-then-got.html#

Blitzer, J. (2017, March 23). After an immigration raid, a city's students vanish. *The New Yorker.* Retrieved from www.newyorker.com/news/news-desk/after-an-immigration-raid-a-citys-students-vanish

Bocknek, E. L., Sanderson, J., & Britner, P. A. (2009). Ambiguous loss and posttraumatic stress in school-age children of prisoners. *Journal of Child and Family Studies, 18*(3), 323–333. Retrieved from link.springer.com/article/10.1007/s10826-008-9233-y

Bowdler, J., Quercia, R., & Smith, D. A. (2010). *The foreclosure generation: The long-term impact of the housing crisis on Latino children and families.* Washington, DC: National Council of La Raza.

Brabeck, K., & Xu, Q.. (2010). The impact of detention and deportation on Latino immigrant children and families: A quantitative exploration. *Hispanic Journal of Behavioral Sciences, 32*(3), 341–361.

Brooklyn Defender Services. (2015, March 17). Testimony of . . . presented before the New York City Council, Committees on General Welfare, Women's Issues, and Juvenile Justice, preliminary budget hearing. Retrieved from bds.org/wp-content/uploads/ACS-DHS-Testimony-0315.pdf

Brown, C. S., & Stone, E. A. (2016). Gender stereotypes and discrimination: How sexism impacts development. In S. S. Horn, M. D. Ruck, & L. S. Liben (Eds.), *Advances in child development and behavior: Vol. 50. Equity and justice in developmental science: Theoretical and methodological issues* (pp. 105–133). Amsterdam, The Netherlands: Academic Press/ Elsevier.

Brown, S. R. (2017, November 15). Courthouse arrests of immigrants by ICE agents have risen 900% in New York this year: Immigrant defense project. *The New York Daily News.* Retrieved from www.nydailynews.com/new-york/ice-courthouse-arrests-immigrants-900-n-y-2017-article-1.3633463

Cammarota, J., & Fine, M. (Eds.). (2008). *Revolutionizing education: Youth participatory action research in motion.* New York, NY: Routledge.

Campos, P. F. (2017, July 29). White economic privilege is alive and well. *New York Times.* Retrieved from www.nytimes.com/2017/07/29/opinion/sunday/black-income-white-privilege.html

Capps, R., Fix, M., & Zong, J. (2016, January). *A profile of U.S. children with unauthorized immigrant parents.* (MPI Fact Sheet). Washington, DC: Migration Policy Institute.

Capps, R., Hooker, S., Koball, H., Pedroza, J. M., Campetella, A., & Perreira, K. (2015, September). *Implications of immigration enforcement activities for the well-being of children in immigrant families: A review of the literature.* Washington, DC: Urban Institute.

Carson, C. (1981). *In struggle: SNCC and the Black awakening of the 1960s.* Cambridge, MA: Harvard University Press.

Casella, R. (2010). Safety or control? The security fortification of schools in capitalist society. T. Monahan & R. D. Torres (Eds.), In *Schools under surveillance: Cultures of control in public education* (pp. 73–86). New Brunswick, NJ: Rutgers University Press.

Charbonneau, S. M. (2011, Summer). Claims to be heard: Young self-expressivity, social change, and the Educational Video Center. *Jump Cut: A Review of Contemporary Media, 53.* Retrieved from www.ejumpcut.org/archive/jc53.2011/charbnYouthMedia/index.html

Charles, L., & Ward, N. (2007, January). *Generating change through research: Action research and its implications* (Centre for Rural Economy Discussion Paper Series No. 10). New Castle upon Tyne, United Kingdom: Centre for Rural Economy, University of New Castle upon Tyne.

Charron, K. M. (2009). *Freedom's teacher. The life of Septima Clark.* Chapel Hill, NC: University of North Carolina Press.

Chetty, R., Hendren, N., Jones, M. R., & Porter, S. R. (2018, March). *Race and economic opportunity in the United States: An intergenerational perspective.* Equality of Opportunity Project. Retrieved from http://www.equality-of-opportunity.org/assets/documents/race_paper.pdf

Child Trends Databank. (2015). *Foster care.* Retrieved from www.childtrends.org/indicators/foster-care/

Child Welfare Information Gateway. (2016, November). *Racial disproportionality and disparity in child welfare* (Issue brief). Washington, DC: U.S. Department of Health and Human Services, Children's Bureau. Retrieved from www.childwelfare.gov/pubPDFs/racial_disproportionality.pdf

City of New York. (2015). *Safety with dignity: Complete report by the Mayor's leadership team on climate and discipline. Phase 1 recommendations.* Retrieved from www1.nyc.gov/assets/sclt/downloads/pdf/safety-with-dignity-final-complete-report-723.pdf

Clark, S. P. (1964, Winter). Literacy and liberation. *Freedomways: A Quarterly Review of the Negro Freedom Movement, 4*(1), 113–124.

Coates, T.-N. (2014, June). The case for reparations. *The Atlantic.* Retrieved from www.theatlantic.com/features/archive/2014/05/the-case-for-reparations/361631/

Cobb, C. (1963). Prospectus for a summer freedom school program in Mississippi. *Student Nonviolent Coordinating Committee Papers, 1959–1973.* Retrieved from www.educationanddemocracy.org/FSCfiles/B_05_ProspForFSchools.htm

Cobb, C. (2011). Freedom's struggle and freedom schools. *Monthly Review, 63*(3). Retrieved from monthlyreview.org/2011/07/01/freedoms-struggle-and-freedom-schools/

Coleman-Jensen, A., Gregory, C., & Singh, A. (2014, September). *Household food security in the United States in 2013* (Report summary of Economic Research Report No. ERR-173). Washington, DC: United States Department of Agriculture, Economic Research Service. Retrieved from www.ers.usda.gov/publications/pub-details/?pubid=45268

Collins, K., Connors, K., Donohue, A., Gardner, S., Goldblatt, E., Hayward, A., ... Thompson, E. (2010). *Understanding the impact of trauma and urban poverty on family systems: Risks, resilience and interventions.* Baltimore, MD: Family-Informed Trauma Treatment Center. Retrieved from www.quantumunitsed.com/materials/1431_0221_Trauma-Urban_Poverty.pdf

Courtney, M. E., Barth, R. P., Berrick, J. D., Brooks, D., Needell, B., & Park, L. (1996). Race and child welfare services: Past research and future directions. *Child Welfare, 75*(2), 99–136.

Courtney, M. E., Roderick, M., Smithgall, C., Gladden, R. M., & Nagaoka, J. (2004, December). *The educational status of foster children* (Issue Brief #102). Chicago, IL: Chapin Hall Center for Children.

Crowley, S. (2003, Winter). The affordable housing crisis: Residential mobility of poor families and school mobility of poor children. *The Journal of Negro Education, 72*(1), 22–38.

Dominus, S. (2016, September 7). An effective but exhausting alternative to high-school suspensions. *New York Times*. Retrieved from www.nytimes.com/2016/09/11/magazine/an-effective-ut-exhausting-alternative-to-high-school-suspensions.html

Dilulio, J. J., Jr. (1995, November 27). The coming of the super-predators. *The Weekly Standard*. Retrieved from http://www.weeklystandard.com/the-coming-of-the-super-predators/article/8160

Dreby, J. (2012). The burden of deportation on children in Mexican immigrant families. *Journal of Marriage and Family, 74*(4), 829–845.

Duckworth, A. L. (2016). *Grit: The power of passion and perseverance*. New York, NY: Scribner.

Duckworth, A. L., & Eskreis-Winkler, L. (2013). True grit. *Association for Psychological Science, 26*(4). Retrieved from www.psychologicalscience.org/index.php/publications/observer/2013/april-13/true-grit.html

Duckworth, A. L., Peterson, C., Matthews, M. D., & Kelly, D. R. (2007). Grit: Perseverance and passion for long-term goals. *Journal of Personality and Social Psychology, 92*(6), 1087–1101.

Duncan-Andrade, J. M. R. (2006). Urban youth, media literacy, and increased critical civic participation. In S. Ginwright, P. Noguera, & J. Cammarota (Eds.), *Beyond resistance: Youth activism and community change* (pp. 149–169). New York, NY: Routledge.

Duncan-Andrade, J. M. R. (2009). Note to educators. Hope required when growing roses in concrete. *Harvard Educational Review, 79*(2), 181–194.

Duncan-Andrade, J. M. R., & Morrell, E. (2008). *The art of critical pedagogy: Possibilities for moving from theory to practice in urban schools*. New York, NY: Peter Lang.

Durso, L. E., & Gates, G. J. (2012). *Serving our youth: Findings from a national survey of service providers with lesbian, gay, bisexual, and transgender youth who are homeless or at risk of becoming homeless*. Los Angeles, CA: The Williams Institute with True Colors Fund and The Palette Fund.

Dweck, C. S. (2006). *Mindset: The new psychology of success*. New York, NY: Random House.

Eastern Research Group. (2014, December). *The social and economic effects of wage violations: Estimates for California and New York*. Lexington, MA: Author.

Eaton, D. K., Kann, L., Kinchen, S., Shanklin, S., Flint, K. H., Hawkins, J., . . . Wechsler, H. (2012, June 8). Youth risk behavior surveillance—United States, 2011. *MMWR Surveillance Summaries, 61*(4), 1–162. Retrieved from www.cdc.gov/mmwr/pdf/ss/ss6104.pdf

Eccles, J. S., Midgley, C., Wigfield, A., Buchanan, C. M., Reuman, D., Flanagan, C., & Mac Iver, D. (1993). Development during adolescence: The impact of stage–environment fit on young adolescents' experiences in schools and in families. *American Psychologist, 48*(2), 90–101.

Eddy, J. M., & Reid, J. B. (2003). The adolescent children of incarcerated parents: A developmental perspective. In J. Travis & M. Waul (Eds.), *Prisoners once removed: The impact of incarceration and reentry on children, families, and communities* (pp. 233–258). Washington, DC: Urban Institute Press.

Editorial Board. (2017, September 30). America's 8-step program for opioid addiction. *The New York Times*. Retrieved from www.nytimes.com/2017/09/30/opinion/opioid-addiction-treatment-program.html

Educational Video Center (Producer). (1986). *2371 Second Avenue: An East Harlem story* [Video file]. New York, NY: EVC.

Educational Video Center (Producer). (1990). *Hard times in Cypress Hills* [Video file]. New York, NY: EVC.

Educational Video Center (Producer). (1991). *To serve and protect?* [Video file]. New York, NY: EVC.

Educational Video Center (Producer). (1992). *Unequal education: Failing our children* [Video file]. New York: NY: EVC.

Educational Video Center (Producer). (1994). *Someplace to call home: Surviving the foster care system* [Video file]. New York, NY: EVC.

Educational Video Center (Producer). (1997). *Young gunz* [Video file]. New York, NY: EVC.

Educational Video Center (Producer). (1998). *Out youth in schools* [Video file]. New York, NY: EVC.

Educational Video Center (Producer). (2003). *Not me, not mine: Adult survivors of foster care* [Video file]. New York, NY: EVC.

Educational Video Center (Producer). (2005). *Alienated: Undocumented immigrant youth* [Video file]. New York, NY: EVC.

Educational Video Center (Producer). (2007). *Losing ground: The new face of homelessness* [Video file]. New York, NY: EVC

Educational Video Center (Producer). (2009). *Another part of me: Youth views on drugs and incarceration in our community* [Video file]. New York, NY: EVC.

Educational Video Center (Producer). (2010a). *As the sun comes up, the bricks fall down* [Video file]. New York, NY: EVC.

Educational Video Center (Producer). (2010b). *Shadows of ignorance: The love that's feared* [Video file]. New York, NY: EVC.

Educational Video Center (Producer). (2011). *Mortgage mayhem: Living inside fraud* [Video file]. New York, NY: EVC.

Educational Video Center (Producer). (2012). *Life under suspicion: Youth perspectives on the NYPD's stop and frisk policy* [Video file]. New York, NY: EVC.

Educational Video Center (Producer). (2013). *Breathing easy: Environmental hazards in public housing* [Video file]. New York, NY: EVC.

Educational Video Center (Producer). (2014a). *Gender power: Street harassment in NYC* [Video file]. New York, NY: EVC.

Educational Video Center (Producer). (2014b). *High on perceptions* [Video file]. New York, NY: EVC.

Educational Video Center (Producer). (2014c). *What's your beautiful?* [Video file] New York, NY: EVC.

Educational Video Center (Producer). (2015a). *Growing apart: The politics of family separation* [Video file]. New York, NY: EVC.

Educational Video Center (Producer). (2015b). *Policing the times: Youth perspectives on police brutality* [Video file]. New York, NY: EVC.

Educational Video Center (Producer). (2016). *New visions: A deeper look at the American dream* [Video file]. New York, NY: EVC.

Educational Video Center (Producer). (2017). *Moving without direction* [Video file]. New York, NY: EVC.

Ehrenreich, B., & Hochschild, A. R. (2002). Introduction. In B. Ehrenreich & A. R. Hochschild (Eds.), *Global women: Nannies, maids, and sex workers in the new economy* (pp. 1–14). New York, NY: Henry Holt.

Elisa W. v. City of New York, 1:15-cv-05273 (S.D.N.Y. 2015).

Emirbayer, M., & Mische, A. (1998, January). What is agency? *American Journal of Sociology*, *103*(4), 962–1023.

Espelage, D. L. (2015). Bullying and K–12 students. In G. L. Wimberly (Ed.), *LGBTQ issues in education: Advancing a research agenda* (pp. 105–119). Washington, DC: American Educational Research Association.

Fausset, R., & Southall, A. (2015, October 26). Video shows officer flipping student in South Carolina, prompting inquiry. *New York Times*. Retrieved from www.nytimes .com/2015/10/27/us/officers-classroom-fight-with-student-is-caught-on-video.html

Federal Deposit Insurance Corporation. (n.d.). Foreclosure statistics: Homeowners facing foreclosure. *NeighborWorks America*. Retrieved August 19, 2015 from www.fdic.gov /about/comein/files/foreclosure_statistics.pdf

Fisher, E. S., & Kennedy, K. S. (2012). *Responsive school practices to support lesbian, gay, bisexual, transgender, and questioning students and families*. New York, NY: Routledge.

Fredrickson, B. L., & Roberts, T. A. (1997). Objectification theory: Toward understanding women's lived experiences and mental health risks. *Psychology of Women Quarterly*, *21*, 173–206.

Freire, P. (1970). *Pedagogy of the oppressed*. New York, NY: Continuum.

Fronius, T., Persson, H., Guckenburg, S., Hurley, N., & Petrosino, A. (2016, February). *Restorative justice in U.S. schools: A research review*. San Francisco, CA: WestEd.

Fullilove, M. T. (2004). *Root shock: How tearing up city neighborhoods hurt America and what we can do about it*. New York, NY: Ballantine Books.

Fullilove, M. T. (2013, September 12). Urban restructuring and inequity. In *Valuing the intersection between arts, culture and community: An exchange of research and practice*. Symposium conducted by NOCD-NY, New York, NY.

Fullilove, M. T., & Wallace, R. (2011, June). Serial forced displacement in American cities, 1916–2010. *Journal of Urban Health*, *88*(3), 381–389.

Gabrielson, R., Grochowski Jones, R., & Sagara, E. (2014, October 10). Deadly force in black and white: A ProPublica analysis of killings by police shows outsize risk for young black males. *ProPublica*. Retrieved from www.propublica.org/article/deadly-force-in-black-and-white

Garcia, O. (2009, June). Emergent bilinguals and TESOL. What's in a name? *TESOL Quarterly*, *43*(2), 322–326.

Garcia, O., & Kleifgen, J. A. (2010). *Educating emergent bilinguals: Policies, programs and practices for English language learners*. New York, NY: Teachers College Press.

Gay, G. (2010). *Culturally responsive teaching: Theory, research, and practice*. New York, NY: Teachers College Press.

Ginwright, S. (2008). Collective radical imagination: Youth participatory action and the art of emancipatory knowledge. In J. Cammarota, & M. Fine (Eds.), *Revolutionizing education: Youth participatory action research in motion* (pp. 13–22). New York, NY: Routledge.

Goff, P. A., Jackson, M. C., Culotta, C. M., Di Leone, B. A. L., & DiTomaso, N. A. (2014). The essence of innocence: Consequences of dehumanizing Black children. *Journal of Personality and Social Psychology*, *106*(4), 526–545.

Gonnerman, J. (2014, October 6). Before the law. *The New Yorker*. Retrieved from www .newyorker.com/magazine/2014/10/06/before-the-law

Gonzalez-Barrera, A., & Krogstad, J. M. (2017, March 2). What we know about illegal immigration from Mexico. *Fact tank: News in the numbers*. Washington, DC: Pew Research Center. Retrieved from www.pewresearch.org/fact-tank/2017/03/02/what-we-know-about -illegal-immigration-from-mexico/

Goodman, S. (1994). Talking back: The portrait of a student documentary on school inequity. In F. Pignatelli & S. W. Pflaum (Eds.), *Experiencing diversity: Toward educational equity* (pp. 47–69). Thousand Oaks, CA: Corwin Press.

Goodman, S. (2003). *Teaching youth media: A critical guide to literacy, video production, and social change*. New York, NY: Teachers College Press.

Goodman, S., & Cocca, C. (2013, February 1). Youth voices for change: Building political efficacy and civic engagement through digital media literacy. *Journal of Digital and Media Literacy, 1*(1). Retrieved from www.jodml.org/2013/02/01/youth-voices-for-change/

Goodman, S., & Cocca, C. (2014, December). Spaces of action: Teaching critical literacy for community empowerment in the age of neoliberalism. *English Teaching: Practice and Critique, 13*(3), 210–226. Retrieved from education.waikato.ac.nz/research/files/etpc/files/2014v13n3dial1.pdf

Gorski, P. (2013). *Reaching and teaching students in poverty: Strategies for erasing the opportunity gap*. New York, NY: Teachers College Press.

Gramsci, A. (1971). *Selections from the prison notebooks* (Q. Hoare & G. N. Smith, Eds. & Trans.). New York, NY: International Publishers.

Greene, M. (1988). *The dialectic of freedom*. New York, NY: Teachers College Press.

Greene, M. (1995). *Releasing the imagination: Essays on education, the arts, and social change*. San Franciso, CA: Jossey-Bass.

Greene, M. (2001). *Variations on a blue guitar: The Lincoln Center Institute lectures on aesthetic education*. New York, NY: Teachers College Press.

Gross, K. (2017). *Breakaway learners. Strategies for post-secondary success with at-risk students*. New York, NY: Teachers College Press.

Gruber, J., & Fineran, S. (2016). Sexual harassment, bullying, and outcomes for high school girls and boys. *Violence Against Women, 22*(1), 112–133. Retrieved from journals.sagepub.com/doi/pdf/10.1177/1077801215599079

Hagen, E., Peppard, P., Barnet, J., Young, T., Finn, L., & Teodorescu, M. (2013, December). Asthma predicts 8-year incidence of obstructive sleep apnea in the Wisconsin sleep cohort. *Sleep Medicine, 14*(1), e26. Retrieved from www.sleep-journal.com/article/S1389-9457(13)01239-2/pdf

Harris, E. A. (2017, October 10). 10% of New York City public school students were homeless last year. *New York Times*. Retrieved from www.nytimes.com/2017/10/10/nyregion/one-in-10-new-york-city-public-school-students-are-homeless.html

Herbert, B. (2007, April 9). 6-year-olds under arrest. *New York Times*. Retrieved from www.nytimes.com/2007/04/09/opinion/09herbert.html

Hess, A., & O'Neill, S. (2017, December 22). Internetting with Amanda Hess: The ugly business of beauty apps. *New York Times*. Retrieved from www.nytimes.com/video/arts/100000005615408/the-ugly-business-of-beauty-apps.html

Hesson, S., Seltzer, K., & Woodley, H.W. (2014, December). *Translanguaging in curriculum & instruction: A CUNY-NYSIEB guide for educators*. New York, NY: CUNY-NYSIEB.

Horton, M. (with Kohl, J., & Kohl, H.). (1990). *The long haul: An autobiography*. New York, NY: Doubleday.

Human Rights Watch. (2016, December 7). *"Like walking through a hailstorm": Discrimination against LGBT youth in US schools*. New York, NY: Human Rights Watch. Retrieved from www.hrw.org/report/2016/12/07/walking-through-hailstorm/discrimination-against-lgbt-youth-us-schools

Hunt, J., & Moodie-Mills, A. C. (2012, June 29). The unfair criminalization of gay and transgender youth. An overview of the experiences of LGBT youth in the juvenile justice system. Retrieved from www.americanprogress.org/issues/lgbt/reports/2012/06/29/11730/the-unfair-criminalization-of-gay-and-transgender-youth/

Huynh-Hohnbaum, A-L, Bussell, T., & Lee, G. (2015). Incarcerated mothers and fathers: How their absences disrupt children's high school graduation. *International Journal of*

Psychology and Educational Studies, 1(2), 1–11. Retrieved from www.ijpes.com/frontend/articles/pdf/v02i02/v02i02-01.pdf

Jargowsky, P. A. (2015). *Architecture of segregation: Civil unrest, the concentration of poverty, and public policy.* Camden, NJ: The Century Foundation and the School of Arts and Sciences at Rutgers University.

Jones, J., Schmitt, J., & Wilson, V. (2018, February 26). 50 Years after the Kerner commission: African Americans are better off in many ways but are still disadvantaged by racial inequality. *Economic Policy Institute.* Retrieved from www.epi.org/publication/50-years-after-the-kerner-commission/

Jones, R. L., Homa, D. M., Meyer, P. A., Brody, D. J., Caldwell, K. L., Pirkle, J. L., & Brown, M. J. (2009). Trends in blood lead levels and blood lead testing among US children aged 1 to 5 years, 1988–2004. *Pediatrics, 123*(3), e376–385. Retrieved from www.researchgate.net/publication/24171355_Trends_in_Blood_Lead_Levels_and_Blood_Lead_Testing_Among_US_Children_Aged_1_to_5_Years_1988-2004

Kang, C. (2017, June 13). Court strikes Obama-era rule capping cost of phone calls from prison. *New York Times.* Retrieved from www.nytimes.com/2017/06/13/technology/fcc-prison-phone-calls-regulations.html

Kann, L., Olsen, E. O., McManus, T., Harris, W. A., Shanklin, S. L., Flint, K. H., . . . Zaza, S. (2016, August 12). Sexual identity, sex of sexual contacts, and health-related behaviors among students in grades 9–12—United States and selected sites, 2015. *MMWR Surveillance Summaries, 65*(9), 1–202. Retrieved from www.cdc.gov/mmwr/volumes/65/ss/ss6509a1.htm?s_cid=ss6509a1_w

Kearl, H. (2014, Spring). *Unsafe and harassed in public spaces: A national street harassment report.* Reston, VA: Stop Street Harassment. Retrieved from www.stopstreetharassment.org/our-work/nationalstudy/

Kelling, G., & Wilson, J. Q. (1982, March). Broken windows: The police and neighborhood safety. *The Atlantic.* Retrieved from www.theatlantic.com/magazine/archive/1982/03/broken-windows/304465/

Ketteringham, E. S. (2017, August 22). Live in a poor neighborhood? Better be a perfect parent. *New York Times.* Retrieved from https://nyti.ms/2vUiDgb

Keuroghlian, A. S., Shtasel, D., &. Bassuk, E. L. (2014). Out on the street: A public health and policy agenda for lesbian, gay, bisexual, and transgender youth who are homeless. *American Journal of Orthopsychiatry, 84*(1), 66–72.

Kosciw, J. G., Greytak, E. A., Giga, N. M., Villenas, C., & Danischewski, D. J. (2016). *The 2015 national school climate survey: The experiences of lesbian, gay, bisexual, transgender, and queer youth in our nation's schools.* New York, NY: GLSEN.

Kozol, J. (1991). *Savage inequalities: Children in America's schools.* New York, NY: Random House.

Krebs, B., & Pitcoff, P. (2004). Reversing the failure of the foster care system. *Harvard Women's Law Journal, 27,* 357–366.

Krebs, B., & Pitcoff, P. (2006). *Beyond the foster care system: The future for teens.* New Brunswick, NJ: Rutgers University Press.

Kreiger, J., & D. L. Higgins. (2002). Housing and health: Time again for public health action. *American Journal of Public Health, 92*(5), 758–768.

Kucsera, J. (with Orfield, G.). (2014, March 26). *New York State's extreme school segregation: Inequality, inaction and a damaged future.* Los Angeles, CA: The Civil Rights Project at UCLA. Retrieved from civilrightsproject.ucla.edu/research/k-12-education/integration-and-diversity/ny-norflet-report-placeholder/Kucsera-New-York-Extreme-Segregation-2014.pdf

Kupchik, A. (2010). *Homeroom security: School discipline in an age of fear.* New York, NY: New York University.

Ladson-Billings, G. (1995). Toward a theory of culturally relevant pedagogy. *American Educational Research Journal, 32,* 465–491.

Ladson-Billings, G. (2009). *The dreamkeepers: Successful teachers of African American children* (2nd ed.). San Francisco, CA: Jossey-Bass.

Ladson-Billings, G. (2017). The (r)evolution will not be standardized: Teacher education, hip hop pedagogy, and culturally relevant pedagogy 2.0. In D. Paris & H. S. Alim (Eds.), *Culturally sustaining pedagogies: Teaching and learning for justice in a changing world* (pp. 141–156). New York, NY: Teachers College Press.

La Vigne, N. G., Davies, E., & Brazell, D. (2008, February). *Broken bonds. Understanding and addressing the needs of children with incarcerated parents.* Washington, DC: Urban Institute Justice Policy Center.

Levin, J. (2013, December 19). The welfare queen. *Slate.com* Retrieved from longform.org /posts/the-welfare-queen

Lifting the Veil. (2016, August 20). Public advocate's lawsuit dealt a well deserved setback. Retrieved from blog.liftingtheveil.org/2016/08/20/public-advocates-lawsuit-dealt-well -deserved-setback/

Lipsky, M. (1980). *Street-level bureaucracy: Dilemmas of the individual in public services.* New York, NY: Russell Sage Foundation.

Losen, D. J. (Ed.). (2015). *Closing the school discipline gap: Equitable remedies for excessive exclusion.* New York, NY: Teachers College Press.

Lugg, C. A., & Adelman, M. (2015). Sociolegal contexts of LGBTQ issues in education. In G. L. Wimberly (Ed.), *LGBTQ issues in education: Advancing a research agenda.* (pp. 43–73). Washington, DC: American Educational Research Association.

Lynd, S. (1965). Freedom schools: Concept and organization. *Freedomways: A Quarterly Review of the Negro Freedom Movement, 5*(2), 302–309. Retrieved from www.crmvet.org /info/fschool1.htm

MacFarquhar, L. (2017, August 7 & 14). When should a child be taken from his parents? *The New Yorker.* Retrieved from www.newyorker.com/magazine/2017/08/07/when -should-a-child-be-taken-from-his-parents

Maeckelbergh, M. (2012, July). Mobilizing to stay put: Housing struggles in New York City. *International Journal of Urban and Regional Research, 36*(4), 655–673.

Marcuse, P. (1986, August). The beginnings of public housing in New York. *Journal of Urban History, 12*(4), 353–390.

Massey, D. (2008). Origins of economic disparities: The historical role of housing segregation. In J. H. Carr & N. K. Kutty (Eds.), *Segregation: The rising costs for America* (pp. 39–80). New York, NY: Routledge.

Massey, D., & Denton, N. A. (1993). *American apartheid: Segregation and the making of the underclass.* Cambridge, MA: Harvard University Press.

Mastin, D., Metzger, S., & Golden, J. (2013, April). *Foster care and disconnected youth: A way forward for New York.* New York, NY: Community Service Society and The Children's Aid Society.

McCoy, T. (2015, April 29). Freddie Gray's life, a study on the effects of lead paint on poor Blacks. *The Washington Post.* Retrieved from www.washingtonpost.com/local/freddie-grays -life-a-study-in-the-sad-effects-of-lead-paint-on-poor-blacks/2015/04/29/0be898e6 -eea8-11e4-8abc-d6aa3bad79dd_story.html

McDonald, J. P., Mohr, N., Dichter, A., & McDonald, E. C. (2013). *The power of protocols: an educator's guide to better practice* (3rd ed.). New York, NY: Teachers College Press.

McKenna, T. (2016, November 24). Let us teach you how to teach us: What is education? *Bread Loaf Teacher Network Journal.* Retrieved from sites.middlebury.edu/bltnmag/2016/11/24/what-is-education/

McKenney, S. J., & Bigler, R. S. (2016). High heels, low grades: Internalized sexualization and academic orientation among adolescent girls. *Journal of Research on Adolescence, 26* 30–36.

McKoy, D. L., & Vincent, J. M. (2008). Housing and education: The inextricable link. In J. H. Carr & N. K. Kutty (Eds.), *Segregation: The rising costs for America* (pp. 125–150). New York, NY: Routledge.

Meier, D. (1995). *The power of their ideas: Lessons for America from a small school in Harlem.* Boston, MA: Beacon Press.

Meier, D. (2009). Educating for what? The struggle for democracy in education. *PowerPlay, 1*(1), 20–27.

Meng, Y., Babey, S. H., & Wolstein, J. (2012, May 17). Asthma-related school absenteeism and school concentration of low-income students in California. *Preventing Chronic Disease: Public Health Research, Practice and Policy, 9*(110312). Retrieved from www.cdc.gov/pcd/issues/2012/11_0312.htm

Menken, K. (2013, October). Emergent bilingual students in secondary school: Along the academic language and literacy continuum. *Language Teaching, 46*(4), 438–476.

Merikangas, K. R., He, J. P., Burstein, M., Swanson, S. A., Avenevoli, S., Cui, L., . . . Swendsen, J. (2010, October). Lifetime prevalence of mental disorders in U.S. adolescents: Results from the national comorbidity survey replication—Adolescent supplement (NCS–A). *Journal of the American Academy of Child and Adolescent Psychiatry, 49*(10), 980–989.

Moll, L. C., Amanti, C., Neff, D., & Gonzales, N. (1992). Funds of knowledge for teaching: Using a qualitative approach to connect to homes and classrooms. *Theory into Practice, 32*(2), 132–141.

Morgenthau, R. M. (2014, August 13). The US keeps 34,000 immigrants in detention each day simply to meet a quota. *The Nation.* www.thenation.com/article/us-keeps-34000-immigrants-detention-each-day-simply-meet-quota/

Morrell, E. (2008). Six summers of YPAR: Learning, action, and change in urban education. In J. Cammarota & M. Fine (Eds.), *Revolutionizing education: Youth participatory action research in motion* (pp. 155–184). New York, NY: Routledge.

Morris, M. W. (2016). *Pushout: The criminalization of Black girls in schools.* New York, NY: The New Press.

Moyers, B. (Executive Editor). (2016). *Rikers: An American jail.* [Video file] New York, NY: Schumann Media Center.

Mukherjee, E. (2007). *Criminalizing the classroom: The overpolicing of New York City schools.* New York, NY: New York Civil Liberties Union (NYCLU).

Myers, C., Walters, S., & Perez-Rivera, B. (2012, July). Preventing and treating childhood asthma in New York City. *NYC Vital Signs, 11*(4), 1–4.

Nadal, K. L. (2008). Preventing racial, ethnic, gender, sexual minority, disability, and religious microaggressions: Recommendations for promoting positive mental health. *Prevention in Counseling Psychology: Theory, Research, Practice and Training, 2*(1), 22–27.

Nance, J. P. (2016). Students, police, and the school-to-prison pipeline. *Washington University Law Review, 93*(4), 919–987. Retrieved from openscholarship.wustl.edu/cgi/viewcontent.cgi?referer=&httpsredir=1&article=6209&context=law_lawreview

National Center for Victims of Crime. (2012). Action partnership on interventions for Black children exposed to violence and victimization. Retrieved from victimsofcrime.org/our-programs/other-projects/youth-initiative/interventions-for-black-children%27s-exposure-to-violence

National Coalition of Anti-Violence Programs. (2017). *Lesbian, gay, bisexual, transgender, queer, and HIV-affected hate violence in 2016.* New York, NY: New York City Gay and Lesbian Anti-Violence Project. Retrieved from avp.org/wp-content/uploads/2017/06 /NCAVP_2016HateViolence_REPORT.pdf

National Institute of Mental Health. (2014). *Eating disorders: About more than food* (NIH Publication No.TR 14-4901). Retrieved from www.nimh.nih.gov/health/publications /eating-disorders/eating-disorders-pdf_148810.pdf

National Scientific Council on the Developing Child. (2015). *Supportive relationships and active skill-building strengthen the foundations of resilience* (Working Paper 13). Retrieved from 46y5eh11fhgw3ve3ytpwxt9r.wpengine.netdna-cdn.com/wp-content/uploads/2015 /05/The-Science-of-Resilience1.pdf

New York City Administration for Children's Services. (2016). *Report on youth in foster care.* Retrieved from www1.nyc.gov/assets/acs/pdf/data-analysis/2016/ACSReportOnYouthIn FosterCareLL1452016.pdf

New York City Department of Investigation. (2017, November 14). *DOI investigation reveals NYCHA failed to conduct mandatory lead paint safety inspections for four years* [Press release]. Retrieved from www1.nyc.gov/assets/doi/press-releases/2017 /nov/27NYCHALeadPaint11-14-2017_UL.pdf

New York City Housing Authority (NYCHA). (2015, January 1). *Special tabulation of resident characteristics.* Retrieved from www1.nyc.gov/assets/nycha/downloads/pdf/res_data.pdf

New York City Housing Authority (NYCHA). (2017, April 13). *NYCHA 2017 fact sheet.* Retrieved from www1.nyc.gov/assets/nycha/downloads/pdf/factsheet.pdf

New York City Housing Authority (NYCHA). (2018). *About NYCHA.* Retrieved from www1 .nyc.gov/site/nycha/about/about-nycha.page

New York City Independent Budget Office. (2012, September). Table 6: Class of 2009 graduation, dropout, and discharge rate by country of origin. *Graduates, dropouts, discharges: Tracking four-year outcomes for the class of 2009.* Retrieved from www.ibo.nyc.ny.us /iboreports/gradrates2012.html

New York City School–Justice Partnership Task Force. (2013, May). *Keeping kids in school and out of court: Report and recommendations.* Albany, NY: New York State Permanent Judicial Commission on Justice for Children.

New York Civil Liberties Union (NYCLU). (n.d.). *Nicholson v. Williams (Defending parental rights of mothers who are domestic violence victims).* Retrieved from www.nyclu.org/en /cases/nicholson-v-williams-defending-parental-rights-of-mothers-who-are-domestic -violence-victims

New York Civil Liberties Union (NYCLU). (2016, July 21). *NYPD releases complete school safety data for the first time* [Press release]. Retrieved from https://www.nyclu.org/en /press-releases/nypd-releases-complete-school-safety-data-first-time

New York State Division of Criminal Justice Services. (2010). *New York State felony drug arrest, indictment and commitment trends 1973–2008. Report no. 1.* Retrieved from www.criminaljustice.ny.gov/pio/annualreport/baseline_trends_report.pdf

New York State Education Department (NYSED). (2018, February 7). Slide 11: Statewide, the graduation rate achievement gap by racial/ethnic group persists, particularly for the advanced designation diploma. *June graduation rates for 2013 cohort.* Retrieved from www.nysed.gov/news/2018/state-education-department-releases-2013-cohort -high-school-graduation-rates

Nir, S. M. (2015a, May 7). The price of nice nails. *New York Times.* Retrieved from nyti.ms /1KOuiMq

Nir, S. M. (2015b, May 8). Perfect nails, poisoned workers. *New York Times.* Retrieved from nyti.ms/1JvkhCJ

Nir, S. M. (2015c, May 11). Cuomo orders emergency measures to protect workers at nail salons. *New York Times*. Retrieved from nyti.ms/1KWxsO2

Noguera, P. (2003, Autumn). Schools, prisons, and social implications of punishment: Rethinking disciplinary practices. *Theory Into Practice, 42*(4), 341–350.

Noguera, P. (2008). The trouble with Black boys: . . . And other reflections on race, equity and the future of public education. San Francisco, CA: Jossey-Bass.

Nolan, K. (2011). *Police in the hallways: Discipline in an urban high school.* Minneapolis: University of Minnesota Press.

Oakes, J., & Rogers, J. (with Lipton, M.). (2006) *Learning power: Organizing for education and justice.* New York, NY: Teachers College Press.

O'Donoghue, J. L. (2006). Taking their own power: Urban youth, community-based youth organizations, and public efficacy. In S. Ginwright, P. Noguera, & J. Cammarota (Eds.), *Beyond resistance! Youth activism and community change.* (pp. 229–245). New York, NY: Routledge.

Office of Juvenile Justice and Delinquency Prevention. (2017, July). *The number of juveniles in residential placement reached a new low in 2015.* Retrieved from www.ojjdp.gov/ojstatbb /snapshots/DataSnapshot_CJRP2015.pdf

Office of the New York City Public Advocate Letitia James. (2014, September). Policy report: Foster care part I. Improving the outcomes for youth aging out of foster care in New York City. Retrieved from pubadvocate.nyc.gov/sites/advocate.nyc.gov/files/report _foster_care_part_i_aging_out_youth.pdf

Orfield, G., & McArdle, N. (2006, August). *The vicious cycle: Segregated housing, schools and intergenerational inequality* (W06-4). Cambridge, MA: Joint Center for Housing Studies of Harvard University. Retrieved from www.jchs.harvard.edu/research/publications /vicious-cycle-segregated-housing-schools-and-intergenerational-inequality

Oyserman, D., & Markus, H. R. (1990). Possible selves and delinquency. *Journal of Personality and Social Psychology, 59*(1), 112–125.

Pettit, B. (2004, June). Moving and children's social connections: Neighborhood context and the consequences of moving for low-income families. *Sociological Forum, 19*(2), 285–331.

Pettit, K. L. S., & Comey, J. (2012, January). The foreclosure crisis and children: A three-city study. Washington, DC: The Urban Institute. Retrieved from www.urban.org/sites/default /files/publication/25151/412517-The-Foreclosure-Crisis-and-Children-A-Three-City -Study.PDF

Prangley, E. (2016, July 12). *Two-thirds of public schools reported zero incidents of sexual harassment in 2013–14.* Washington, DC: AAUW. Retrieved from www.aauw.org/article /schools-report-zero-sexual-harassment/

Pribesh, S., & Downey, D. B. (1999). Why are residential and school moves associated with poor school performance? *Demography, 36*(4), 521–534.

Public Counsel. (2015, September 30). Our stories: Historic ruling in landmark complaint on unique needs of children affected by trauma. Retrieved from www.publiccounsel.org /stories?id=0172

Ransom, J. (2014, January 29). East Harlem tenants paying low rents say they're living with rats, leaks and mold because their landlord wants them out. *New York Daily News*. Retrieved from www.nydailynews.com/new-york/uptown/tenants-landlords-article-1.1596108

Ream, G. L., & Forge, N. (2014). Homeless lesbian, gay, bisexual and transgender (LGBT) youth in New York City: Insights from the field. *Child Welfare, 93*(2), 7–22.

Reardon, S. F., & Bischoff, K. (2011, November). *Growth in the residential segregation of families by income, 1970–2009.* (US2010 Project of Russell Sage Foundation and American Communities Project of Brown University). Retrieved from www.s4.brown.edu/us2010 /Data/Report/report111111.pdf

Rehabs.com. (2012). *Dying to be Barbie: Eating disorders in the pursuit of the impossible.* Retrieved from www.rehabs.com/explore/dying-to-be-barbie/

Reilly, T. (2003). Transition from care: Status and outcomes of youth who age out of foster care. *Child Welfare, 82*(6), 727–746.

Reyes, C. (2016, January 12). 100,000 NYC school children face airport style security screening every day. *ProPublica.* Retrieved from www.propublica.org/article/nyc-school-children-face-airport-style-security-screening-every-day

Roberts, D. E. (2012). Prison, foster care, and the systemic punishment of Black mothers. *UCLA Law Review, 59*, 1474–1500.

Rosario, M., Schrimshaw, E. W., & Hunter, J. (2012). Risk factors for homelessness among lesbian, gay, and bisexual youths: A developmental milestone approach. *Children and Youth Services Review, 34*(1), 186–193.

Rothstein, R. (2004). *Class and schools: Using social, economic, and educational reform to close the Black-White achievement gap.* New York, NY: Economic Policy Institute.

Rothstein, R. (2017). *The color of law: A forgotten history of how our government segregated America.* New York, NY: Liveright.

Rudacille, D. (2005). *The riddle of gender: Science, activism, and transgender rights.* New York, NY: Pantheon Books.

Ruiz Soto, A. G., Hooker, S., & Batalova, J. (2015, June). *States and districts with the highest number and share of English language learners.* Washington, DC: Migration Policy Institute. Retrieved from www.migrationpolicy.org/research/states-and-districts-highest-number-and-share-english-language-learners

Scanlon, E., & Devine, K. (2001). Residential mobility and youth well-being: Research, policy, and practice issues. *Journal of Sociology and Social Welfare, 28*(1), 119–138.

Schwartz, A. (2010). *Housing policy in the United States* (2nd ed.). New York, NY: Routledge.

Schwirtz, M., Winerip, M., & Gebeloff, R. (2016, December 3). The scourge of racial bias in New York State's prisons. *New York Times.* Retrieved from www.nytimes.com/2016/12/03/nyregion/new-york-state-prisons-inmates-racial-bias.html

Seelye, K. Q., & Bidgood, J. (2017, April 6). 'Don't open the door': How fear of an immigration raid gripped a city. *The New York Times.* Retrieved from www.nytimes.com/2017/04/06/us/immigration-raid-fear-brockton-massachusetts.html

The Sentencing Project. (2017). *Criminal justice facts.* Retrieved from www.sentencingproject.org/criminal-justice-facts/Sherman, F. T., & Balck, A. (2015). *Gender injustice: System-level juvenile justice reforms for girls.* Portland, OR: National Crittenton Foundation.

Sickmund, M., & Puzzanchera, C. (Eds.). (2014, December). *Juvenile offenders and victims: 2014 National report.* Pittsburgh, PA: National Center for Juvenile Justice.

Simon. J. (2007). *Governing through crime: How the war on crime transformed American democracy.* New York, NY: Oxford University Press.

Smithgall, C., Gladden, R. M., Howard, E., Goerge, R. M., & Courtney, M. E. (2004). *Educational experiences of children in out-of-home care.* Chicago, IL: Chapin Hall Center for Children at the University of Chicago.

Stern, L. (2013, December 30). *Valuing the intersection between arts, culture, and community: An exchange of research and practice* (A summary essay from NOCDNY.org). Retrieved from nocdny.org/2014/03/17/valuing-the-intersection-between-arts-culture-and-community-an-exchange-of-research-and-practice-2/

Stoloff, J. A. (2004, August 14). *A brief history of public housing.* Paper presented at the annual meeting of the American Sociological Association, San Francisco, CA. Retrieved from www.researchgate.net/profile/Jennifer_Stoloff/publication/228789405_A_brief_history_of_public_housing/links/5643a68008ae9f9c13e05df6/A-brief-history-of-public-housing.pdf

Stringer, S. M. (2016, September 22). *Diploma disparities: High school graduation rates in New York City.* Office of New York City Comptroller. Retrieved from https://comptroller.nyc.gov/reports/diploma-disparities-high-school-graduation-rates-in-new-york-city/

Suárez-Orozco, C., Bang, H. J., O'Connor, E., Gaytán, F. X., Pakes, J., & Rhodes, J. (2010). Academic trajectories of newcomer youth. *Developmental Psychology, 46*(3), 602–618.

Suárez-Orozco, C., Rhodes, J., & Milburn, M. (2009). Unraveling the immigrant paradox: Academic engagement and disengagement among recently arrived immigrant youth. *Youth & Society, 41,* 151–185.

Suárez-Orozco, C., Suárez-Orozco, M. M., & Todorova, I. (2008). *Learning in a new land: Immigrant students in American society.* Cambridge, MA: Belknap Press of Harvard University Press.

Suárez-Orozco, C., Todorova, I., & Louie, J., (2002). Making up for lost time: The experience of separation and reunification among immigrant families. *Family Process, 41*(4), 625–643.

Teachers Unite (Producer). (2012). *Growing fairness: Building community and resisting the school-to-prison pipeline with restorative justice in schools* [Video file]. New York, NY: Teachers Unite.

Thronson, D. B. (2008). Creating crisis: Immigration raids and the destabilization of immigrant families. *Wake Forest Law Review, 43,* 391–418.

Tobis, D. (2013). *From pariahs to partners: How parents and their allies changed New York City's child welfare system.* New York, NY: Oxford University Press.

Torre, M. E., & Fine, M. (with Alexander, N., Billups, A. B., Blanding, Y., Genao, E., Marboe, E., Salah, T., & Urdang, K.). (2008). Participatory action research in the contact zone. In J. Cammarota & M. Fine (Eds.), *Revolutionizing education: Youth participatory action research in motion* (pp. 23–44). New York, NY: Routledge.

Tough, P. (2012). *How children succeed: Grit, curiosity, and the hidden power of character.* New York, NY: Houghton Mifflin Harcourt.

Trice, A. D., & Brewster, J. (2004). The effects of maternal incarceration on adolescent children. *Journal of Police and Criminal Psychology, 19*(1), 27–35. Retrieved from www.researchgate.net/publication/225570820_The_Effects_of_Maternal_Incarceration_on_Adolescent_Children

Urban Institute. (2017, October 5). *Nine charts about wealth inequality in America.* Retrieved from datatools.urban.org/Features/wealth-inequality-charts/

U.S. Department of Education, National Center for Education Statistics (NCES). (2012). Table 129. Percentage of high school dropouts among persons 16 through 24 years old (status dropout rate), by income level, and percentage distribution of status dropouts, by labor force status and years of school completed: 1970 through 2011. *Digest of Education Statistics.* Retrieved from nces.ed.gov/programs/digest/d12/tables/dt12_129.asp

U.S. Department of Education, National Center for Education Statistics (NCES). (2015, May). Public school safety and discipline: 2013–14. First look. Retrieved from nces.ed.gov/pubs2015/2015051.pdf

U.S. Department of Education, National Center for Education Statistics (NCES). (2016, May). Indicators of school crime and safety. Indicator 20: Safety and security measures taken by public schools. Retrieved from nces.ed.gov/programs/crimeindicators/ind_20.asp

U.S. Department of Education, National Center for Education Statistics (NCES). (2018, March). Trends in high school dropout and completion rates in the United States: 2014. Retrieved from https://nces.ed.gov/pubsearch/pubsinfo.asp?pubid=2018117

U.S. Department of Education, Office for Civil Rights. (2014, March 21). *Civil rights data collection: Data snapshot: school discipline* (Issue Brief No. 1). www2.ed.gov/about/offices/list/ocr/docs/crdc-discipline-snapshot.pdf

U.S. Department of Health and Human Services, Administration on Children, Youth and Families, Children's Bureau. (2017, October 20). *The AFCARS report: Preliminary fy2016 estimates as of October 20, 2017* (No. 24). Retrieved from www.acf.hhs.gov/sites/default/files/cb/afcarsreport24.pdf

U.S. Department of Health and Human Services, Health Resources and Services Administration, Maternal and Child Health Bureau. (2014). *Child Health USA 2014.* Retrieved from mchb.hrsa.gov/chusa14/population-characteristics/children-immigrant-parents.html

U.S. Department of Health and Human Services, National Institutes of Health, National Institute on Drug Abuse (NIDA). (2010). Comorbidity: Addiction and other mental illnesses. *Research Report Series.* Retrieved from www.drugabuse.gov/sites/default/files/rrcomorbidity.pdf

U.S. Department of Homeland Security, Office of Immigration Statistics. (2016, August). Table 41. Aliens removed by criminal status and region and country of nationality: Fiscal years 2005 to 2014. *2014 Yearbook of immigration statistics.* Retrieved from www.dhs.gov/sites/default/files/publications/DHS%202014%20Yearbook.pdf

U.S. Department of Justice, United States Attorney, Southern District of New York. (2014, August 4). *CRIPA investigation of the New York City Department of Corrections jails on Rikers Island.* Retrieved from www.justice.gov/sites/default/files/usao-sdny/legacy/2015/03/25/SDNY%20Rikers%20Report.pdf

Vitale, A. S. (2017). *The end of policing.* London, United Kingdom: Verso.

Walls, N. E., Kane, S. B., & Wisneski, H. (2010). Gay–straight alliances and school experiences of sexual minority youth. *Youth & Society, 41*(3), 307–332.

Wasylkiw, L., Emms, A., Meuse, R., & Poirier, K. F. (2009). Are all models created equal? A content analysis of women in advertisements of fitness versus fashion magazines. *Body Image, 6,* 137–140.

Weiss, L., & Fine, M. (2004). *Working method: Research and social justice.* New York, NY: Routledge.

Williams, W. R. (2009). Struggling with poverty: Implications for theory and policy of increasing research on social class-based stigma. *Analyses of Social Issues and Public Policy, 9*(1), 37–56.

Wilson, D. (2009, December 11). Poor children likelier to get antipsychotics. *New York Times.* Retrieved from www.nytimes.com/2009/12/12/health/12medicaid.html

Wilson, J. P., Rule, N. O., & Hugenberg, K. (2017). Racial bias in judgments of physical size and formidability: From size to threat. *Journal of Personality and Social Psychology, 113*(1), 59–80.

Wimberly, G. L., Wilkinson, L., & Pearson, J. (2015). LGBTQ student achievement and educational attainment. In G. L. Wimberly (Ed.), *LGBTQ issues in education: Advancing a research agenda* (pp. 121–139). Washington, DC: American Educational Research Association.

Wright, C. L., & Levitt, M. J. (2014). Parental absence, academic competence, and expectations in Latino immigrant youth. *Journal of Family Issues, 35*(13), 1754–1779.

Yan, H. (2017, January 4). Video shows North Carolina school officer slamming girl, 15, to floor. *CNN.* Retrieved from www.cnn.com/2017/01/04/us/north-carolina-officer-body-slams-student/index.html

Yee, V. (2015, July 7). Suit to accuse New York City and state of keeping children in foster care too long. *New York Times.* Retrieved from www.nytimes.com/2015/07/08/nyregion/suit-accuses-new-york-city-and-state-of-keeping-children-in-foster-care-too-long.html

Zong, J., Batalova, J., & Hallock, J. (2018, February 8). Frequently requested statistics on immigrants and immigration in the United States. *Migration Information Source.* Retrieved from www.migrationpolicy.org/article/frequently-requested-statistics-immigrants-and-immigration-united-states

Index

The letter *f* or *n* in a page reference refers to a figure or note, respectively.